T0224788

PMI-ACP Exam Prep Study Guide

EXTRA PREPARATION FOR PMI-ACP CERTIFICATION EXAMINATION

VIVEK VAISHAMPAYAN, PMP, MCTS, PMI-ACP

PMI-ACP EXAM PREP STUDY GUIDE
EXTRA PREPARATION FOR PMI-ACP CERTIFICATION EXAMINATION

Copyright © 2014 Vivek Vaishampayan, PMP, MCTS, PMI-ACP.

All rights reserved. No part of this book may be used or reproduced by any means, graphic, electronic, or mechanical, including photocopying, recording, taping or by any information storage retrieval system without the written permission of the author except in the case of brief quotations embodied in critical articles and reviews.

iUniverse books may be ordered through booksellers or by contacting:

iUniverse
1663 Liberty Drive
Bloomington, IN 47403
www.iuniverse.com
1-800-Authors (1-800-288-4677)

Because of the dynamic nature of the Internet, any web addresses or links contained in this book may have changed since publication and may no longer be valid. The views expressed in this work are solely those of the author and do not necessarily reflect the views of the publisher, and the publisher hereby disclaims any responsibility for them.

Any people depicted in stock imagery provided by Thinkstock are models, and such images are being used for illustrative purposes only.
Certain stock imagery © Thinkstock.

ISBN: 978-1-4917-3556-5 (sc)
ISBN: 978-1-4917-3557-2 (e)

Print information available on the last page.

iUniverse rev. date: 01/05/2016

Dedicated To my wife Manjiri and our son Amit and our daughter Isha

Contents

PART V   Overview: PMI-ACP Sample PMI-ACP Cert Exam

PART VI   Overview: PMI-ACP Appendices

Acknowledgements

Vivek Vaishampayan would like to thank his wife Manjiri for her patience while writing the original book and now this revised second edition of the book. She is the inspiration to write the first book and also gave the encouragement to complete this second edition. Vivek would also like to extend his gratitude for his entire family; his wife Manjiri and their son Amit and daughter Isha. Vivek would like to thank all his family friends in Crystal Lake for their continuous support and encouragement.

Vivek would like to acknowledge a number of students who have been attending his PMI-ACP certification courses, asking numerous questions, and listening to his lectures during PMI-ACP boot camp sessions. Practical solutions addressed in this book were inspired by such questions. Special thanks to John Potter, one of my best students, who reviewed my manuscript in short period of time and provided valuable feedback on all contents. Last but not least, Vivek would like to sincerely thank Sanjay Kumar MBA, director of COMNET group, Crystal Lake, Illinois for showing the confidence in him to submit ACP curriculum based on this book to PMI to obtain REP for his training institute and encouraging him to conduct the PMI-ACP certification prep courses at various locations.

Vivek would also like to thank the editorial board who went through entire manuscript multiple times till it came out perfect. Vivek takes this opportunity to thank *iUniverse* and all their staff in helping to publish the first edition and now this second edition book to keep up with time.

PART I

Overview: PMI-ACP
All About Agile

Introduction

Welcome to the *PMI-ACP Exam Prep Study Guide* book. This book is designed to help those interested in preparing and passing the Project Management Institute's revised certification exam for Agile Certified Practitioner (PMI-ACP). This test preparation guide book will also provide a handy reference to the team members who are implementing practices of Agile Project Management. This handbook consists of an introduction to the PMI-ACP exam process, various agile methodologies, the agile manifesto, detail study notes covering the agile tools and techniques in ten areas, explanations on thirty three knowledge and skill areas, handy tips for taking exam, and sample exam questions that can be used for practice.

THE PMI-ACP CERTIFICATION EXAMINATION

The Project Management Institute (PMI) has created a certification for project management practitioners who are using agile practices in their projects, or whose organizations are adopting Agile approaches to project management. PMI created PMI-ACP certification for those who believe in and apply agile principles and practices on projects. It requires a combination of training, experience and an exam. It also bridges agile approaches such as SCRUM, XP, LEAN and Kanban. This certification has been designed to:

- Demonstrate to employers the practitioner's level of professionalism in agile practices of project management.
- Increase the practitioner's versatility in project management tools and techniques,
- Show that the practitioner has the capacity to lead basic Agile project teams, and
- Provide a framework for agile training and professional development initiatives.

Overview of the PMI-ACP Certification

Timeline of the PMI-ACP Certification Process

Step #1: The PMI-ACP Application Submission

You have 90 days to complete the application once you started it.

To take the PMI-ACP exam, you need to fill up an application on pmi.org with certain details. PMI encourages you to use the online certification system to apply for all certifications and credentials.

To be eligible for PMI-ACP certification, you must meet the following educational and professional experience requirements:

Educational Background	+	General Project Experience	+	Agile Project Experience	+	Training in Agile Practices
Secondary degree (high school diploma, associate's degree or global equivalent)		*2,000 hours (12 months) working on project teams This experience must have been earned in the last 5 years		1,500 hours (8 months) working on project teams using agile methodologies This experience must have been earned in the last 3 years These hours are in addition to the 2,000 hours required in general project experience.		21 contact hours Hours must have been earned in agile practices

*Note: for those who hold a PMP and/or PgMP credentials, PMI has already verified you have exceeded the project experience requirements. In other words, PMP and/or PgMP credential holders will be accepted as fulfilling the general project experience requirements.

Step #2: Application Completeness Review

You may have to wait up to 10 calendar days (once your application is submitted online). PMI will inform you about acceptance of your application.

NOTE: This processing timeline does not apply if your application has been selected for PMI's audit process (refer to the PMI Audit Process section in the PMI-ACP handbook for more details).

Step #3: Applicant Payment Process

You can't schedule examination until you submit payment of certification fees. Please check PMI website for exact amount of certification fees to be paid to PMI.

PMI will inform you about acceptance of your payment of certification fees.

The proper fees for payment are determined by your PMI membership status and the examination delivery type (computer-based versus paper-based) for your geographic location. Refer to the Examination Administration section in the handbook to see if you qualify for paper-based exam delivery. Otherwise, plan on taking a computer-based exam and submitting the associated fees. Use the chart provided in the PMI-ACP handbook to determine the certification fee.

Step #4: Audit Process

(This process happens ONLY if your application is selected for Audit).

You have 90 days to send your audit material. Typically there is missing information or overlapping experience or inconsistency in your application, for which further clarification may be required.

PMI processes audit material in 5-7 days and will inform you about the status of your application. Please refer to the section of "PMI Audit Process" in the PMI-ACP handbook for further details.

Step #5: Multiple-Choice Examination Eligibility

You have 1 year from the date your application is accepted, to appear for the certification exam.

You can take the exam up to 3 times during this 1 year. You may need to pay exam fees again.

Here are more details about the PMI-ACP certification examination.

The PMI-ACP Exam Information

The PMI-ACP exam is comprised of 120 multiple-choice questions with 3 hours allotted time to answer. Of the 120 questions, 20 are considered pretest questions. Pretest questions do not affect the score and are used in examinations as an effective and legitimate way to test the validity of future questions. All questions are randomly placed throughout the exam.

No. of Scored Questions	No. of Pretest (Unscored) Questions	Total Examination Questions
100	20	120

Computer-based testing (CBT) is the standard method
of administration for PMI examinations.
The allotted time to complete the computer-based examination is **_three hours_**.

Allotted Examination Time
3 hours

It may take some candidates less than the allotted three hours to complete the examination.

There are **no scheduled breaks** during the exam, although you are allowed to take a break if needed. If you take a break during the exam, your exam clock continues to count down.

The examination is **preceded by a tutorial and followed by a survey,** both of which are optional and both of which can take up to 15 minutes to complete. The time used to complete the tutorial and survey is not included in the examination time of three hours.

Exam Content Outline (as per PMI)

PMI-ACP Exam Blueprint

The PMI-ACP certification exam is developed based on the _PMI-ACP Examination Content Outline_. The exam blueprint details the topic areas (or domains) in which exam questions will focus. The allocation of questions will be as follows:

Domain	Percentage of Items on Test
Domain I. Agile Principles and Mindset	16%
Domain II. Value-driven Delivery	20%
Domain III. Stakeholder Engagement	17%
Domain IV. Team Performance	16%
Domain V. Adaptive Planning	12%
Domain VI. Problem Detection and Resolution	10%
Domain VII. Continuous Improvement (Product, Process, People)	9%
TOTAL	**100%**

Domain I. Agile Principles and Mindset (9 tasks)
Explore, embrace, and apply agile principles and mindset within the context of the project team and organization.

Domain II. Value-Driven Delivery (4 sub-domains, 14 tasks)
Deliver valuable results by producing high-value increments for review, early and often, based on stakeholder priorities. Have the stakeholders provide feedback on these increments, and use this feedback to prioritize and improve future increments.

Domain III. Stakeholder Engagement (3 sub-domains, 9 tasks)
Engage current and future interested parties by building a trusting environment that aligns their needs and expectations and balances their requests with an understanding of the cost/effort involved. Promote participation and collaboration throughout the project life cycle and provide the tools for effective and informed decision making.

Domain IV. Team Performance (3 sub-domains, 9 tasks)
Create an environment of trust, learning, collaboration, and conflict resolution that promotes team self-organization, enhances relationships among team members, and cultivates a culture of high performance.

Domain V. Adaptive Planning (3 sub-domains, 10 tasks)
Produce and maintain an evolving plan, from initiation to closure, based on goals, values, risks, constraints, stakeholder feedback, and review findings.

Domain VI. Problem Detection and Resolution (5 tasks)
Continuously identify problems, impediments, and risks; prioritize and resolve in a timely manner; monitor and communicate the problem resolution status; and implement process improvements to prevent them from occurring again.

Domain VII. Continuous Improvement (Product, Process, People) (6 tasks)
Continuously improve the quality, effectiveness, and value of the product, the process, and the team.

The entire PMI-ACP exam is covered by these 7 domains, spread over T&T (Tools & Techniques) and K&S (Knowledge and Skills). It is imperative that the PMI-ACP exam accurately reflects the agile practices, tools, and techniques being used by project management practitioners.

Approximately 20 questions will be asked on first domain covering "Agile Principles and Mindset".

Approximately 24 questions will be asked on second domain covering "Value-driven Delivery".

Approximately 20 questions will be asked on third domain covering "Stakeholder Engagement".

Approximately 20 questions will be asked on fourth domain covering "Team Performance".

Approximately 14 questions will be asked on fifth domain covering "Adaptive Planning".

Approximately 12 questions will be asked on sixth domain covering "Problem Detection and Resolution".

Approximately 10 questions will be asked on seventh domain covering "Continuous Improvement (Product, Process, and People".

Pay most attention to Value-driven Delivery, Agile Principles & Mindset, Stakeholder Engagement and Team Performance. Then pay attention to Adaptive Planning, Problem Resolution and Continuous Improvement.

The PMI Agile Certified Practitioner (PMI-ACP) Certification has been designed to:

- Demonstrate to employers the practitioner's level of professionalism in Agile practices of project management.
- Increase the practitioner's versatility in project management tools and techniques.
- Show that the practitioner has the capacity to lead basic Agile project teams, and
- Provide a framework for Agile training and professional development initiatives.

Candidates are urged to use the PMI-ACP *Examination Content Outline* as a guide to the areas included on the examination, and to study current references in agile, such as those on the PMI-ACP *examination preparation reference list*. Please use the following links to obtain latest information from PMI website.

http://www.pmi.org/~/media/PDF/Certifications/exam-outline/agile-certified-exam-outline.ashx

http://www.pmi.org/~/media/PDF/Certifications/ACP_Reference_list_v2.ashx

This book is based on the PMI-ACP Examination Content Outline as well as extracts from numerous books listed under PMI *reference list* and agile related preparation content references available online. It will NOT be possible to list each and every reference used directly and/or indirectly in the preparation of this book due to space constraints, however the author deeply extends his gratitude towards all those authors and publishers providing tons of valuable information everywhere.

I wish you all the best in your preparation for PMI-ACP certification examination. I am sure this book will help you as a supplement to your other preparation material. This is my sincere attempt to help the candidates to prepare for the PMI-ACP certification exam based on my own preparation for the exam followed by multiple training sessions I instructed and the vast information I compiled together. Enjoy reading the book!!

Vivek Vaishampayan, PMP, MCTS, PMI-ACP, CSM

CHAPTER ONE

All About Agile

This chapter provides an overview about agile and also covers "barely sufficient" details about PMI-ACP certification examination. Part I contains introduction and all about agile. Part II consists of 10 chapters related to agile tools and techniques. Part III consists of 3 chapters related to agile knowledge and skills. Part IV consists of agile domains and tasks to be used by agile trainers. Part V consists of a sample PMI-ACP certification examination. Part VI consists of agile terms, acronyms, appendix and other useful information.

This chapter covers the following:

> **PMI-ACP Certification**
> **What is Agile?**
> **Introduction to Agile**
> **Agile Project**
> **Agile Manifesto**
> **Agile Practices**
> **Agile Principles**
> **Agile Methodologies**
> **Agile Project Management**
> **Agile References**

Overall the PMI-ACP exam is divided into 2 broad categories. The first category is all about agile tools and techniques (T&T). The second category is all about agile knowledge and skills (K&S).

Looking at the PMI ACP certification examination content outline, it is stated that there will be 120 questions which are distributed equally among 2 categories. Part II of this book consisting of 10 chapters will help you to prepare for those questions based on tools and techniques, the first category of exam.

Part III of this book, consisting of 3 chapters will help you to prepare for those questions based on thirty three agile knowledge and skills, the second category of exam.

PMI-ACP Certification

PMI-ACP is different from the PMP credential in that the PMI-ACP specifically validates a practitioner's ability to understand and apply agile principles and practice, whereas the PMP credential recognizes demonstrated competence leading and directing project teams.

The PMI-ACP certification recognizes practitioners for their understanding of agile principles and practices. The certification represents an important facet of a practitioner's professional development.

What are the eligibility requirements for the PMI-ACP?

Since PMI is the authority providing the final eligibility requirements for the PMI-ACP, it is strongly recommended that you should visit http://www.pmi.org/ for further details.

Please check the above website to obtain up-to-date details for PMI-ACP Certification examination about:

- Experience eligibility requirements
- Education eligibility requirements
- Application process and fees
- PMI-ACP certification examination expectations
- Certification schedule and payment information
- How to register to take PMI-ACP certification exam at centers administered by Prometrics.
- Continuing certification requirements (CCR)

PMI-ACP Exam Question Allocation

The PMI-ACP examination will consist of total 120 questions, to be answered in 3 hours.

Specifics:

- 120 Multiple-choice questions
- 20 pre-test questions (unscored) included at random
- 100 scored questions
- 3 hours allotted time

The allocation of questions will be as follows:

Tools & Techniques (50%)	Knowledge & Skills (50%)

Exam Blueprint: Tools & Techniques

The PMI-ACP examination will consist of 60 questions from following Tools & Techniques:

Agile Analysis and Design	Including but not limited to:
	Product roadmap
	User stories/backlog
	Story maps
	Progressive Elaboration
	Wireframes
	Chartering
	Personas
	Agile modeling
	Workshops
	Learning cycle
	Collaboration games
Agile Estimation	**Including but not limited to:**
	relative sizing/story points/T-shirt sizing
	wide band Delphi/planning poker
	affinity estimating
	ideal time
Communications	**Including but not limited to:**
	information radiator
	team space agile tooling
	osmotic communications for co-located and/or distributed teams
	two-way communications (trustworthy, conversation driven)
	social media–based communication
	active listening
	brainstorming
	feedback methods

Interpersonal Skills	**Including but not limited to:** emotional intelligence collaboration adaptive leadership servant leadership negotiation conflict resolution
Metrics	**Including but not limited to:** velocity/throughput/productivity cycle time lead time EVM for agile projects defect rate approved iterations work in progress
Planning, Monitoring, and Adapting	**Including but not limited to:** reviews Kanban board task board time-boxing iteration and release planning variance and trend analysis WIP limits daily stand ups burn down/up charts cumulative flow diagrams backlog grooming/refinement product-feedback loop
Process Improvement	**Including but not limited to:** Kaizen the Five WHYs retrospectives, intraspectives process tailoring/hybrid models value stream mapping control limits pre-mortem (rule setting, failure analysis) fishbone diagram analysis

Product Quality	**Including but not limited to:**
	frequent verification and validation
	definition of done
	continuous integration
	testing, including exploratory and usability
Risk Management	**Including but not limited to:**
	risk adjusted backlog
	risk burn down graphs
	risk-based spike
	architectural spike
Value-Based Prioritization	**Including but not limited to:**
	ROI/NPV/IRR
	compliance
	customer valued prioritization
	requirements reviews
	minimal viable product (MVP)
	minimal marketable feature (MMF)
	relative prioritization/ranking
	MoSCoW
	Kano analysis

Exam Blueprint: Knowledge & Skills

The PMI-ACP examination will consist of 60 questions from following Knowledge & Skills:

Note: All three levels are equally important and they carry same weight in the ACP examination. These are divided into three levels for simplicity and ease of presentation. These are also arranged in alphabetical order.

Level I Knowledge & Skills	Level II Knowledge & Skills	Level III Knowledge & Skills
Agile contracting methods	Assessing and incorporating community and stakeholder values	Physical and virtual co-location
Agile discovery	Communication management	PMI's Code of Ethics and Professional Conduct
Agile Frameworks and terminology	Continuous improvement	Principles of systems thinking (complex, adaptive, chaos)

Agile hybrid models	Developmental mastery models (Tuckman, Dreyfus, Shu Ha Ri)	Prioritization
Agile Manifesto values and principles	Facilitation methods	Problem-solving strategies, tools and techniques
Agile methods and approaches	Global, cultural, and team diversity	Process analysis
Agile project accounting principles	Incremental Delivery	Regulatory compliance
Agile project chartering	Knowledge Sharing / written communication	Self-assessment tools and techniques
Agile sizing and estimation	Leadership tools and techniques	Stakeholder management
Agile values and principles	Managing with agile KPIs	Training, coaching, and mentoring
Building agile teams	Participatory decision models (convergent, shared collaboration)	Value-based analysis and decomposition

What is Agile?

Agile is a philosophy that uses organizational models based on people, collaboration and shared values. The Agile Manifesto outlines tenets of agile philosophy. Agile uses rolling wave planning; iterative and incremental delivery; rapid and flexible response to change; and open communication between teams, stakeholders and customers. There are many agile methodologies that adhere to these tenets, such as Scrum, XP, Lean and Test-driven Development (TDD), etc.

Agile principles and practices are topics of growing importance in project management. Project management practitioners can use agile principles and practices to successfully manage change, improve communication, reduce cost, increase efficiency and demonstrate value to customers and stakeholders. Here are basic definitions for some common terms associated with agile principles and practices.

Introduction to Agile

Agile Manifesto is a philosophy about software development – a way of thinking.

Agile Methods are processes that support agile philosophy. Method or process is – a way of working.

Agile software development is NOT a specific process you can follow. Practices are an expression of underlying agile principles. Understand those 12 agile principles to choose the right practices. Agile methods combine practices in unique way, which supports agile philosophy.

Agility is more attitude than process, more environment than methodology.

Agile Practices are the "Activities that are the application of agile principles".

Agile Principles are the "Fundamental truths and shared values that drive behavior in agile methodologies".

Agile Methodologies are "Frameworks and processes whose practices support the Agile Manifesto principles". Examples include: SCRUM, XP, Crystal, DSDM, and FDD etc.

Agile Manifesto is a public declaration of the philosophy and principles of agile software development.

Where can you learn more about agile?

Visit the PMI web site for additional information on Agile Community of Practice.

Agile Project

An agile project is a project that is planned and executed based on tenets of Agile Manifesto. One of the best practices to execute long term agile projects is using sequential releases consisting of collections of iterations. Agile project is kicked off by at least 3 processes: vision, product roadmap and list of product backlogs. The interim phases in agile project are project releases. The release milestone deliverable is a working set of features. A release is made up of several iterations. The final process in agile project is project retrospective, which is equivalent to project postmortem resembling project closing process under traditional project management practices.

Agile project managers must be the champions of the agile process:

- Understands the principles of agile and seeks to encourage them within the team.
- Holds team accountable to seek anything and everything that adds value.
- Understands that a process needs to be continually re-evaluated and re-examined.
- Builds ownership in the process so that growth is more guidance than enforcement, moves from traditional management of "command-and-control" style to effective leadership with "servant leadership" style.
- Empowers continuous improvement in the product, process, team and self.

Agile Manifesto

This is very important section for PMI-ACP certification examination. You need to <u>remember all words</u> as are mentioned below. There will be multiple questions on this section, where the exam has multiple choices with twisted or wrong terms and just one with correct wording. Eliminate all those with wrong / incorrect / inappropriate order and you score 100% on these questions!!

- Individuals and Interactions <u>over</u> Processes and Tools
- Working Software <u>over</u> Comprehensive Documentation
- Customer Collaboration <u>over</u> Contract Negotiation
- Responding to Change <u>over</u> Following a Plan

Note: While there is value in the items on right, we value the items on left more

Key Point: Remember exact wording and sequence of all 4 above.

What is Agile Manifesto?

Agile Manifesto is a public declaration of the philosophy and principles of agile software development, created in February 2001 in Snowbird, Utah. Visit <u>http://www.AgileManifesto.org/</u> to learn more.

1. **Individuals and Interactions <u>over</u> Processes and Tools**
   Software Development Life Cycles are centered on people, processes and tools. The processes and tools are good and required. But there is a limit to what extent these tools should be used and processes must be followed. Ultimately projects are accomplished through people utilizing those tools and processes.

   Agile projects put heavy emphasis on the team work, thereby on the individuals and interaction between the individuals. The agile team will eventually tailor the processes and will use automated tools if needed. Agile methodologies will work with strong team and positive interaction which must be valued more than the fact that processes and tools may or may not add that much value.

2. **Working Software <u>over</u> Comprehensive Documentation**
   Traditional project management is plan driven. As per PMI PMBOK Fifth Edition, a project management plan consists of 16 subsidiary plan documents involving 10 knowledge areas and processes. All this leads to a very detailed comprehensive documentation which may or may not be needed or used at all.

   On the contrary agile strongly supports creating "barely sufficient" documentation but get the working, deliverable and shippable software. The working software must have self-documented code. The working software is what brings most value to the customers whereas the comprehensive documentation only shows what is intended to be delivered. For a customer the working software is more valuable than mere documentation.

3. **Customer Collaboration <u>over</u> Contract Negotiation**

   A contract is needed between customer and agile teams to have a positive starting point, whether it's in the form of contract statement of work (SOW), or project charter or requirements document. It is mainly to be used to collaborate with customers whenever there are variances and how best the differences can be resolved so that there will be always the product delivered to the customer which is desirable by the customer. Definitely there is a value in doing this.

   The contract document should not be used to negotiate on what is promised, what is delivered and why the customer can't make changes to the contract. The contract negotiation has a value to the extent that the deliverables are in accordance with initial contract. The customer collaboration brings more value by leading to win-win situation by making the customer collaboration in positive direction, acknowledging what the customer wants and working collaboratively to deliver those changes rather than fighting over what gets delivered is what the customer asked whether it carries values or not now. There is more value in delivering what the customer wishes and collaborating with customer at various stages such as planning meetings, reviews, product demos. The most valuable approach in agile is adapting ATDD – Acceptance Test Driven Development, whereby all increments are demonstrated to the customer and verified and accepted by the customer before the team moves forward to next iteration. Customer gets minimally marketable features (MMF) delivered at very short duration rather than waiting all the way to the end of project duration to get all deliverables, if at all those get delivered.

4. **Responding to Change <u>over</u> Following a Plan**

   Traditional project management makes a plan and then makes sure to follow that plan. Entire efforts are oriented towards following that plan to deliver as per requirements, no more and no less. In fact the terms like "gold plating" and "scope creep" are detrimental in following a plan. Plan driven project management doesn't advocate changes. There is a very rigorous process known as "integrated change control" to find impact of change on triple constraints and then approve/reject the change. There is a value in that the overall impact is assessed before actually implementing the approved change but it involves so many processes and updates to so many documentation that the value is lost in the process.

   Agile always and any time welcome changes. In fact the agile methodology implementation is done such that the agile team will adapt and change the strategies to implement the changes in the code or deliverables that will bring value to the customer. The relatively smaller iterations of deliverables under agile are all meant to take care the changes requested by the customers. The basic assumption is that the deliverables are subject to change and the customer is going to request to make changes to the products. Agile team acknowledges those changes the customer wants and works collaboratively to deliver those rather than fighting over on why these can't get delivered. There is more value in responding to changes and delivering what the customer wishes and collaborating with an openness of supporting "you will be happy if you get what you want with all desirable changes" attitude.

Agile Practices

Agile practices are the activities that are the application of agile principles. This is another very important section for PMI-ACP certification examination. There will be lots of questions on this section. You need to remember all roles and important concepts under

- XP
- SCRUM
- Lean

Key Point: Remember agile practices. Read books on SCRUM, XP, Lean and TDD listed under references.

What are some examples of agile principles and practices?

o Early, measurable return on investment (ROI) through defined, iterative delivery of product increments.
o High visibility of project progress allows early identification and resolution or monitoring of problems.
o Continuous involvement of the customer throughout the product development cycle.
o Empowerment of the business owner to make decisions needed to meet goals.
o Adaptation to changing business needs, giving more influence over requirement changes.
o Reduced product and process waste.
o Seek to manage change through flexibility, adaptation, and direct communication.
o Agile principles and practices are disciplined and value driven.
o Agile principles are different than practices.

Agile Principles

Agile principles are fundamental truths and shared values that drive behavior in agile methodologies. This is another very important section for PMI-ACP certification examination. You need to remember all words as are mentioned below. There will be multiple questions on this section, where the exam has multiple choices with twisted or wrong terms and just one with correct wording. Eliminate all those with wrong / incorrect / inappropriate order and you score 100% on these questions!!

Key Point: Remember exact wordings and meanings of all 12 agile principles.

- Our highest priority is <u>to satisfy the customer</u> through <u>early and continuous delivery of valuable software</u>.
- <u>Welcome changing requirements</u>, even late in development. Agile processes harness change for the customer's competitive advantage.
- <u>Deliver working software frequently</u>, from a couple of weeks to a couple of months, with a preference to the shorter timescale.
- Business people and developers <u>must work together daily</u> throughout the project.
- Build projects around <u>motivated individuals</u>. Give them the environment and support they need, and trust them to get the job done.
- The most efficient and effective method of conveying information to and within a development team is <u>face-to-face conversation.</u>
- <u>Working software</u> is the primary measure of progress.
- Agile processes promote sustainable development. The sponsors, developers, and users should be able to <u>maintain a constant pace</u> indefinitely.
- <u>Continuous attention</u> to technical excellence and good design enhances agility.
- <u>Simplicity</u>—the art of maximizing the amount of work not done—is essential.
- The best architectures, requirements, and designs <u>emerge from self-organizing teams</u>.
- At regular intervals, the team reflects on <u>how to become more effective,</u> then tunes and adjusts its behavior accordingly.

PRINCIPLE # 1
Our highest priority is <u>to satisfy the customer</u> through <u>early and continuous delivery of valuable software</u>.

Each and every word of this principle is very important from examination point of perspective. The agile team strives to deliver software that is valuable to the customer. The delivery has to be early, as soon as the increment (or piece of working software) is "done" and ready. The delivery must be continuous, with fixed frequency, in most cases after every 4 weeks or lesser. The delivery of valuable software should satisfy customer and this must be the highest priority of the agile team. Remember all these points.

PRINCIPLE # 2
<u>Welcome changing requirements</u>, even late in development. Agile processes harness change for the customer's competitive advantage.

This principle is completely different than what has been rigorously followed under traditional plan driven project management practices. The plan driven approach discourages the changes, especially towards late in development, tries to find root cause of the change and follows a process of integrated change control to assess the impact. Agile welcomes changing requirements at any stage of development, even late. The foundation of agile is to adapt to changes as quickly and as efficiently as possible. Agile teams will change their strategy and process to harness changes requested by the customer. The agile team understands that these requested changes in requirements are for the customer's competitive advantage and it is the most important thing customer wants to get as part of deliverable, preferably with minimum impact on cost, schedule and other constraints. Remember this principle and concept to answer questions in the examination by thinking differently.

PRINCIPLE # 3
Deliver working software frequently, from a couple of weeks to a couple of months, with a preference to the shorter timescale.

This principle is again completely different than what has been rigorously followed under traditional plan driven project management practices. The plan driven approach delivers the final product at the close of project or phase. Nothing gets delivered before that closing process and a customer may become skeptical or even nervous as to what gets delivered at the end.

The expectation from agile team is that they will deliver software. This is mainly to make sure that the product gets delivered and it might have come from past experiences where nothing got delivered at the closing of a project or phase by following traditional plan. The delivery must be of working software. What is the value of software that is non-working or works with caveats or even not fit for use? The agile team's responsibility is to deliver working software and that too verified / accepted by customer. There is maximum value if the delivery of working software is with fixed frequency, in most cases from couple of weeks to couple of months, typically after every 4 weeks or lesser. Customer preference is to the shorter timescale for shorter increments and shorter overall time to deliver shippable product. Remember this principle and concept to answer questions in the examination by thinking timescales, frequency of delivery to be shorter and most importantly the working software.

PRINCIPLE # 4
Business people and developers must work together daily throughout the project.

This principle is again completely different than what has been normally followed under traditional plan driven project management practices. Under the plan driven approach probably the developers will never see business people and won't be even talking or working together on the project. There is always a layer of architect or business analyst between developers and business people (or end users).

The expectation from agile team is that they will get the requirements from the business people right at the inception of the project or during project charter. The developers can ask direct questions to business people, get clarifications on issues, try to understand business rules and discuss face-to-face anything that needs further explanation from business. The gap between business people and developers is diminished and both parties feel confident as well as comfortable with each other. This also reduces the interpretation and incorrect assumptions on both sides.

The business people can see what the developers are doing, how the system is built, and at what pace the development is progressing. The business people feel much better that they are consulted and informed at major milestones during the project deliverables. The development community also feels good that their efforts are appreciated by real people and they are building a system which real people will be using and those business people are actually looking forward for the project deliverables. This provides mutual satisfaction and sense of responsibility for both parties.

In many organizations, it may not be possible to have the business people available to talk to developers on 24x7 bases. Normally the business people make themselves available on certain days at specific time, e.g. there will be a business-to-developer meeting every Monday from 2-3pm in conference room #2. There is no meeting invite or mandatory roll call. Whoever has doubts or needs further additional information from business show up at the meeting. Business people don't necessarily mean the end users or actual business stakeholders; it can be the representative from business unit or subject matter expert or spokesperson.

This principle is a new concept in project management and will reap many benefits if followed properly.

<u>PRINCIPLE # 5</u>
Build projects around <u>motivated individuals</u>. Give them the environment and support they need, and trust them to get the job done.

This principle is supplementing to what has been normally followed under traditional plan driven project management practices. Under the plan driven approach the projects are normally build around the iron triangle of scope, schedule and cost. Individuals are treated as a very small part of the entire project under human resource management and certain motivational theories are proposed to get the work done.

Under agile projects, everything is entrusted on the motivated individuals who will make the project successful. The material, tools, and other resources are useful only if these are used at maximum capacity by the motivated individuals. What is the use of very sophisticated tools and high tech material and advanced technology if the people who are going to use these are not motivated at all? Under new servant leadership style, these intelligent and motivated workers need an environment which will favor their imagination and will give faith and freedom to explore their fullest potential.

A full faith and trust is needed when a task is assigned to these motivated individuals. There may be some mentoring and coaching needed, but definitely any kind of macro and micro-management on what is being done on every hour is not tolerated. Assign the task, tell the expectations, discuss the challenges and leave it to the individual to accomplish the best way the person can achieve the end result. They don't need supervision; they need collaboration; working brain-to-brain and not even shoulder-to-shoulder.

PRINCIPLE # 6
The most efficient and effective method of conveying information to and within a development team is <u>face-to-face conversation.</u>

This principle is based on the reality and years of observation in normal plan driven project management. The usual way of communication used to be informing the manager about a problem, sometimes pointing fingers to other development units in the organization and many times assuming that the problem will get resolved by itself.

As a member of an agile team, everyone shares the responsibility of completing the tasks as a team. Everyone knows that it's a joint cohesive effort to convert the user stories into features which become part of big picture. There is a time box and no one can waste time unproductive. All the tasks need to be getting done within the team. No wonder face-to-face communication is the most effective and efficient method of exchanging information among the team members.

If there is a problem or there is something new that gets discovered, everyone in the team wants everyone else to be informed and involved in sharing the information. This can happen in the meetings, at the water cooler or in the war room. But the information is conveyed in-person face-to-face. This also brings some sort of brainstorming and forming of the high performance teams. Everyone knows what everyone else knows and there are no hidden secrets. Everyone is sharing the knowledge they possess.

There are challenges in face-to-face conversation such as tone, language, presentation, content and repetition. However at technical level, the development team understands the language of coding and any kind of drawbacks in the face-to-face communications are ignored. That's why the most efficient and effective method of conveying information to and within a development team is face-to-face communication.

PRINCIPLE # 7
<u>Working software</u> is the primary measure of progress.

This principle is again completely different than what has been normally followed under traditional plan driven project management practices. Under the plan driven approach the documentation and the PM plan are primarily focused. It advocates that first lay down the solid rails (or permanent paths) and then drive your project on this well-defined railroad (or paths). If this approach is followed, then automatically the end product will be your working software or application or system.

In reality the plan driven approach spends so much time and energy that the main objective of delivering something gets side tracked. That's why the agile methodology reminds all to think of the end product and always deliver something which is working. The progress is measured not on how many documents are prepared and how perfect those are, but how much working software is delivered at the end of every day / iteration / sprint.

This is almost like a lawn mower boy giving you all the information, probably 50 pages document about grass height, temperature, sun shine, best time to cut the grass, angle of blades etc. but ultimately you are looking at whether the grass is cut or not. The product owner and stakeholders are more interested in seeing the working software rather than those thick binders of documentation and PM plans with 16 sub plans.

This is a radical change in the outlook of what needs to be delivered verses what needs to be prepared for delivery. Hopefully the agile teams will understand this principle in the right perspective and keep delivering working software to show the progress and allow them to be measured that way.

PRINCIPLE # 8
Agile processes promote sustainable development. The sponsors, developers, and users should be able to <u>maintain a constant pace</u> indefinitely.

This principle is supplementing to what has been normally followed under traditional plan driven project management practices. Under the plan driven approach the projects are normally executed, monitored and controlled so that the project deliverables are on track and many times are brought back in case any kind of variance is observed.

The agile processes promote sustainable development, there are no ups and down, no too high and too lows, no peaks and valleys. This is normally achieved by keeping the velocity constant, turning the user stories into deliverables at same speed and ensuring resource levelling so that nobody gets over-burdened and tired.

It's the responsibility of sponsors, developers and users to maintain a constant pace indefinitely. Nobody wants to work for 60-80 hours per week in consecutive weeks. This burns out the development teams; they get exhausted and loose the tempo of good work. Over exertion also brings fatigue and unproductive nature in the development. Team members can't concentrate on the work and loose the grip on the project.

The sponsors should not bring in too many changes, the developers should not take too many challenges and users should not put extra pressure on development efforts. All are supposed to keep and maintain a constant pace in the best interest to deliver working software meeting all requirements of users and meeting expectations of sponsors. The word indefinitely here means till the end of project.

PRINCIPLE # 9
Continuous attention to technical excellence and good design enhances agility.

This principle is based on the reality and years of observation in normal plan driven project management. In plan driven project management, perhaps this factor of technical excellence and good design was lost somewhere in the documentation.

The development team is responsible to pay close and continuous attention to technical excellence. The person who is doing the work is the best judge of the work done and knows what needs to be done to make it better and best. As member of agile team, everyone is responsible to pay continuous attention to technical details of the working software. There are many techniques like refactoring, pair programming, frequent validation which can definitely bring the technical excellence. The agile team members must be on constant lookout for technical advancements and new tools and new versions in technology. They must not be afraid to do prototyping to implement these excellent methods into their working software.

Design is the blue print of the final product. Improving the design and making enhancements to the design will eventually lead to excellent final product. The agile team members must always pay continuous attention to incorporate good design and make improvements to the design to make it better.

PRINCIPLE # 10
Simplicity—the art of maximizing the amount of work not done—is essential.

This principle is supplementing to what has been normally followed under traditional plan driven project management practices. Under the plan driven approach the projects are normally executed, monitored and controlled so that there is no scope creep and no gold plating.

Under agile approach, instead of saying that do what is important; it's better to say that don't do anything that is not needed. This way you will do only what is needed. This is called as the art of maximizing the amount of work not done. In traditional plan driven, nothing gets delivered if it's not in the WBS or work package. The plan driven approach always said – deliver what is there in the scope baseline – nothing less and nothing more.

Agile approach goes one step further and insists that it is absolutely essential to maximize the amount of work not done. Everything has to be done well done. Don't leave anything which is half way done or you would like to come back to that later or you think that it may be useful some other time in future. In common language, don't create clutter and clear the clutter if any. This brings unproductive work and need to be removed. The agile team makes it simple by not creating anything that is not needed in the first place.

PRINCIPLE # 11
The best architectures, requirements, and designs <u>emerge from self-organizing teams</u>.

This principle is supplementing to what has been normally followed under traditional plan driven project management practices. Under the plan driven approach the requirements comes from stakeholders and/or end users. The architecture is built based upon those requirements by experienced architects and design is also made by those data designers and/or architects. This is all subject to interpretations and assumptions.

The best architectures, requirements, and designs emerge from self-organizing teams. These teams know ins-and-outs of the final delivers and live the life of project. That's the reason why the person who is doing the job can make it the best and nobody else can do that. There is motivation and self-organization to do the best in what you are doing. This brings satisfaction, pride and ownership which are traits of any self-organizing team. The best always comes from the self-organizing teams.

PRINCIPLE # 12
At regular intervals, the team reflects on <u>how to become more effective,</u> then tunes and adjusts its behavior accordingly.

This principle is supplementing to what has been normally followed under traditional plan driven project management practices. Under the plan driven approach the projects are normally undergoing changes outlined in (PIP) process improvement plan.

The agile team follows the approach of rugby game. At any given interval, the team takes a snapshot, examines it very carefully and decides on strategies for improvements. In many organizations, during the retrospective meetings, the team lists what was done right and what was done wrong and how can this be improved. After that the team selects one area and vows to be better in that area going forward. This can be reporting, communication, inspection or anything that needs improvements. This may come from the knowledge about removing impediments.

In the next retrospective, the team again uses the magnifying glass to inspect on what went wrong or pick up the last area of improvement and critically do self-evaluation on whether it is really getting improved. Doing this in every retrospective meeting brings that regular interval of self-evaluation. Since the team is doing this, they reflect on how to become more effective and nobody external to them is enforcing any kind of behavior changes. The team tunes and adjusts themselves in the pursuit of excellence. This brings self-improvement, team improvement and thereby process improvement and overall improvement to the project. This is almost like Dr. Deming's dream comes true on continuous process improvement.

Agile Methodologies

Agile methodologies are frameworks and processes whose practices support Agile Manifesto principles. Examples include: Scrum, Extreme Programming XP), Crystal, Dynamic Systems Development Method (DSDM), Feature Driven Development (FDD) etc. This is another very important section for PMI-ACP certification examination. There will be lots of questions on this section. You need to remember all roles and important concepts under following agile methodologies which are listed here in order of importance:

- XP (eXtreme Programming)
- SCRUM
- Lean Software Development
- Crystal
- DSDM (Dynamic Systems Development Method)
- FDD (Feature Driven Development)
- KANBAN

Key Point: The traditional plan-driven project management processes describe "what should be done during the management of a project". Agile methodologies describe "how to do the things that should be done" – in short, "what" versus "how".

SCRUM: Scrum is a lightweight management framework with broad applicability for managing iterative and incremental projects of all types. Over the last few years in particular, Scrum has garnered increasing popularity in the software community due to its simplicity, proven success and improved productivity, and its ability to act as a wrapper for various engineering practices promoted by other agile methodologies.

XP (eXtreme Programming): XP has emerged as one of the more popular and controversial agile methods. XP is a disciplined approach to delivering high-quality software quickly and continuously. It promotes high customer involvement, rapid feedback loops, continuous testing, continuous planning, and close teamwork to deliver working software at very frequent intervals, typically every 1-3 week.

The original XP recipe is based on four simple values – simplicity, communication, feedback, and courage – and twelve supporting practices: Planning Game, Small Releases, Customer Acceptance Tests, Simple Design, Pair Programming, Test-Driven Development, Refactoring, Continuous Integration, Collective Code Ownership, Coding Standards, Metaphor and Sustainable Pace.

CRYSTAL: The Crystal methodology is one of the most lightweight, adaptable approaches to software development. Crystal is actually comprised of a family of methodologies (Crystal Clear, Crystal Yellow, Crystal Orange, etc.) whose unique characteristics are driven by several factors such as team size, system criticality, and project priorities. This Crystal family addresses the realization that each project may require a slightly tailored set of policies, practices, and processes in order to meet the project's unique characteristics.

DSDM (Dynamic Systems Development Method): DSDM grew out of the need to provide an industry standard project delivery framework for what was referred to as Rapid Application Development (RAD) at the time. DSDM methodology has evolved and matured to provide a comprehensive foundation for planning, managing, executing, and scaling agile and iterative software development projects.

DSDM is based on nine key principles that primarily revolve around business needs/value, active user involvement, empowered teams, frequent delivery, integrated testing, and stakeholder collaboration. DSDM specifically calls out "fitness for business purpose" as the primary criteria for delivery and acceptance of a system, focusing on the useful 80% of the system that can be deployed in 20% of the time.

FDD (Feature Driven Development): FDD is a model-driven, short-iteration process. It begins with establishing an overall model shape. Then it continues with a series of two-week "design by feature, build by feature" iterations. The features are small, "useful in the eyes of the client" results.

FDD designs the rest of the development process around feature delivery using the following eight practices: Domain Object Modeling, Developing by Feature, Component/Class Ownership, Feature Teams, Inspections, Configuration Management, Regular Builds, Visibility of Progress and Results.

Lean Software Development: Lean Software Development is an iterative methodology and owes much of its principles and practices to the Lean Enterprise movement and the practices of companies like Toyota. Lean Software Development focuses the team on delivering value to the customer, and on the efficiency of the "Value Stream," the mechanisms that deliver that value. The main principles of Lean include Eliminating Waste, Amplifying Learning, Deciding as Late as Possible, Delivering as Fast as Possible, Empowering the Team, Building Integrity In, and Seeing the Whole.

Lean eliminates waste by selecting only the truly valuable features for a system, prioritizing those selected, and delivering them in small batches. It emphasizes the speed and efficiency of development workflow, and relies on rapid and reliable feedback between programmers and customers.

KANBAN: Kanban as applied to software development is a pull-based planning and execution method. Rather than planning work items up front and pushing them into the work queue of a team, the team signals when they are ready for more work and pull it into their queue.

Kanban historically uses cards to signal the need for an item. For software development teams, these cards are kept on a Kanban Board which is organized into columns and rows. The columns represent the different states of a work item, from initial planning through customer acceptance. The specific columns a team uses should meet the needs of the team and be tailored to their context. The rows on the Kanban Board represent work items. Work items are sometimes grouped within areas, such as feature sets and category types.

Kanban focuses on maximizing the throughput of a team. One of the ways it achieves this goal is through the application of Work-in-Process (WIP) limits in each of the states of a work item. Under a Kanban (or Lean) approach, queues or inventories of work in any state are seen as waste. The WIP limits enable a team to focus on the optimal flow of work items through the system, minimizing any associated waste. Kanban allows teams to achieve process optimizations while respecting and maintaining a sustainable pace.

Agile Project Management

Successfully developing software is more than simply creating a plan and then attempting to follow it. Agile project management is something you do in practice and then adjust your approach based on experience rather than theory.

Under agile project management, we can't assume that we are able to perfectly describe in details every aspect of our product before building anything. However we definitely know that things will change as we progress throughout the development cycle, and treat changes as part of successful path. Whatever we deliver will not be sufficient – the customer always needs something more than delivered.

The traditional plan-driven project management processes describe "what should be done during the management of a project". Agile methodologies describe "how to do the things that should be done" – in short, "what" versus "how". The approaches defined in the PMBOK Guide – Fifth Edition and in agile are compatible. Agile can be used together with the PMBOK Guide – Fifth Edition because the "how" can be layered on top of the "what". It is up to the project manager to determine which principles and practices to apply to any specific project.

Key Point: Understand how Agile Project Management and agile principles & practices compare to PMBOK Guide – Fifth Edition process groups and how agile can be adopted on top of conventional project management practices and processes as follows:

- The project management principles recommended by the PMBOK Guide – Fifth Edition starts with processes associated with Initiating the project, followed by process groups for Planning, then a recursive cycle of processes for Executing and Controlling & Monitoring while revisiting Planning as necessary. At the end of the project are processes for Closing.
- Agile methodologies start with developing a Product Vision (which corresponds with Initiating); followed by development and prioritization of user stories (which correspond to

Planning); followed by a series of sprint or iterative cycles and reviews (which corresponds to Executing, Control & Monitoring, and Planning); followed by Product Delivery (which corresponds to project Closing).

- While the phases of agile model correspond well to the PMBOK Guide – Fifth Edition process groups, the difference is that each agile sprint or iteration cycle includes the creation of a limited number of product features or components which are completed before proceeding to the next iteration. Therefore, a project managed according to agile principles and practices will have multiple iterations while a project based on the PMBOK Guide – Fifth Edition has only one.

How are agile principles and practices different from waterfall principles and practices?

Agile principles and practices seek to manage change through flexibility, adaptation and direct communication. Waterfall principles and practices, often referred to simply as "waterfall," are sequential, phase-driven project management approaches where each phase must be planned and completed before further work can progress.

Agile principles and practices are suited to projects which require a nimble response to change and continual communication to customers.

Waterfall principles and practices are suited to projects where little to no change in requirements is expected, and where requirements are clear and well-understood by all team members.

Agile principles and practices can be adapted to suit organizations and industries that follow waterfall principles and practices. Agile and waterfall principles and practices are not mutually exclusive - some organizations apply elements of both principles and practices. However, it important to know that not all organizations lend themselves to agile principles and practices.

How are agile principles and practices different from Unified Process principles and practices?

Iterative

The software development process using the iterative approach is mainly based on the component-driven architecture (CDA) or model-driven architecture (MDA). Many organizations used the proprietary Rational Unified Process (RUP) or still continue to use open source Open Unified Process (Open UP) to achieve iterative software development.

Iterative and Incremental

The approach of implementing a work product in successive pieces (increments), while also gradually refining the work product through targeted improvements (iterations). This approach is used for agile project management (ALM – Agile Lifecycle Management).

Agile References

PMI Website

For latest information on PMI – ACP Certification, always refer to official PMI website. http://www.pmi.org/certification/agile-management-acp.aspx

Sample Practice Examination on Chapter I Introduction to Agile

Q1: PMI-ACP certification examination will consist of how many total questions?

A. 175+25
B. 80+20
C. 100+20
D. Variable

Q2: Which is NOT one of the clauses under Agile manifesto?

A. Processes and Tools <u>over</u> Individuals and Interactions
B. Working Software <u>over</u> Comprehensive Documentation
C. Customer Collaboration <u>over</u> Contract Negotiations
D. Responding to Change <u>over</u> Following a Plan

Q3: Agile Manifesto is a public declaration of the philosophy and principles of agile software development. Which statement is true as per this declaration, created in February 2001 in Snobird, Utah?

A. While there is value in the items on left, we value the items on right more.
B. While there is value in the items on right, we value the items on left more.
C. While there is value in the items on left, we value the items on right equally.
D. While there is value in the items on right, we value the items on left equally.

Q4: Agile methodologies can be best described as following closely the:

A. Sequential and overlapping
B. Iterative and unified
C. Adaptive and change-based
D. None of above

Q5: The following may NOT be best suited for Agile practices

    A. XP

    B. SCRUM

    C. Waterfall

    D. Lean

Q6: One of the most popular Agile practices is XP. What does XP stand for?

    A. XP is powerful Microsoft Operating System

    B. XP means eXtremely Powerful methodology

    C. There is no long form for XP just like SCRUM.

    D. XP means eXtreme Programming

Q7: PMI-ACP certification examination considers how many agile principles?

    A. 25

    B. 20

    C. 12

    D. Not sure

Q8: One of the most popular Agile principle (principle #2) states that:

    A. Welcome changing requirements, always at beginning in development.

    B. Welcome changing requirements, even late in development.

    C. Welcome changing requirements, anytime in development.

    D. Welcome changing requirements, by anybody in development.

Q9: One of the most popular Agile principles (principle #3) states that:

    A. Deliver working software, at beginning in development.

    B. Deliver working software, at end of development.

    C. Deliver working software, anytime in development.

    D. Deliver working software, frequently.

Q10: One of the most popular Agile principles (principle #4) states that:

    A. Business people and developers must work together daily throughout the project.

    B. Business people and developers must work together weekly throughout the project.

    C. Business people and developers must work together monthly throughout the project.

    D. Business people and developers must work together frequently throughout the project.

Q11: One of the most popular Agile principles (principle #5) states that:

    A. Build projects around powerful individuals.

B. Build projects around motivated individuals.

C. Build projects around empowered individuals.

D. Build projects around intellectual individuals.

Q12: One of the most popular Agile principle (principle #6) states that the most efficient and effective method of conveying information to and within a development team is

A. Facebook.

B. IM (Instant Messaging).

C. Social Networking.

D. Face-to-face conversation.

Q13: One of the most popular Agile principles (principle #7) states that:

A. Working software is the primary measure of progress.

B. Value-driven software is the primary measure of progress.

C. Best software is the primary measure of progress.

D. User Accepted software is the primary measure of progress.

Q14: One of the most popular Agile principles (principle #8) states that agile processes promote sustainable development. The sponsors, developers, and users should be able to maintain a

A. Fast pace indefinitely.

B. Constant pace indefinitely.

C. Steady pace indefinitely.

D. Consistent pace indefinitely.

Q15: One of the most popular Agile principles (principle #10) states that Simplicity is essential. Simplicity is

A. The art of minimizing the amount of work done

B. The art of maximizing the amount of work done

C. The art of minimizing the amount of work not done

D. The art of maximizing the amount of work not done

Q16: An agile project is a project that is planned and executed based on the

A. Guidelines provided by PMI-ACP

B. Guidelines provided by PMBOK 5th Edition

C. Tenets of the Agile Manifesto

D. Agile principles and methodologies

Q17: Kanban as applied to software development is a _____ planning and execution method. Rather than planning work items up front into the work queue of a team, the team signals when they are ready for more work.

 A. Pull-based
 B. Push-based
 C. Interactive
 D. Lean

Q18: The approach of implementing a work product in successive pieces (increments), while also gradually refining the work product through targeted improvements (iterations). This approach is used for agile project management and is commonly known as _____.

 A. AMDD – Agile Model Driven Development
 B. ALM – Agile Lifecycle Management
 C. APM – Agile Project Management
 D. AUP – Agile Unified Process

Q19: Kanban focuses on maximizing the throughput of a team. One of the ways it achieves this goal is through the application of WIP limits in each of the states of a work item. Under a Kanban (or Lean) approach, queues or inventories of work in any state are seen as waste. The WIP limits enable a team to focus on the optimal flow of work items through the system, minimizing any associated waste. What is WIP under Kanban?

 A. Work-In-Production
 B. Work-In-Procedure
 C. Work-In-Process
 D. Work-In-Phase

Q20: FDD is a model-driven, short-iteration process. It begins with establishing an overall model shape. Then it continues with a series of two-week "design and build" iterations. What is FDD?

 A. Focus Driven Development
 B. Feature Driven Development
 C. Function Driven Development
 D. Framework Driven Development

Answers:

Q1: C (As per PMI, the PMI-ACP examination consists of total 120 questions, out of which 100 are scored and 20 are not).

Q2: A (As per Agile Manifesto, Individuals and Interactions <u>over</u> Processes and Tools)

Q3: B (The original Agile Manifesto states that while there is value in the items on right, we value the items on left more.)

Q4: C (Agile methodologies can be best described as following closely the adaptive and change-based).

Q5: C (Out of all options, the waterfall lifecycle may NOT be best suited for Agile practices).

Q6: D (XP means eXtreme Programming)

Q7: C (PMI-ACP certification examination considers 12 agile principles)

Q8: B (Agile principle #2 states that Welcome changing requirements, even late in development).

Q9: D (Agile principle #3 states that Deliver working software, frequently, from a couple of weeks to a couple of months, with a preference to the shorter timescale).

Q10: A (Agile principle #4 states that Business people and developers must work together daily throughout the project)

Q11: B (Agile principle #5 states that Build projects around motivated individuals.)

Q12: D (One of the most popular Agile principle #6 states that the most efficient and effective method of conveying information to and within a development team is face-to-face conversation)

Q13: A (One of the most popular Agile principle #7 states that Working software is the primary measure of progress).

Q14: B (One of the most popular Agile principle #8 states that agile processes promote sustainable development. The sponsors, developers, and users should be able to maintain a constant pace indefinitely.

Q15: D (One of the most popular Agile principle #10 states that Simplicity is essential. Simplicity is the art of maximizing the amount of work not done, or not required to be done)

Q16: C (An agile project is a project that is planned and executed based on the tenets of the Agile Manifesto)

Q17: A (Kanban as applied to software development is a pull-based planning and execution method. Rather than planning work items up front and pushing them into the work queue of a team, the team signals when they are ready for more work and pull it into their queue.)

Q18: B (The approach of implementing a work product in successive pieces (increments), while also gradually refining the work product through targeted improvements (iterations). This approach is used for agile project management and is commonly known as ALM – Agile Lifecycle Management.)

Q19: C (Kanban focuses on maximizing the throughput of a team. One of the ways it achieves this goal is through the application of Work-in-Process (WIP) limits in each of the states of a work item. Under a Kanban (or Lean) approach, queues or inventories of work in any state are seen as waste. The WIP limits enable a team to focus on the optimal flow of work items through the system, minimizing any associated waste. WIP stands for Work-In-Process under Kanban)

Q20: B (FDD is a model-driven, short-iteration process. It begins with establishing an overall model shape. Then it continues with a series of two-week "design by feature, build by feature" iterations. This is Feature Driven Development)

PART II

Overview: PMI-ACP Tools and Techniques

CHAPTER TWO

Agile Analysis And Design

This chapter covers the following tools and techniques used under "Agile Analysis and Design" Toolkit:

- ➤ **Product Roadmap**
- ➤ **User Stories/backlog**
- ➤ **Story Maps**
- ➤ **Progressive Elaboration**
- ➤ **Wireframes**
- ➤ **Chartering**
- ➤ **Personas**
- ➤ **Agile Modeling**
- ➤ **Workshops**
- ➤ **Learning Cycle**
- ➤ **Collaboration Games**

Agile A&D is the process where the agile teams analyzes the product backlog and designs the solution using certain tools and techniques such as agile modeling, story maps, wireframes, personas etc.

Traditional Analysis and Design phase under waterfall model undertakes the task of analyzing requirements and designing the system with either procedural approach with Component Driven Architecture (CDA) or object oriented approach with Model Driven Architecture (MDA). Agile analysis and design covers agile modeling thereby analyzing the Product Backlog, prioritizing the backlog items, creating story maps and progressively elaborating the product design. Agile A&D supports Service Oriented Architecture (SOA) and also adaptive /change-driven methodology.

Product Roadmap

Product roadmap is the holistic view of product features that create the product vision. The product vision describes the goals for the product and its alignment with the company's strategy. Product Owner of scrum team creates and owns both the vision and product roadmap. The product vision is done at least once in a year whereas the product roadmap is done at least twice in a year.

Product Roadmap planning is one of the processes that is kicked off during agile project planning. Product roadmap is used to categorize requirements, to prioritize them, and to determine a timetable (schedule) for their release.

The five levels of Agile Project Planning are:

- ❖ Vision
- ❖ Product Roadmap
- ❖ Release Planning
- ❖ Iteration Planning and
- ❖ Daily Stand-up meetings.

Product Roadmap is at the second level out of the above mentioned five levels. This is equivalent to PMBOK's "Develop Project Charter" and "Define Scope".

What does the Product Roadmap depict?

- The evolution of the product over time (say over next 3 to 4 releases).
- The definition of what each release "chunk" will look like (high level representation of what features or themes to be delivered in each release).
- The estimate on a timeframe for each release delivery (some calendar time, typically quarters).
- The list of customer targeted features.
- The architecture needed to support the features.
- The business value that the release is expected to meet.

Who is responsible for Revision of Product Roadmap?

Customer or product manager, agile project manager, architect, and executive management meet 2 to 3 time a year to collaborate on the development and revision of product roadmap. Because priorities and values can change, the product roadmap will get updated throughout the project.

The customer has the ownership of Product Roadmap. In many projects the customer is the primary product owner.

User Stories / Backlog

A clear and most effective format to define product requirements is the user story. While the collection of requirements can be called as "backlog" in agile, each requirement can be defined by "user story". The features are estimated at gross level in product backlog. Agile user stories are short descriptions of features; the customer wants and values most. A prioritized, estimated product backlog becomes an input to release planning. The agile PMO is responsible for product backlog control by looking across multiple backlogs across multiple projects.

Why are User Stories written usually on a small index card?

- Goal is not to get into all explicit details at the beginning.
- Write down few key words to capture spirit of the feature
- Why user stories are in short definitions?
  - o Neither sure when the feature will be needed nor whether the feature will be ever or even be needed.
  - o To save time and energy in writing details and redo later (or worst abandon it totally), thereby limiting waste of time and resources.
  - o Defer diving into lower-level details until needed and possibly after directional elaboration has deepened.

Give me an example of User Story?

Student logs in with expired account.

- Validation	- Screen Shots
- Error Checking	- Business Rules
- Terms & Definitions	- Security Requirements

What are the elements of good User Stories?

- It's something of value to the customers.
- It goes from end to end ("slices the cake")
- Remember ***INVEST***

(Independent, Negotiable, Valuable, Estimatable, Small and Testable)

What User Story Template can be used?

As a <type of user>	who	is this story for
I want <some goal>	what	they want to do
So that <some reason>	why	they want to do

What is the difference between User Story and Use Case?

Typically a User Story is written under Agile Projects whereas Use Case is written under projects following Unified Process. User Cases provide written communication, User Story promotes team collaboration.

Use case is more elaborate, good for written communication and there is no restriction on write-up content or length of write-up.

User stories are short due to a simplicity restriction encouraging team collaboration. The restriction is placed so that there will be more verbal communication among team members in developing feature based on the User Story. Not everything is clear / included in the User Story. Keeping the use story simple and brief, promotes team communication and collaboration.

Backlog:

Product Backlog: A product backlog is a list of items to be implemented in the product. Product backlog definition is one of the processes that are kicked off during agile project planning. There is no formal process of requirements gathering under agile project management. Requirements are gathered as user stories. User stories under XP are almost equivalent to product backlogs under SCRUM.

Iteration Backlog: An updated iteration backlog is produced by the agile team while working on its features during the iteration. The iteration backlog provides list of tasks to be performed by individual team member on daily basis and also provides how many hours to complete each task. Adding, removing, and updating tasks are the responsibilities of each agile team member. If one team member is allocated more than 40 hours in a week, another team member self-assigns for over-allocated tasks. A feature deferred under iteration planning is put back on the product backlog.

The product backlog must be updated by the product owner to reflect any changes made during the iteration.

Product backlogs are entered for new features / functionalities / requirements. Defect Backlogs are entered for the bugs, defects, issues, changes, or enhancements.

Story Maps

Story Maps are used to get a bigger picture through a high level overview. Story maps enable the team members to obtain considerable insight in their collaborative efforts on each user story.

Story mapping is a way to organize numerous small stories to portray a bigger vision to depict the software and system. The user story map provides a useful tool for the entire team to **understand the big picture** to see the entire breadth of the system and its diverse set of users and uses.

How does a "user story map" arrange user stories into a useful model?

- to help understand the functionality of the system,
- identify holes and omissions in the backlog, and
- effectively plan holistic releases that deliver value to users and to the business with each release
- The story map works just like a physical geographical map allowing one to quickly find a "place" in the system's process flow where the specific story you're working on is located.
- Each Story Map may affix an EPIC of User Stories to represent a large piece of functionality.

Progressive Elaboration

Progressive Elaboration is what happens in the rolling wave planning process. Progressive Elaboration means that over time the team's knowledge manifests to support more elaborate detail in the **work packages**. It may further contribute to the team's work velocity definition. The features in product backlog are estimated at gross level, with no detail tasks or resources. During iteration, features slated for that iteration and only for that iteration, are elaborated into tasks representing development plan for the feature. This is just-in-time elaboration. The PMBOK supports this idea of "rolling wave planning".

Rolling wave planning is the process of planning a project in waves (phases) as the project progresses and things (like mappings, features, contents, and team interplay) become clearer.

Initially the team can see clearly what is in close proximity, but looking further ahead our vision is less clear. Depending upon the project - its length and complexity - we may be able to plan as much as a few weeks or even a few months in advance with a fair amount of clarity.

Rolling Wave Planning is a multi-step, intermittent process like waves - because we cannot provide the details very far out in our planning. A detailed, well-defined **WBS** is created for that period of clarity, and only milestones are highlighted for the rest of the project. The agile approach advocates not to spend time doing "excessive decomposition" until it's ready to work on.

What is the approach used in Progressive Planning?

- Planning is an iterative process.
- It's difficult to do detail planning of a project in the beginning because things change so often.

- As the project evolves, and more specific and accurate details are available, the planning gets more detailed.
- The ability to plan, manage, and control the work is enhanced.
- With each successive iteration of the planning process, the project plan becomes more elaborate and complete.
- This approach to planning is known as Progressive Elaboration.
- Some projects only plan for 2 iterations, the current one and next one.

Wireframes

The main focus lies in functionality, behavior, and priority of content.

In other words, it focuses on "what a screen does, not what it looks like."

Aside from websites, wireframes are utilized for the prototyping of mobile sites, computer applications, or other screen-based products that involve human-computer interaction.

What does the Wireframes focus on?

- The kinds of information displayed
- Wireframes signify a "bare bones" aesthetic
- The range of functions available
- The relative priorities of the information and functions
- The rules for displaying certain kinds of information
- The effect of different scenarios on the display

Uses of wireframes

Wireframes may be utilized by different disciplines.

- Developers use wireframes to get a more tangible grasp of the site's functionality,
- Designers use them to push the user interface (UI) process.
- User experience designers and information architects use wireframes to show navigation paths between pages.
- Business stakeholders use wireframes to ensure that requirements and objectives are met through the design and track functioning completeness.
- Other professionals who create wireframes include business analysts, information architects, interaction designers, user experience designers, graphic designers, programmers, and product managers.

Chartering

The project charter is a formal document used to justify, explain, define, and ultimately authorize a project.

Two ways to develop project charter in agile:

- Continue along traditional route of preparing paperwork to gather support and get approval.
- Barely sufficient is just good enough.

A useful project charter contains three key elements:

1. **Vision:** The vision defines the "Why" of the project. This is the higher purpose, or the reason for the project's existence.
2. **Mission:** This is the "What" of the project and it states what will be done in the project to achieve its higher purpose.
3. **Success Criteria:** The success criteria are management tests that describe effects outside of the solution itself.

Personas

A **persona**, in the word's everyday usage, is a role or a character played by an actor. Persona is a fictional character that is created to represent the attributes of a group of the product's users. Personas are helpful tools to use as a guide when deciding on a product's features, functionality, or visual design. The agile team can identify possible end users of the product.

Personas can be described as the various roles played in the agile projects and what are their responsibilities and what are their expectations?

Why are Personas used in agile projects?

- Personas are good for getting to know your customers.
- Personas provide descriptions of the people who are going to use your systems.
- Just like Actor under traditional Use Cases.
- Think of a persona as a character in a book or movie.
- They help bring some personality to the system.
- These are real people, with real problems, and system is expected to meet their needs.
- Support user story alignment to vision and reduce rework.

Agile Modeling

Agile Modeling (AM) is a practice-based methodology for effective modeling and documentation of software-based systems. Communication, simplicity, feedback, and courage are the four Values of Agile Modeling.

Simply, Agile Modeling (AM) is a collection of values, principles, and practices for modeling software that can be applied on a software development project in an effective and light-weight manner.

What are the four values of agile modeling?

- Communication: Typical agile practices such as pair programming (two programmers collaborating), estimating tasks, and unit testing rely heavily on good communication.
- Simplicity: Simplicity for software development means that we will begin with the simplest possible thing we can do. We don't become overwhelmed with the complexity and bigness of the task. It is commonly said that "you cannot run until you know how to walk and you cannot walk until you know how to stand".
- Feedback: Feedback is the third basic value that is important. Good and concrete feedback that is useful to the programmer, analyst, and customer can occur within seconds, minutes, days, weeks, or months, depending on what is needed, who is communicating, and what will be done with the feedback.
- Courage: Courage is the fourth value enunciated in agile programming. The value of courage has to do with a level of trust and comfort that must exist in the development team. It means not being afraid to throw out an afternoon or a day of programming and begin again if all is not right. Courage means being able to stay in touch with one's instincts (and test results) concerning what is working and what is not. Courage is a high-risk, high-reward value that encourages experimentation that can take the team to its goal more rapidly, in an innovative way.

How to do Agile Modeling?

- AM is meant to be tailored into other, full-fledged methodologies such as XP or RUP, to develop a software process which truly meets project needs.
- With an Agile Model Driven Development (AMDD) approach you typically do just enough high-level modeling at the beginning of a project to understand the scope and potential architecture of the system,
- Then during development iterations you do modeling as part of your iteration planning activities and take a just in time (JIT) model storming approach where you model for several minutes as a precursor to several hours of coding.

Workshops

WORKSHOPS, TRAINING AND SEMINARS

In traditional courses, people listen to the presenter without interrupting. More and more, this approach is giving way to a much more dynamic and stimulating group learning process. This may involve a workshop, training session or seminar. The trend in learning activities is now for people to interact with their peers. People share what they know. People discuss things. People benefit from each other's views and experiences. A presenter no longer leads these meetings. A facilitator does. The facilitator's mandate is to guide the various activities and discussions throughout the event. Several knowledge-sharing methods can be used in a seminar, training session or workshop. These methods can be tailored to your needs.

Learning cycle

Agile teams strive to deliver functionality that can be touched or even used by the customer at the end of the first iteration. Sometimes, however, it does make sense for the team to focus on building its foundation before delivering functionality. This may be the case for larger applications, for teams new to agile development, or for projects where the features are still extremely fuzzy. These are perfect opportunities to execute an iteration zero.

An iteration zero does not deliver any functionality to the customer. Instead, the project team focuses on the simple processes that will be required for the adoption and use of most agile practices. From a programming point of view the features delivered in an iteration zero may include:

- Source control system installed and operational
- Initial build script written and checked into source control
- Initial promotion and deployment scripts written and checked into source control
- Automated test framework selected and implemented with an empty test suite
- Construction of a rudimentary continuous integration process

Collaboration Games

Innovation Games are powerful qualitative research and problem solving techniques focused on the use of collaborative play with customers, colleagues, partners and the community at large. Used both in-person and online. The techniques include both open-ended and more focused methods for achieving actionable insights and results.

What are the 13 games invented by Luke Hohmann?

- Buy a Feature
- Give Them a Hot Tub
- Me and My Shadow
- Product Box
- Prune the Product Tree
- Remember the Future
- Show and Tell
- Speed Boat
- Spider Web
- Start Your Day
- The Apprentice
- New Game: "My Worst Nightmare", which was just introduced in 2010.

Regardless of how the games are used, one can apply a very standard approach consistently to ensure a quality result. The basic process in using these innovative games includes planning, playing, processing, and acting. Each game is useful in solving problems under specific scenarios. The author, Luke Hohmann, encourage the teams to learn about each of the games and to consider how they might best be applied to agile project situation either individually or collectively. Please visit the website to do so: http://innovationgames.com/resources/the-games/

The two most commonly used innovative games under agile are "buy a feature" and "product box". In the "buy a feature" game, the team can decide which features will bring more value by evaluating its cost versus benefits. This game is similar to the very popular game of monopoly. In the "product box" game, the team takes pride in designing the logo, slogan, three important features and three important selling points.

SUMMARY

Although just eleven tools and techniques are mentioned under this toolkit, these are very important from PMI-ACP exam point of view. The students are encouraged to understand the importance of analysis and design phase to be achieved under agile.

Sample Practice Examination on Chapter II Agile Analysis and Design

Q1: Agile Analysis & Design supports more closely which architecture?

    A. Service Oriented Architecture (SOA)
    B. Component Driven Architecture (CDA)
    C. Model Driven Architecture (MDA)
    D. Open Architecture (OpenUpA)

Q2: The product vision is done at least once in a year whereas the product roadmap is done .....

    A. also once in a year
    B. at least twice in a year
    C. at least thrice in a year
    D. at least four times in a year

Q3: Who from the Scrum team creates and owns both the vision and product roadmap?

    A. All.
    B. None.
    C. Product Owner.
    D. Scrum Master.

Q4: What is a clear and most effective format to define product requirements in the Agile analysis & design?

    A. Requirements Documentation
    B. Requirements Traceability Matrix (RTM)
    C. Use Case
    D. User Story

Q5: The user stories are usually written on a

    A. Notepad
    B. Kanban Board
    C. Small Index Card
    D. Bulletin Board

Q6: The elements of a good user story can be described by mnemonics of INVEST. Which element is not in the INVEST?

    A. Independent
    B. Negotiable
    C. Variable
    D. Testable

Q7: A product backlog is a list of items?

    A. That were not completed from previous sprint
    B. To be implemented in the product
    C. That will be postponed for implementation
    D. That are part of change / issue log

Q8: Innovation Games are powerful qualitative research and problem solving techniques focused on the use of collaborative play with customers, colleagues, partners and the community at large. The following is one of those famous 13 games invented by Luke Hohmann, while others are not.

    A. Monopoly
    B. Buy a feature
    C. XBox
    D. My First Nightmare

Q9: In which innovative game, the team takes pride in designing the logo, slogan, three important features and three important selling points?

    A. Product Box
    B. Feature Box
    C. Start a Day
    D. Show and Tell

Q10: In the case for larger applications, for teams new to agile development, or for projects where the features are still extremely fuzzy, there are perfect opportunities to execute an iteration that does not deliver any functionality to the customer. What is this iteration known as?

    A. Initiating Iteration
    B. Sample Iteration
    C. Start-up Iteration
    D. Zero Iteration.

Q11: What is AMDD under Agile Analysis and Design?

    A. Agile Method Design Development
    B. Agile Model Driven Development
    C. Agile Model Design Development
    D. Agile Method Driven Development

Q12: What is JIT, which is commonly used in lean manufacturing?

    A. Job In Transit
    B. Just In Training
    C. Just In Time
    D. Just In Transform

Q13: What is NOT covered in the daily stand-up meeting?

    A. What was achieved in last 24 hours?
    B. What will be achieved in next 24 hours?
    C. What are the roadblocks / impediments?
    D. What is the solution of the problem in details?

Q14: The Product Roadmap doesn't depict the following:

    A. The list of customers targeted.
    B. The list of customer targeted features.
    C. The architecture needed to support the features.
    D. The evolution of the product over time.

Q15: The collection of requirements can be called as _____ in agile software development.

    A. Requirements Document
    B. Requirements Traceability Matrix
    C. Backlog
    D. User Stories

Q16: A clear and most effective format to define product requirements and to describe the features in short is _____.

    A. Excel spreadsheet
    B. Product Scope
    C. Backlog
    D. User Stories

Q17: User stories are in short definition and the goal is not to get into all explicit details at the beginning. That's the reason why user stories are usually written on _____.

    A. Large Notepad
    B. Small Index Card
    C. Wall paper
    D. Information Radiator

Q18: The typical user story template is not used for

    A. Who is the story for?
    B. What they want to do?
    C. Why they want to do?
    D. When they want to do?

Q19: An acronym called as INVEST is used to depict the elements of good user stories. What is NOT one of the elements depicted normally by INVEST?

    A. Interdependent
    B. Negotiable
    C. Valuable
    D. Testable

Q20: It is said that use case is more elaborate whereas user story is deliberately kept small and the user story is "told" to the agile team members mainly to promote the _____ among the team.

    A. Written communication
    B. Nonverbal communication
    C. Team communication
    D. Miscommunication

Answers:

Q1: A (Agile Analysis & Design supports more closely the Service Oriented Architecture - SOA).

Q2: B (The product vision is done at least once in a year whereas the product roadmap is done at least twice in a year)

Q3: C (The Product Owner from the Scrum team creates and owns both the vision and product roadmap.)

Q4: D (A clear and most effective format to define product requirements is the user story).

Q5: C (The user stories are usually written on a small index card)

Q6: C (The elements of a good user story can be described by mnemonics of INVEST which stands for Independent, Negotiable, Valuable, Estimatable, Small and Testable)

Q7: B (A product backlog is a list of items to be implemented in the product)

Q8: B (Buy a feature is one of those famous 13 games invented by Luke Hohmann, while others are not).

Q9: A (In the "product box" game, the team takes pride in designing the logo, slogan, three important features and three important selling points.)

Q10: D. (An iteration that does not deliver any functionality to the customer is known as Zero Iteration)

Q11: B (AMDD under Agile Analysis and Design stands for Agile Model Driven Development)

Q12: C (JIT stands for Just In Time, a concept used in lean manufacturing to reduce waste and inventory)

Q13: D. The problem solution in detail is NOT discussed in the quick 15-minutes scrum meeting.

Q14: A. The Product Roadmap doesn't depict the list of customers targeted. All remaining three items are depicted in the product roadmap.

Q15: C. The collection of requirements can be called as Backlog in agile software development. The short description of the feature / requirement is achieved by user story.

Q16: D. A clear and most effective format to define product requirements and to describe the features in short is User Story whereas the collection of requirements is known as backlog in agile software development.

Q17: B. User stories are in short definition and the goal is not to get into all explicit details at the beginning. That's the reason why user stories are usually written on a small index card.

Q18: D. The typical user story template is not used for when they want to use the user story.

Q19: A: The INVEST stands for Independent, Negotiable, Valuable, Estimatable, Small and Testable.

Q20: C. It is said that use case is more elaborate whereas user story is deliberately kept small and the user story is "told" to the agile team members mainly to promote the team communication and collaboration among the team. There will be more verbal communication.

CHAPTER THREE

Agile Estimation

This chapter covers the following tools and techniques used under "Agile Estimation" in agile:

- ➤ **Relative sizing**
- ➤ **Story points / T-shirt sizing**
- ➤ **Wide band Delphi**
- ➤ **Planning poker**
- ➤ **Affinity estimating**
- ➤ **Ideal time**

Agile estimating is the process where the agile teams perform estimating using certain tools and techniques such as relative sizing, planning poker etc.

Relative Sizing

There are 2 ways of estimating, one is to estimate relatively and the other is to estimate absolutely.

Example of relative estimating: How long it takes to eat 10 cookies if eating 1 cookie takes 10 seconds? Example of absolute estimating: How long it takes to find 2 missing cards in the deck of 52 cards?

The challenge in estimation: With 2 stones, side by side, one can tell which stone is bigger than the other (relative), but to tell precisely how much bigger one stone is than the other is a challenge (estimating absolutely).

The simple principle of relative sizing forms the cornerstone of agile estimation and planning. A simple easy-to-use point-based system is used to estimate relatively and then to track progress.

Decide 1 user story as base with some size (and points) and compare all others, relative to this base story. Typically the sizes are sorted as small, medium, or large.

How Relative Sizing is used for Agile Estimation?

- Estimating or scoring backlog items on value and effort is the first key step for prioritizing the requirements.
- Agile estimation is done using simple point-based system.
- Agile teams often use the Fibonacci sizing sequence for estimating the scores. Keep it simple. Don't use all numbers in Fibonacci sequence.

How Relative Sizing is used for Agile Planning?

- Two things are used for Agile Planning
  o Relative Sizing of User Stories using story points (point-based system)
  o Team Velocity (how fast these user stories can be converted into increments of deliverables?).
- Relative priority can be calculated by using a simple formula: Relative priority = Value / Efforts. Higher the number, better to move it in top position on the priority list.
- The Agile Planning and Estimation is subject to change in every iteration since one of the factors is the Team's Velocity. The teams may work slower or faster than originally estimated velocity per release at initial planning / estimation time.

What are the advantages of Relative Sizing for Agile Planning?

- The units of measure don't matter. The measure is one of relativity – not absolute, since the sizing is based on simple point-based system.
- Trying to capture the bigness of a task (or story) with a "number" and "size it" relatively to all others.
- It evens out ultimately – for every story that is over-estimated, there will be one with under-estimate.

2 Simple Agile Estimation Techniques:

There are 2 simple Agile Estimation Techniques:

- **Triangulation**: is about taking a few sample reference stories and sizing other stories relatively to these. One of each S, M and L (small, medium, and Large sizes)
- **Planning Poker**: is a game where agile development team estimates stories individually first (using a deck of cards with 1, 3 and 5 points on them) and then compares the results collectively together after with the team. A team consensus derives the final point estimate. Often the team will self-review individual sizing estimates for the final determination.

What do you do after Estimation?

- After initial relative sizing, look further for
  - o Logical Groupings
  - o Stories that go end-to-end (to flesh out architecture)
  - o Stories that relate to and may encompass the entire application (a piece cutting through all layers of cake)
  - o Commonality or anything typical to the application that you would use throughout the life of project.
- You may re-estimate your stories based on this practice.
- Caution: Don't continuously resize user stories; it will affect team velocity, which then needs to be recalibrated.

What is a Spike?

During estimation, you haven't done something before and you don't know how to size it...do a *spike*.

- Spike: is a time-boxed experiment where just enough investigation is done to come up with an estimate and then stop. (Don't actually do the story!!)
- Spikes are typically no more than couple of days and are great ways to try something fast.
- Then inform the customer of the estimated efforts (money, time and resources).
- The Customer can then decide whether it's worth the investment and set priorities accordingly.

How is Epic and Theme different than Spike?

- **Agile Epic**: Some authors describe an Epic as "a large user story" and others as "a group of related User Stories". The 'very large' stories are broken down into smaller stories to minimize complexity and reduce uncertainty, thereby making Epic as a group of related user stories. It is quite common not to release the individual stories until the full epic is 'done'.

- **Agile Theme**: A Theme is a **top-level objective that may span projects and products**. Themes may be broken down into sub-themes, which are more likely to be product-specific. At its most granular form, a Theme may be an Epic.

Story Points

The user story is a simple description of a product requirement in terms of what that requirement must accomplish for whom. Story point is a unit of measure for measuring user stories under agile estimation and planning. Instead of using absolute sizing in terms of calendar days, hours or any other tangible measures, the agile teams use relative sizing in terms of Story Points to measure the user stories.

The story point measure is based on Fibonacci sequence, but to keep it simple, use only 3 sizes, Small (with 1 point), Medium (with 3 points) and Large (with 5 points).

Take 3 user stories, each of 1 pt., 3 pts., and 5 pts. and make those as "base stories". Compare all other user stories with respect to these base stories and assign "story points" to each user story. Add the points of all user stories selected under iteration to measure team velocity. Based on the team Velocity, the Product Owner chooses the user stories to be implemented in subsequent iterations with consensus from agile development team members. You may re-estimate your user stories, but it may affect the velocity if done continuously.

T-shirt Sizing

Instead of using absolute sizing in terms of calendar days, hours or any other tangible measures, the agile teams use relative sizing like T-shirt sizing for agile estimation of work to be done.

- The T-shirt size concept is in play. T-shirts are typically sold in Small, Medium, and Large sizes.
- Relative estimating uses a simple, easy-to-use point-based system, mapped to sizing.
- Small: 1 point: No Sweat
- Medium: 3 points: Nothing we can't handle
- Large: 5 points: Going to take some efforts

The story point measure is based on Fibonacci sequence, but to keep it simple, use only 3 sizes, Small (with 1 point), Medium (with 3 points) and Large (with 5 points).

Wideband Delphi

The **Wideband Delphi** estimation method is a consensus-based technique for estimating effort. It derives from the Delphi Method which was developed in the 1940s at the RAND Corporation as a forecasting tool. The Delphi technique is a way to reach consensus of experts participating in this technique anonymously. This technique helps reduce bias in the estimation data and keeps any one person from having undue influence on the estimates.

It is called as "wideband" because, compared to the existing Delphi method, the new method involved greater interaction and more communication between those participating. It is also known as "wisdom of crowds".

Describe the steps under Wideband Delphi?

Step1. Coordinator or facilitator presents each expert with a specification and an estimation form.

Step 2: Coordinator calls a group meeting in which the experts discuss any estimation issues with the coordinator and each other.

Step 3: Experts fill out forms anonymously with individual estimates.

Step 4: Coordinator prepares and distributes a summary of the estimates.

Step 5: Coordinator calls a group meeting, specifically focusing on having the experts discuss points where their estimates vary widely.

Step 6: Experts fill out forms, again anonymously, and steps 4 to 6 are repeated for as many rounds as appropriate. Consensus may be reached in a few rounds of this process.

The Wideband Delphi method of estimation is very similar to the "Planning Poker" method of estimation used in many agile and scrum project environments.

Both Wideband Delphi and Planning Poker methods are effective since the people who are estimating are the people who are committed to the work. The estimates are NOT made by the people who are typical project planners or project managers or schedulers as used to be under plan driven project management approaches.

Planning Poker

Planning Poker game is one of the two Agile Estimation Techniques. It is based on Fibonacci sequence and also calls upon the collaborative consensus in deciding story size during the agile estimation process.

When we play planning poker for agile estimation, we look to harness the wisdom of crowds with regard to our estimates. We are betting that the agile team (crowd) will be able to come up with a better guess than any one, single expert/individual.

- Team discusses user stories to identify their baseline.
- Customer/Product Owner then reads/describes the user story to the group and allows for brief discussion. There may or may not be open discussion about the user story (aka requirement) at this time.
- Everyone estimates the story points by picking a card and then places their card face down.
- All team members show their cards at the same time.
- If everyone's estimate is more or less same, that estimate is kept.

- If there is difference, team discusses and estimates again till consensus is reached.
- Planning poker works because the people, who are going to do the work, are the ones estimating.
- It's powerful due to group discussions and consensus.
- Keep it simple with 1, 3 and 5 points. Don't use all numbers in Fibonacci sequence.

Affinity Estimating

Affinity Estimating is another sizing / estimation technique. This can be similar to mind-mapping techniques in that the stories are used to generate ideas about estimation that can be linked to form organized pattern of thoughts about the estimated size.

In this technique stories are read out to the whole team and then the team is asked to arrange the stories horizontally on a wall in order of size, **without talking**.

- It's quick and easy; it feels very natural; and, the entire decision making process is made very visible.
- Finally, "Affinity Estimating" helps make estimating a positive experience rather than a confrontational one.
- Those who lack communication skills or are intimated by others in group discussions, find this technique most effective.
- Although Affinity Estimating and Magic Estimating seem to be fast and fun, they seem to be missing the detailed discussions of Planning Poker.

Ideal Time

In agile estimation process, some agile teams do estimate in days, calling them "ideal days". Ideal Time is part of Planning Poker and Agile Estimation techniques.

An ideal day is the perfect day where you have no interruptions and are able to work for eight hours straight in uninterrupted bliss. Ideal time (ideal days) are just another form of story point.

- We never get ideal days at work.
- Wit points, we don't have to worry about my ideal day not equaling yours.

SUMMARY

Although just six techniques are mentioned under this tools and techniques, these are very important from PMI-ACP exam point of view. The students are encouraged to understand the importance of estimation process under agile.

Sample Practice Examination on Chapter III Agile Estimation

Q1: There are two ways of estimating in agile estimation. If you have a deck of 52 cards and you want to estimate how long it takes to find 2 missing cards, then this example is of what type of estimating?

    A. Relative Estimating
    B. Absolute Estimating
    C. Near Estimating
    D. Guess Estimating

Q2: You are managing a project in agile environment. Your team has estimated 200 user stories. Out of those user stories, 20 are very complex and it seems that each complex user story may take 24-30 hours. If you want to find out how long it will take to accomplish just the complex stories, what kind of estimating you will be using?

    A. Random Estimating
    B. Beta Estimating
    C. Relative Estimating
    D. Absolute Estimating

Q3: This is a game where agile development team estimates stories individually first (using a deck of cards with 1, 3 and 5 points on them) and then compares the results collectively together after with the team. A team consensus derives the final point estimate. Often the team will self-review individual sizing estimates for the final determination.

    A. Relative sizing
    B. Random sizing
    C. Planning Poker
    D. Triangulation

Q4: During estimation, you haven't done something before and you don't know how to size it. You are going to experiment on it just to come up with estimate and then stop there. What is this known as?

    A. Known Unknown
    B. Unknown Unknown
    C. Ad-hoc experimentation
    D. Spike

Q5: Spike is _____experiment where just enough investigation is done to come up with an estimate and then stop.

    A. On-going
    B. Never ending
    C. Time Boxed
    D. First-hand

Q6: Instead of using absolute sizing in terms of calendar days, hours or any other tangible measures, the agile teams use relative sizing to measure the user stories. What is a unit of measure for measuring user stories under agile estimation and planning?

    A. Story Points
    B. Velocity
    C. Team Capacity
    D. Numerical

Q7: You are facilitating a meeting to estimate story points for ten user stories inviting novice as well as experts from various departments. You are engaging team members to improve estimate accuracy and to reach a consensus on estimates anonymously. You would like to keep the newcomers from having undue influence on the outcome from experts and to reduce bias in the data. What estimation technique are you using?

    A. Delhi technique
    B. Facilitation technique
    C. Daily stand-up technique
    D. Wide band Delphi technique

Q8: Planning Poker is a game that is widely used under agile estimation techniques. It is based on _____, although all numbers are not used.

    A. Normal Distribution
    B. Random Numbers

C. Sequential Numbers
D. Fibonacci Sequence

Q9: You as an agile team member are attending an estimation meeting to estimate story sizes of multiple user stories. The agile expert distributed a deck of cards and asked you to show your card at end of discussions. Your card didn't match with many others in the group. You started discussions on why you choose that card. This happened multiple times before you reached / agreed upon final story size. What is this game called as?

A. Playing Cards
B. Planning Poker
C. Monopoly Cards
D. Pick your card

Q10: You are attending an estimation meeting. The agile coach is reading out the stories to the whole team. Individual team member is asked to arrange the stories horizontally on a wall in order of size, **without talking.** There are no detail discussions but you can move around the story size cards. What is this kind of estimating known as?

A. Affinity Estimating
B. Anonymous Estimating
C. Three-point Estimating
D. War-room Estimating

Q11: In agile estimation process, some agile teams do estimate in days, where you have no interruptions and are able to work for eight hours straight in uninterrupted bliss. What is this day called as?

A. Perfect Day
B. Ideal Day
C. Work Day
D. Dream Day

Q12: The agile team has taken 3 stories as base stories. The "No big deal" story uses 1 point. The story with "little more efforts" has 3 points and the story that "needs considerable efforts" is awarded 5 points. A database related user story was discussed and it was agreed that there are multiple databases that will need considerable integration than just usual efforts. How many points will you award for this user story?

A. One Point
B. Three Points
C. Five Points
D. Not Sure

Q13: You were estimating sizes on various user stories. Suddenly you came across "a large user story", which needs to be broken down into smaller stories to minimize complexity and reduce uncertainty. What is this large story known as under agile estimation?

A. Agile Theme
B. Agile Epic
C. Agile Top Story
D. Agile Work Package

Answers:

Q1: B This is an example of Absolute Estimating.

Q2: C. This is an example of Relative Estimating.

Q3: C. Planning Poker is a game where agile development team estimates stories individually first (using a deck of cards with 1, 3 and 5 points on them) and then compares the results collectively together after with the team. A team consensus derives the final point estimate. Often the team will self-review individual sizing estimates for the final determination.

Q4: D. During estimation, you haven't done something before and you don't know how to size it. You are going to experiment on it just to come up with estimate and then stop there. This is known as Spike.

Q5: C. Spike is a time-boxed experiment where just enough investigation is done to come up with an estimate and then stop. Spikes are typically no more than couple of days and are great ways to try something fast.

Q6: A. Story point is a unit of measure for measuring user stories under agile estimation and planning. Instead of using absolute sizing in terms of calendar days, hours or any other tangible measures, the agile teams use relative sizing in terms of Story Points to measure the user stories.

Q7: D. The **Wideband Delphi** estimation method is a consensus-based technique for estimating effort. It is called as "wideband" because, compared to the existing Delphi method, the new method involved greater interaction and more communication between those participating. It is also known as "wisdom of crowds".

Q8: D. Planning Poker game is used for agile estimation of story points and it is based on Fibonacci sequence.

Q9: B. An estimation meeting to estimate story sizes of multiple user stories using a deck of cards and coming up with the group consensus on the story sizes is known as Planning Poker game.

Q10: A. When an individual team member is asked to arrange the stories horizontally on a wall in order of size, **without talking,** it is known as Affinity Estimating. Although this estimating seems to be fast and fun, it lacks the detailed discussions of Planning Poker. This technique is most effective for those who lack communication skills or are intimated by others in group discussions.

Q11: B. In agile estimation process, some agile teams do estimate in days, calling them "ideal days", where you have no interruptions and are able to work for eight hours straight in uninterrupted bliss. We never get ideal days at work. With points, we don't have to worry about my ideal day not equaling yours.

Q12: C. Based on the scenario, it seems these will be considerable efforts for this user story, so I will award 5 points.

Q13: B. "A large user story", which needs to be broken down into smaller stories to minimize complexity and reduce uncertainty, is known as Agile Epic under agile estimation. It is quite common not to release the individual stories until the full epic is "done".

CHAPTER FOUR
Communications

This chapter covers the following tools and techniques used under "Communications" in agile:

- ➤ **Information Radiator**
- ➤ **Team Space for co-located and/or distributed teams**
- ➤ **Agile Tooling**
- ➤ **Osmotic Communications**
- ➤ **Two-way communications (trustworthy, conversation driven)**
- ➤ **Social media-based communication**
- ➤ **Active Listening**
- ➤ **Brainstorming**
- ➤ **Feedback methods**

The most important concepts to understand under this chapter are related to communications management. Please focus on those. Agile teams are different from traditional teams due to their team dynamics. The Agile Manifesto sets the framework for how agile project team members work together: The very first item of value in the manifesto is *individuals and interactions* over processes and tools.

Information Radiator

An *information radiator* is a very effective communication tool that physically displays information to the agile team and any stakeholders in the team's work area. In agile it is necessary to have excellent communication among agile team members and one of the most effective ways to achieve this in co-located team is using Information Radiator. Display in most visible manner, the information which everyone needs to know.

Information radiator concept is derived from the information display boards at airports. The most up-to-date information about all flights arriving, departing, on-time, delayed, cancelled is displayed in most visible way. The passengers are supposed to look at the display billboards and gather information on their own. This also avoids keeping information booths and passengers relying on limited places to seek latest information. In agile projects, this concept is mainly used to let the team members understand that it is their responsibility to derive latest information about the project from the "information radiator" and there won't be any kind of notifications regarding this. The initiative is to implement the "pull" technology rather than "push" technology to retrieve the information. This reduces the burden on communication channels and also avoids potential miscommunication. No one can blame anyone that they didn't receive information on timely manner, since everyone is responsible to not only obtain the latest information but also update the information as and when it changes.

Real time communication occurs throughout the project via use of "highly visible information radiators". Information radiators can include Kanban boards, white boards, bulletin boards, burn-down charts that show the iteration's status, and any other sign with details about the project, the product, or team. This concept is derived from lean manufacturing or Kanban.

What are the advantages of an Information Radiator?

- The information is placed in most visible places like Task/Kanban boards.
- All team members in the co-located teams can see it all the time.
- Real time communication occurs throughout the project.
- Information only needs to be updated in one place.
- Remote / distant teams can see the information via web cameras, wiki, share point or other web accessible options.
- The information radiators may show graphs, tables, burn-down charts, task boards, other metrics, meetings, schedules and most importantly show current status of project.
- Team updates the status and then the stakeholders can see it at any time.

Team Space

Team space design is gaining popularity for agile teams. Newer team space design considers co-location of team members so that their working with each other supports active and open collaboration. The main point is ease of communication among team members and removing any obstacles in the team communication. The team space must promote open space for free discussions. This also helps in osmotic communication.

Team space is a new term very popular in young generation. This is mainly used to provide the proximity in work places still keeping the distance so as to have personal privacy. It is gaining popularity in agile teams due to new challenges in communications and to cope up with those.

Agile flourishes when agile team members work closely together in an environment that supports the process.

For Co-located Teams:

- No separate cubicles: The walls and partitions are disappearing. There will be no designated cubicles for resources. Similar groups can sit and work together.
- Open workspace for easy communication: Ideally all team members should be able to walk to other team members to discuss and exchange views. There must not be any kind of hindrances that prevents the open communication. At the same time each team member should have own team space – the privacy and personal freedom to work as an individual.

For Distributed Teams:

- Virtual open workspace: All the team members are reachable by electronic media at ease and can communicate the thoughts as well as share information. Team members can be global or telecommuting using modern means of communications such as IM (instant messaging), text messaging, chat and others.
- Video conferencing: This is mainly for effective communication with most cost reduction. This eliminates the travel requirements and still can provide personal touch. It also allows participants to share documents on-line instantaneously and get approval. The video conferencing can assist in sharing information, reviewing documents on-line, making updates in group presence, getting approval and in fact digitally signing the papers.
- Gathering all team members physically at the beginning of projects: This allows the team members to know all other team members by face. It also helps to see the face behind phone in later conversations. This improves drastically the team understanding and team communication at the inception of projects which needs to be sustained throughout the project. This also supports the diversity and any challenges due to time zones and physical boundaries which may exist in project.

If possible, the agile team should have its own room, sometimes called as *war room* or *project room* or *scrum room*. The team members must be able to create the setup and environment that fosters the open communication using this room – putting white boards, Kanban boards, bulletin boards and posters / sticky notes on the walls and moving furniture etc. By arranging the team space for productivity, it becomes part of how they work and communicate. The right space allows team to be fully functional and immersed in solving problems and crafting solutions. The same project room can be used for next project or for multiple projects, with higher and quicker efficiency gains paying for the investment needed to create such team space.

Agile Tooling

Agile tooling is to bring better team communication. There are multiple tools that can be used effectively to understand and manage team communications in much better way. These can be physical tools such as war room/billboards or these can be advanced agile technical tools used for better team communication such as build/deployment tools.

Whatever tools are used, these are primarily used to enhance team communication and provide least roadblocks in collecting, maintaining and disseminating the information among team members as well as with stakeholders.

For Co-located Teams:

- common work area (war room) is needed to openly discuss the team issues. This becomes a place to gather, discuss, put your thoughts and make team decisions.
- Reserved conference room provides the best communication it can have with all that wall space, whiteboards and communal work space. The team can have full freedom to discuss, make changes, and simulate if there is a reserved conference room where the information is retained and can be looked at any time of the day.

For Distributed Teams:

Virtual shared space is needed for better communications. This can be one or all of the following

- Wikis: A wiki is a website whose users can share information by adding, modifying or deleting its content via any web browser.
- Instant messaging, Skype, web camera, web conferencing: This is to make internet calls for free, send instant messages and make free video.
- Planning Poker: Tool used to present stories for estimation.
- Card Meeting: Brainstorm and plan using 3x5 index cards.
- Xplanner: Planning and tracking tool for agile teams following XP or Scrum.
- CVS: This is a free software revision control system to handle configuration management. Please search on google.com to obtain more information.
- Fitnesse: A software development collaboration tool.
- Agile tools to build/configure/deploy the deliverables accessible to all.

Osmotic Communications

Osmotic communication relies on team members overhearing conversations. A listener learns many things just due to presence, not necessarily participating. Active listening plays key role in communications.

A listener learns many things just due to presence, by active listening. Osmotic communication expects the listener's participation. This happens automatically as and when a topic of interest or a topic in which the listener is an expert is brought into conversation during meeting.

What are salient features of Osmotic Communications?

- Ask people from different teams to sit together in the discussions, meetings and listen to the conversations.
- Sit close enough to each other so that you can have a quick discussion without getting up from your desk or shouting.
- Teams that sit together not only get rapid answers to their questions, they experience what calls *osmotic communication.*
- Increased communication effectiveness of sitting together.
- Even though a person is focusing on his/her own activity, the brain is paying attention to all the other conversations happening in and around the room.

Two-way communications

Communications include the processes that are required to ensure timely and appropriate collection, creation, distribution, storage, retrieval, manage, control, monitor and ultimate disposition of project information. The agile team spends most of their time communicating with other team members.

Two-way communications create a bridge between two parties. A basic communication model consists of two parties, defined as the sender and receiver. The sequence of steps in a basic communication model is:

- Encode: Thoughts or ideas are translated (encoded) into language by the sender.
- Transmit Message: This information is then sent by the sender using communication channel (medium). Here medium is the technology medium.
- Decode: The message is translated by the receiver back into meaningful thoughts or ideas.
- Acknowledge: Upon receipt of a message, the receiver may signal (acknowledge) receipt of the message but it doesn't mean agreement with or comprehension of the message.
- Feedback/Response: The receiver encodes thoughts and ideas into a feedback or response message and transmits to the original sender.

To achieve effective communication between agile team members, either face-to-face communication or interactive communication is strongly suggested. In interactive communication, two or more parties perform a multidirectional exchange of information. It is the most effective way to ensure a common understanding by all participants on specific topics, and including meetings, phone calls, instant messaging, video conferencing, etc.

Social media-based communication

With the advancement in technology, the agile teams are using the social media based communication methods. Some of the accepted social media based communications include but not limited to:

- FaceTime
- Facebook
- LinkedIn
- WhatsApp
- Video Conferencing
- Instant Messaging
- On-line chat
- On-line meetings

Few years back, these were prohibited at work places. With technological advancement, these mediums are now accepted for communications.

Active Listening

Active listening is an important skill that every agile team member must acquire to improve the communication and performance. This skill is required during all communications, meetings, reviews, and briefings. Active listening is a way of listening and responding to another person that improves mutual understanding. The listener must take care to attend to the speaker fully, and then repeats, in the listener's own words, what he or she thinks the speaker has said. The listener does not have to agree with the speaker--he or she must simply state what they think the speaker said by providing feedback. This enables the speaker to find out whether the listener really understood. If the listener did not, the speaker can explain some more. It is important for a listener to observe the speaker's behavior and body language. Having the ability to interpret a person's body language lets the listener develop a more accurate understanding of the speaker's message.

Active listening has several benefits, such as:

- First, it forces people to listen attentively to others.
- Second, it avoids misunderstandings, as people have to confirm that they do really understand what another person has said.
- Third, it tends to open people up, to get them to say more.
- Fourth, and most important, it can reduce confusion and conflict on teams.

What are three primary elements that comprise active listening?

- **Comprehension:** This is the first step. Comprehension is "shared meaning between parties in a communication transaction". This is the important step for understanding.
- **Retaining:** This is second step in the listening process. Memory is essential to the listening process because the information we retain when involved in the listening process is how we create meaning from words.
- **Responding:** Listening is an interaction between speaker and listener. It adds action to a normally passive process. The speaker looks for verbal and nonverbal responses from the listener to determine if the message is being listened to.

The active listener may take notes on the conversation to retain for records and later to review for better understanding/comprehension and then utilize it even to respond actively.

Active listening must lead to effective listening. Active listener takes active steps to make sure that the message was understood. To be effective listener, it requires receiver's full thoughts and attention. An effective listener provides feedback and confirms the message was received clearly.

Brainstorming techniques

Brainstorming is a general data gathering and group creativity technique that can be used to identify risks, ideas, or solutions to issues by using a group of team members or subject matter experts.

Brainstorming (roughly defined as any group activity involving the pursuit of new ideas) is a popular method of gathering ideas from a group. A typical brainstorming session brings people together into the creative process, and increases the social nature of the project. These sessions bring the ideas on the table based on the collective wisdom of the entire group participating in the brainstorming sessions. Large pool of ideas can be created within very short time interval.

Brainstorming begins by taking the problem at hand. As ideas begin to flow, it is recommended to note down those ideas first and then analyze those later in details. The brainstorming is not to criticize anyone for throwing out a bad idea. Bad ideas can turn into great ideas. Start to bounce ideas off of each other; even a simple thought is worth the pitch. It is possible that a simple thought can spark in another person's creative mind and a new perspective may bring better imagination.

These brainstorming techniques are useful for engaging team members to improve estimate accuracy and commitment to the emerging estimates. By involving the agile team members who are close to the technical execution of the work in the estimation process, additional information is gained and more accurate estimates are obtained. Additionally, when people are involved in the estimation process, their commitment towards meeting the resulting estimates increase.

This is normally done during the release and iterative planning meetings. When doing the brainstorming during these meetings, the moderator keeps repeating the problem statement frequently to remind everyone and keep the discussions on track. Brainstorming techniques must foster creativity involving entire team. It should not matter who was the originator of the idea but what matters most is the idea itself.

Feedback Methods

Feedback means basically understanding the pros and cons of a product from users' perspective. These can be characteristics, constructive suggestions, criticisms, comments or even encouragements. There are multiple feedback techniques for product. Some of those techniques which are applicable to agile are as follows:

1. Prototyping
2. Simulation
3. Demonstrations
4. Evaluations

Prototyping or software prototyping refers to the activity of creating prototypes of software applications which may produce incomplete versions of the software program being developed.

Paper Prototyping: Instead of presenting only one foremost design, it is recommended that the team rapidly produces multiple prototypes utilizing number of different designs and options. The team achieves this quickly using cheap and inexpensive paper prototype. After that, the team then presents these prototypes by demonstrating various "what-if" scenarios to the customers and seeks constructive feedback from the customers.

The major benefit of prototyping is that the software designer and implementer can get valuable feedback from the users early in the project. The other benefit of the prototype review is that the customers, including end-users, examine the prototype and provide feedback on additions or changes which are valuable to them.

Simulation is the imitation of some real thing, state of affairs, or process. The act of simulating something generally entails representing certain key characteristics or behaviors of a selected physical or abstract system. The main purpose of the simulation is to get the *early feedback* from end users and customers about those key features.

Demonstration or *showcase* is the opportunity to show the work to the world and get some real down-to-earth feedback from the customer. Gather sprint review feedback informally.

Whether the company needs to close a sale, gather end-user feedback, show progress to potential customers, or simply explain how the new product works, it will be needed to demo the software product.

Invite only those people to the demo, whose *feedback* is truly valuable.

- Demonstration shows what the team has been doing so far.
- Demonstration shows how far the team is from final shippable product
- Demonstration shows what can be deployed today if the product owner really had to, since it's done.
- Demonstration is a good way to close out last iteration's work done.
- Demonstration must be driven by the customers so that the team can watch how the customers plan to use the software.

Evaluation is basically giving away a fully developed software copy to prospective customers and allowing them to use it at their leisure. During the evaluation period, keep asking for their feedback. These are generally experts who had used many other competitive products. Normally a questionnaire or point method is followed which is simple but effective in evaluating the pros and cons of the product. Evaluations are used to get some real honest-to-goodness feedback from the customers.

SUMMARY

Although only nine tools and techniques are mentioned under this toolkit, these are very important from PMI-ACP exam point of view. The students are encouraged to understand the importance of communications under agile.

The following Agile Principles support valuing people on the project team and how they work together:

1. Business people and developers must work together daily throughout the project.
2. Build projects around motivated individuals. Give them the environment and support they need, and trust them to get the job done.
3. Agile processes promote sustainable development. The sponsors, developers, and users should be able to maintain a constant pace indefinitely.
4. The best architectures, requirements, and design emerge from self-organizing teams.
5. At regular intervals, the team reflects on how to become more effective, then tunes and adjusts its behavior accordingly.

Sample Practice Examination on Chapter IV Agile Communications

Q1: Instead of sending the updates on the progress made by the team and any outstanding issues, the agile coach decided to communicate this information in most visible manner displaying it in the team's work area, where everyone can access and see it. What communication tool is being used in this scenario?

    A. Information Distribution
    B. Information Display Board
    C. Information Radiator
    D. Information Dashboard

Q2: _____ is a new term that is gaining popularity in agile teams due to new challenges in communications and to cope up with those. This is mainly used to provide the proximity in work places still keeping the distance so as to have personal privacy.

    A. Open Space
    B. Team Space
    C. Cubicles
    D. Round Table

Q3: If possible, the agile team should have its own room, sometimes called as *project room* or *scrum room*. The team members must be able to create the setup and environment that fosters the open communication using this room – putting white boards, Kanban boards, bulletin boards and posters / sticky notes on the walls and moving furniture etc. What is this room commonly known as in agile teams?

    A. War room
    B. Conference room
    C. Open room
    D. Corner room

Q4: What is primarily used to enhance team communication and provide least roadblocks in collecting, maintaining and disseminating the information among team members as well as with stakeholders?

- A. Agile Methodology
- B. Agile Manifesto
- C. Agile Collaboration
- D. Agile Tooling

Q5: A new member joined the agile team. The agile coach asked her just to attend few meetings. The new member informed the coach that she learnt many things just due to presence, not necessarily participating. Active listening played key role in communications. She also participated in topics she knew. What is this kind of communication known as under agile?

- A. Direct Communication
- B. Osmotic Communication
- C. On-the-job communication
- D. Indirect Communication

Q6: In interactive communication, two or more parties perform a multidirectional exchange of information. It is the most effective way to ensure a common understanding by all participants on specific topics, and including meetings, phone calls, instant messaging, video conferencing, etc. What is this type of communications known as?

- A. One-way communications
- B. Two-way communications
- C. Broadcasting
- D. Publishing

Q7: The agile teams are communicating nowadays using mediums like IM (Instant Messaging), Video Conferencing, On-Line team meetings, Facetime etc. What are these communications called as?

- A. Technology Communications
- B. Social media based communications
- C. Ultimate communications
- D. Internet based communications

Q8: In active listening, the listener must take care to attend to the speaker fully, and then repeats, in the listener's own words, what he or she thinks the speaker has said. However,

- A. The listener does not have to agree with the speaker.
- B. The listener must have to agree with the speaker.

    C. The speaker does not have to care about listener.

    D. The speaker need not find out what the listener understood.

Q9: This is not one of the primary elements that comprise active listening:

    A. Comprehension

    B. Restraining

    C. Retaining

    D. Responding

Q10: The agile coach is bringing team members together with the honest attempt to bring the ideas on the table based on the collective wisdom of the entire group participating in the process. What is this technique called as?

    A. Status Meeting

    B. Scrum Meeting

    C. Brainstorming Meeting

    D. Information Exchange

Q11: When doing the brainstorming during these meetings, who keeps repeating the problem statement frequently to remind everyone and keep the discussions on track?

    A. Scrum Master

    B. Agile Coach

    C. Product owner

    D. Moderator

Q12: Feedback means basically understanding the pros and cons of a product from users' perspective. There are multiple feedback techniques for product. One of the following techniques which are NOT applicable to agile is:

    A. Simulation

    B. Demonstration

    C. Evaluations

    D. Deployment

Q13: In which SCRUM meeting, the goal is to get feedback from the product owner or any users or other stakeholders who have been invited to the meeting?

    A. Sprint Planning Meeting

    B. Sprint Review Meeting

    C. Sprint Retrospective Meeting

    D. Sprint Stand-up Meeting

Q14: Your product is almost ready. You would like to get excellent feedback from the users. You are ready to provide an evaluation copy. Whom should you send the evaluation copy to get effective and real honest-to-goodness feedback?

    A. New Customers
    B. Expert Customers
    C. Potential Customers
    D. Competitors

Q15: The skill of active listening involves more than just hearing the sounds. Which of the following is a characteristic of a good active listener?

    A. Takes good notes
    B. Repeats some of the things
    C. Finishes speaker's sentences
    D. Agrees with the speaker

Answers:

Q1: C. An *information radiator* is a very effective communication tool that physically displays information to the agile team and any stakeholders in the team's work area.

Q2: B. Team Space is a new term that is gaining popularity in agile teams due to new challenges in communications and to cope up with those. This is mainly used to provide the proximity in work places still keeping the distance so as to have personal privacy.

Q3: A. This room is commonly known as *war room* in agile teams.

Q4: D. Agile Tooling is primarily used to enhance team communication and provide least roadblocks in collecting, maintaining and disseminating the information among team members as well as with stakeholders.

Q5: B. Osmotic communication relies on team members overhearing conversations. A listener learns many things just due to presence, not necessarily participating. Active listening plays key role in communications. A listener learns many things just due to presence, by active listening.

Q6: B. In interactive communication, two or more parties performs a multidirectional exchange of information. It is the most effective way to ensure a common understanding by all participants on specific topics, and including meetings, phone calls, instant messaging, video conferencing, etc. This is an example of two-way communications.

Q7: B. The agile teams are communicating nowadays using mediums like IM (Instant Messaging), Video Conferencing, On-Line team meetings, Facetime etc. These communications are social media based.

Q8: A. In active listening, the listener must take care to attend to the speaker fully, and then repeats, in the listener's own words, what he or she thinks the speaker has said. However the listener does not have to agree with the speaker.

Q9: B. The three primary elements that comprise active listening are Comprehension, Retaining and Responding.

Q10: C. Brainstorming (roughly defined as any group activity involving the pursuit of new ideas) is a popular method of gathering ideas from a group. A typical brainstorming session brings people together into the creative process, and increases the social nature of the project. These sessions bring the ideas on the table based on the collective wisdom of the entire group participating in the brainstorming sessions. Large pool of ideas can be created within very short time interval.

Q11: D. When doing the brainstorming during these meetings, the moderator keeps repeating the problem statement frequently to remind everyone and keep the discussions on track.

Q12: D. Feedback means basically understanding the pros and cons of a product from users' perspective. There are multiple feedback techniques for product. Some of those techniques which are applicable to agile are: Prototyping, Simulation, Demonstrations and Evaluations

Q13: B. In Sprint Review Meeting, the goal is to get feedback from the product owner or any users or other stakeholders who have been invited to the meeting.

Q14: B. Your product is almost ready. You would like to get excellent feedback from the users. You are ready to provide an evaluation copy. You should send the evaluation copy to Experts who had used many other competitive products to get effective and real honest-to-goodness feedback.

Q15: B. Active listening is an important skill for all agile team members. One of the best ways to be active listener is by repeating some of the key things that are said. Summarizing helps you to understand better.

CHAPTER FIVE

Interpersonal Skills

This chapter covers the following tools and techniques used under "Interpersonal Skills" aka "Soft Skills Negotiations" in agile:

> ➤ **Emotional Intelligence**
> ➤ **Collaboration**
> ➤ **Adaptive Leadership**
> ➤ **Servant Leadership**
> ➤ **Negotiation**
> ➤ **Conflict Resolution**

Soft skills are gaining importance especially in agile world mainly due to face-to-face communication and co-located teams working together. The "soft skills" are now known as "interpersonal skills" in work places.

Interpersonal skills are behavioral competencies that include proficiencies such as communication skills, emotional intelligence, conflict resolution, negotiation, influence, team building, and group facilitation. These soft skills are valuable assets when developing agile team.

Emotional Intelligence

Emotional intelligence (EI) is an ability or skill to identify, assess, monitor and control or influence the emotions and feelings of oneself, of others, and of groups. Traditional definitions of intelligence emphasized cognitive aspects such as memory and problem-solving. The non-cognitive aspect such as social intelligence describes the skill of understanding and managing other people and the exclusive human capacity to effectively navigate and negotiate complex social relationships and environments. This understanding must be used to have more satisfying and productive relationships.

The project management team can use emotional intelligence to reduce tension and increase cooperation by identifying, assessing, and controlling the sentiments of agile team members, anticipating their actions, acknowledging their concerns, and following up on their issues.

Emotional intelligence plays an important part in soft skills negotiations. It provides the perceived abilities (which an individual aspires or dreams about) as well as actual abilities (which an individual has demonstrated multiple times consistently).

What are the 3 main models of EI?

- **Ability EI model**: The revised definition of Ability EI model is the ability
  - ➤ to perceive emotion,
  - ➤ to integrate emotion to facilitate thought,
  - ➤ to understand emotions,
  - ➤ to regulate emotions to promote personal growth.
- **Mixed models of EI** (usually subsumed under trait EI): Trait EI model describes *self-perceived abilities* whereas "Ability EI" model refers to *actual abilities*. E.g. claiming to have finished 20-miles Chicago Marathon can be *self-perceived abilities* whereas in reality, running in a local 5-mile community mini-marathon is *actual abilities*.
- **Trait EI model**: This "Trait EI" model refers to an individual's self-perceptions of their emotional abilities.

Anyone can have a better "EI" by practicing a few skills. Here are some:

1. Try encouraging others to speak first and give them your full attention.
2. Eliminate the idea of good and bad personality types at work. Instead, look for the part of their personality that represents positivity and is well-meaning.
3. If there is a conflict or friction between you and a coworker look at where you may be coming up short in communicating and address that first.
4. The next time you find yourself focused solely on winning or on retribution, take a step back and look for ways to achieve your goal that also benefit others.

Collaboration

Collaboration means working together. Communication means sharing together. Coordination means putting together. Collaboration includes communication and communication needs coordination.

Two types of collaboration are important: Customer Collaboration and Team Collaboration.

What is the difference between Communication, Coordination and Collaboration?

- Communication is providing available information and sharing that information.
- Coordination is extending a helping hand in the areas guidance is sought.
- Collaboration is team work, making sure all members agree, resolve conflicts, create a win-win situation and move forward with a group consensus.

One of the most important agile manifestos out of four is: "Customer Collaboration over Contract Negotiations".

Another most valued agile principle out of twelve is: "Business People and Developers must work together daily throughout the project".

Adaptive Leadership

Agile project managers are expected to follow adaptive leadership. They are expected to be adapting "servant leadership" style versus the traditional "command-and-control" leadership style. They would be followers of "Theory Y" in managing knowledge workers as compared to "Theory X" used in managing industrial workers.

Agile project manager must possess following characteristics in order to support teams of "knowledge workers" under agile approach:

- Allows teams to self-manage and adapt their process empirically.
- Assumes different leadership styles for different stages of team formation.
- Leads by serving
- Possesses self-awareness
- Facilitates collaboration
- Removes impediments

Servant Leadership

The typical managerial relationship with team members involving the "command-and-control" style is changing. The agile team members are mostly "knowledge workers" and self-motivated. Agile project managers try to follow McGregor's "Theory Y" which is used for self-motivated happy active participant, rather than "Theory X" being used for non-direction, less effective, and more instructional workers.

- Agile project manager's relationship with team is changing towards "servant leader" meaning "Leads by Serving".

- Agile project manager's role within team is becoming like someone who ensures that "other people's highest priority needs are being served".
- Agile project manager's responsibility towards the team is like somebody who embodies an ideal that "whatever the team needs to be productive, the team gets it".

The agile project manager works in the capacity of a "Servant Leader" meaning "leads by serving". The manager removes the impediments and works as a coach. In the knowledge management area, what had been considered a soft skill and secondary to book smarts, now takes front seat. In an environment of self-managed and empowered teams, the agile PM must practice continuous improvement in order to support the agile teams. Agile project manager must also demonstrate fluency in job-specific responsibilities and should continuously self-assess and adapt to grow in the areas of soft skills as well as technical areas.

What are the responsibilities under servant leader role?

- Protecting the team from outside distractions
- Educating others who interact with the team
- Establishing agreed upon boundaries of operation
- Interacting with those who may affect the team's performance
- Removing impediments to the team's progress

All this needs

- A high level of political support,
- Personal and professional communication
- Intelligence to perform.

Agile project manager must also

- Serve each individual,
- Meet with team members on regular basis
- Help them resolve personality clashes
- Improve their skill base
- Map a career path
- Gather feedback into how they think you are doing?
- Embrace the agile manifesto principles

Negotiation

Negotiation is a dialogue between two or more people or parties, intended to reach an understanding, resolve point of difference, or gain advantage in outcome through dialogue, to produce agreed courses of action, to bargain for individual or collective advantage, to craft outcomes to satisfy various interests of two people/parties involved in negotiation process.

A negotiation for agile projects is that the agile team members are committed for full time 100 percent till the end of project. No team member can work part-time, or on multiple projects, or under multiple managers. This is the kind of negotiated terms at the beginning of the project.

Staff assignments are negotiated on many projects. An agile project manager may need to negotiate with:

- ✓ Functional Managers to ensure appropriate competent staff will be working full time on the project until their responsibilities are completed.
- ✓ Other project management teams to appropriately assign scarce or specialized human resources
- ✓ External organizations, vendors, suppliers, contractors to acquire specialized, qualified, certified or other such specified human resources needed as part of the agile team.

How is the "Integrative Negotiation" useful under agile soft skills?

- Integrative negotiation implies some cooperation, or a joining of forces to achieve something together. The team members can use this to work together on deliverables.
- It usually involves a higher degree of trust and a forming of a relationship. Both parties (team member to another team member) want to walk away feeling they've achieved something which has value (to the customer and agile team) by getting what each wants.
- This negotiation may be in conjunction with creative problem solving and is often described as the win-win scenario.

Conflict Resolution

Conflict is inevitable in any project environment. Sources of conflict include scarce resources, scheduling priorities, and personal work styles.

Conflict resolution is a wide range of methods in addressing sources of conflict and in finding means to resolve a given conflict. Successful conflict resolution results in greater productivity and positive working relationships. When managed properly, differences of opinion can lead to increased creativity and better decision making. Conflict should be addressed early and usually in private, using a direct, collaborative approach.

It is advised to bring a conflict to the agile session and then come out of that session with several ideas to turn the conflict into a win-win situation. If someone doesn't have any conflicts, one can learn how to help others solve their conflicts as a third person behaving like "systems thinking" consultant.

What is included in the process of conflict resolution?

Processes of conflict resolution generally include negotiation, mediation, diplomacy and creative peace building.

FIVE basic ways of addressing conflict:

- Smooth/Accommodate: Emphasizing areas of agreement rather than areas of difference; conceding one's position to the needs of others to maintain harmony and relationships.
- Withdraw/Avoid: Retreating from an actual or potential conflict situation; postponing the issue to be better prepared or to be resolved by others. Avoid or postpone conflict by ignoring it, or changing the subject. Avoidance can be useful as a temporary measure with very minor, non-recurring conflicts. In more severe cases, conflict avoidance can involve severing a relationship or leaving a group.
- Collaborate/Problem Solve: Incorporating multiple viewpoints and insights from differing perspectives; requires a cooperative attitude and open dialogue that typically leads to consensus and commitment. Focus is to work together to find a mutually beneficial solution through consensus.
- Compromise/Reconcile: Searching for solutions that bring some degree of satisfaction to all parties in order to temporarily or partially resolve the conflict. Focus is to search for resolution by allotting partial satisfaction to all parties often by bringing the problem into the open and then a third person presenting given options and consolidating a solution, sometimes known as lose-lose situation.
- Force/Direct: Pushing one's viewpoint at the potential expense of others; offering only win-lose solutions, usually enforced through a power position to resolve an emergency.

The best approach is to Collaborate / Solve Problem, where there is an open dialogue leading to problem resolution by providing for an opportunity for the parties to give and take in the solution, also referred to as win-win situation.

Conflict resolution under agile environments:

As a coach or a team leader, one may face many conflicts of interests when running retrospectives in almost all environments. The leader is supposed to use the best possible soft skills in conflict resolution. The success of agile coach in managing agile teams often depends a great deal on the ability to resolve conflicts.

SUMMARY

Although just six techniques are mentioned under this tools and techniques, these are very important from PMI-ACP exam point of view. The students are encouraged to understand the importance of soft skills performed under agile as interpersonal skills. There may be scenario based questions in this area.

Sample Practice Examination on Chapter V Interpersonal Skills

Q1: Interpersonal skills are also known as:

    A. Soft Skills
    B. Hard Skills
    C. Project Skills
    D. Management Skills

Q2: An ability or skill to identify, assess, monitor and control or influence the emotions and feelings of oneself, of others, and of groups is known as:

    A. Organizational Behavior
    B. Servant Leadership
    C. Artificial Intelligence
    D. Emotional Intelligence

Q3: Under soft skills negotiations, when the available information is provided and that information is shared. What is this called as?

    A. Communication
    B. Coordination
    C. Collaboration
    D. Cooperation

Q4: Under soft skills negotiations, when a helping hand is extended in the areas guidance is sought. What is this called as?

    A. Communication
    B. Coordination
    C. Collaboration
    D. Cooperation

Q5: Under soft skills negotiations, when making sure all members agree, resolve conflicts, create a win-win situation and move forward with a group consensus. What is this called as?

A. Communication
B. Coordination
C. Collaboration
D. Cooperation

Q6: One of the most important agile manifestos is:

A. Customer Collaboration over Contract Negotiations
B. Customer Cooperation over Contract Negotiations
C. Contract Negotiations over Customer Cooperation
D. Contract Negotiations over Customer Collaboration.

Q7: Agile project managers are expected to follow adaptive leadership. They are expected to be adapting _____ leadership style versus the traditional _____ leadership style.

A. Command-and-control, Servant
B. Servant, Visionary
C. Servant, Command-and-control
D. Coaching, Command-and-control

Q8: In management theories, there is "theory Y", which is used in managing people who are self-motivated and will accomplish tasks on their own. There is also "theory X", which is typically used in managing people who need supervision and constant direction to accomplish their tasks. A third theory known as "theory Z" is also used in managing people. Agile project managers would be followers of which theory?

A. Theory X
B. Theory Y
C. Theory X and Y
D. Theory X or Y

Q9: The agile project manager works in the capacity of a "Servant Leader". This doesn't mean:

A. Agile project manager's relationship with team is changing towards "servant leader" meaning "Leads by Serving".
B. Agile project manager's role within team is becoming like someone who ensures that "other people's highest priority needs are being served".
C. Agile project manager's responsibility towards the team is like somebody who embodies an ideal that "whatever the team needs to be productive, the team gets it".

D. Agile project manager's relationship with team is becoming like someone who will "do anything for the team, like a servant".

Q10: _____ for agile projects is that the agile team members are committed for full time 100 percent till the end of project. No team member can work part-time, or on multiple projects, or under multiple managers.

    A. A Negotiation
    B. An Agreement
    C. An Understanding
    D. A Promise

Q11: Agile project managers use a combination of technical, personal, and conceptual skills to analyze situations and interact appropriately with team members. Using appropriate interpersonal skills allows agile project managers to capitalize on the strengths of all team members. Example of interpersonal skills that a manager must mostly avoid is:

    A. Leadership
    B. Influencing
    C. Effective Decision Making
    D. Command-and-control style

Q12: Your IT manager approaches you about a newly assigned team member to the project. She thinks that the person doesn't have the required skills to complete the work expected and suggests that the person be assigned to a different project. What is your BEST course of action?

    A. Arrange for the team member to get the necessary training.
    B. Tell IT manager to fire the team member
    C. Tell IT manager that it is OK if the team member learns on the job
    D. Arrange for the team member to be assigned to another project

Answers:

Q1: B. Interpersonal skills are also known as soft skills in work places.

Q2: D. ability or skill to identify, assess, monitor and control or influence the emotions and feelings of oneself, of others, and of groups is known as Emotional Intelligence.

Q3: A. Communication is providing available information and sharing that information. Coordination is extending a helping hand in the areas guidance is sought. Collaboration is team work, making sure all members agree, resolve conflicts, create a win-win situation and move forward with a group consensus.

Q4: B. Communication is providing available information and sharing that information. Coordination is extending a helping hand in the areas guidance is sought. Collaboration is team work, making sure all members agree, resolve conflicts, create a win-win situation and move forward with a group consensus.

Q5: C. Communication is providing available information and sharing that information. Coordination is extending a helping hand in the areas guidance is sought. Collaboration is team work, making sure all members agree, resolve conflicts, create a win-win situation and move forward with a group consensus.

Q6: A. One of the most important agile manifestos out of four is: "Customer Collaboration over Contract Negotiations".

Q7: C. Agile project managers are expected to follow adaptive leadership. They are expected to be adapting "servant leadership" style versus the traditional "command-and-control" leadership style.

Q8: B. Agile project managers would be followers of "Theory Y" in managing knowledge workers as compared to "Theory X" used in managing industrial workers.

Q9: D. The agile project manager works in the capacity of a "Servant Leader". This doesn't mean: Agile project manager's relationship with team is becoming like someone who will "do anything for the team, like a servant".

Q10: A. A negotiation for agile projects is that the agile team members are committed for full time 100 percent till the end of project. No team member can work part-time, or on multiple projects, or under multiple managers.

Q11: D. Agile project managers use a combination of technical, personal, and conceptual skills to analyze situations and interact appropriately with team members. Using appropriate interpersonal skills allows agile project managers to capitalize on the strengths of all team members. Example of interpersonal skills that a manager uses most often include: Leadership, Influencing and Effective Decision Making.

Q12: A. You have a responsibility, where possible, to provide training for your team members to acquire necessary skills to perform the work asked of them.

CHAPTER SIX

Metrics

This chapter covers the following tools and techniques used under "Metrics" in agile:

- ❖ **Velocity/throughput/productivity**
- ❖ **Cycle Time**
- ❖ **Lead Time**
- ❖ **Earned Value Management (EVM) for agile projects**
- ❖ **Defect Rate**
- ❖ **Approved Iterations**
- ❖ **Work In Progress**

Metrics means measurement. Although there are many more such tools used for measuring the agile project performances, only those seven tools and techniques listed for PMI-ACP certification examination are discussed in this chapter. Metrics play an important role and they are the primary way to monitor and communicate the status and progress of an agile project to senior stakeholders.

Velocity/throughput/productivity

Velocity is one of the agile metrics. The team velocity is defined as the speed at which user stories are turned into working software. The total number of story points that a team can complete in one iteration is called *velocity*. Although valuable for a team to track their progress over time, it is not a universal measure. One can use velocity as a long range planning tool.

One of the most important measures about time management in agile projects is the use of velocity, a very powerful tool for forecasting long-term project timelines. This is what is used for measuring team's productivity and for setting expectations about delivery dates in the future. The team velocity is also the slope of the burn-down graph.

Example of team velocity: 10 story pts per iteration.

Few Other Agile Metrics:

- CvC: Another metrics called as CvC (Complete vs. Commit) reflects how well a team is able to meet their commitments, an absolutely essential component for agile teams.

  CvC = Story points committed / story points completed.

- Business value delivery: demonstrates to the business the value of the product delivered to date.

- Defects per story point: This metric reflects a team's effectiveness in delivering defect free code into subsequent environments.

Team velocity is used in agile planning along with how much to do – to determine when it is expected to be done. Velocity is the amount of work a team can complete in an iteration, usually given in story points. Team decides and estimates velocity. It's *not* imposed on them and team velocity gets adjusted.

Team velocity feeds data to "project burn-down chart". Velocity is a good trending tool too. The development time and activities remain same from sprint to sprint; therefore velocity can be used to determine future timelines.

Velocity is an empirical observation of the team's capacity to complete work per iteration and not an estimate or a target to aim for.

How is the velocity determined?

- Velocity provides a measure as how rapidly a team can create working features. When a team begins agile development, it takes an educated guess about how much work it can take on in an iteration.
- After 2 or 3 iterations, this guess becomes more solid, and the team begins to confidently pick off the amount of work that it can do. This amount of work is called the team's velocity. Over time, team velocity is derived from actual data.
- As agile teams start delivering, one of the two things is going to happen:
  o The team is going faster than expected ➔ they will be ahead of schedule.
  o The team is going slower than originally thought ➔ team has too much to do and do not have enough time. In this scenario, agile team will do less; they will change the plan usually by reducing scope.

Which factors can affect team velocity?

- Number of resources. (The agile project manager must do negotiations at the inception of the project to have fully dedicated resources on agile project from start-to-delivery)
- Interruption (The agile project manager must provide an Ideal time of at least 6-7 hours to maintain the team velocity at a constant pace indefinitely)
- Multi-tasking. (The agile project manager must ensure that agile team members are dedicated fully to this project and won't be encouraged to do any kind of multi-tasking with other projects).

How can the velocity affect the scope?

In agile you have to be flexible on "delivery date" or "scope". You can plot burn-down chart with efforts remaining on y-axis and time remaining on x-axis. The slope of the chart is "team velocity". Due to various factors, the team velocity can be slower than expected or faster than expected. That affects the delivery and/or scope. To fulfill one of the agile principles of "welcome changing requirements, even late in the development", you have to be flexible on date or scope.

Due to time-boxed concept, agile teams generally prefer being flexible about scope. In traditional plan-driven project management, it is very common pushing out release dates. Under agile, the goal must be shipping working software on time, even if it strips down few features which are probably of less value compared to those which will be shipped as core set of features.

Velocity can naturally increase with each sprint, as the scrum team finds synergy of working together over time, many things become clearer by using progressive elaboration and risk factors get reduced over time. However the following ways can be sought in increasing the velocity:

- ✓ Remove project impediments
- ✓ Avoid project roadblocks
- ✓ Eliminate external and internal distractions
- ✓ Solicit input and feedback from self, team and stakeholders.
- ✓ Keep consistent sprint lengths, work hours and team members.

Cycle Time

Cycle time is another metric used in measuring agile performance. Cycle time is defined as the wall clock time necessary to complete a single item of work, from start-to-finish. One of the key points of Cycle Time is that it needs to be measured between two points in the value chain. It doesn't make sense to say: "Our cycle time is 10 days". Rather, one should say: "Our cycle time from start of development to production release is 10 days".

An empirical formula may be used to calculate cycle time as follows:

Cycle time = WIP/Throughput
WIP = 500; Throughput =50; cycle time=500/50=10.

Cycle time in agile is the elapsed time, where the cycle starts with an idea and ends with a finished product. To improve the agile performance, it is encouraged to reduce the cycle time by reducing the waste.

How do you reduce *cycle time*?

- Make iterative cycles as short as possible.
- Speed up the learning feedback loop, and decrease the time-to-market.
- Understand clearly the definition of done for delivery.
- Identify waste and remove waste from the team's software development process.
- Avoid rework, improve on quality, and perform root-cause analysis.
- Get better at the difficult stuff.
- Employ poly-skilled people with more "generalists" versus specialists.
- Nurture and follow a culture of excellence.

Lead Time

Lead time is a term borrowed from the lean manufacturing method or Toyota Production System, where it is defined as the time elapsed between a customer placing an order and receiving the product ordered. In Software Development, the same can be defined as the time elapsed between identification of a requirement and its fulfilment.

In agile, the lead time is the elapsed time between formulation of a user story and that story being used "in production", by actual users under normal conditions. The agile teams opting for the Kanban approach favor this measure, over the other better known metrics of velocity. Instead of aiming at increasing velocity, improvement initiatives intend to reduce lead time.

Some authors make a distinction between "lead time" and "cycle time". The former is a "user's point of view" measurement - the time between a request being made and being fulfilled - while the latter is from a "developer's point of view" - the time between start of work on a user story and making the feature available for delivery.

To some extent, these definitions are currently fluid and may vary significantly from one software development team to the next, given the great diversity among software efforts. The best approach is probably to pick one type of measurement carefully, and ensure that everyone in team understands how it's being used and why.

EVM for Agile Projects

Earned Value Management (EVM) is a methodology that combines scope, schedule and resource measurements to assess project performance and progress. Traditionally EVM develops and monitors three key dimensions for each work package and control account. This will be compared for agile projects:

- **Planned Value**. Planned Value (PV) defines the physical work that should have been accomplished. For agile environment, the PV can be the "user stories" in the iteration.

Performance measurement baseline (PMB) is the total of the PV. Under agile, this can be total number of User Stories to be completed under iteration.

Budget at Completion (BAC) is the total planned value for the project. Under agile, this can be the total backlog for release.

- **Earned Value**. Earned Value (EV) is often used to calculate the percent complete of a project. Project managers monitor EV, both incrementally to determine current status and cumulatively to determine the long-term performance trends. Under agile, the EV can be number of user stories completed (or "done" or converted into "increments"). The agile coach may monitor EV for current iteration/sprint to determine current status as velocity. The agile coach may monitor EV cumulatively to determine the progress on burn-down / burn-up charts and adjust velocity.

- **Actual Cost**. Actual Cost (AC) is the total cost incurred in accomplishing the work that the EV measured. This is normally monitored by the customer as how much the customer has spent so far. This can be cost per iteration, cost per user story, cost per sprint, etc.

AgileEVM is a valuable technique when cost performance must be measured. EVM simply measures how much the customer has spent relative to the point in time of measurement in the project. Talk to product owner or customer about what value means to them and how they will know it when they see it.

AgileEVM is used to measure cost performance for agile projects. Agile projects are estimated top-down with detail and accuracy appropriate to the time horizon.

What are the basic assumptions when using "AgileEVM"?

- Measure progress at the release level, not at the iteration or product level.
- Measure progress at the end of each iteration, when actual iteration velocity and actual iteration costs are known.
- Measure progress when functionality is "done" at the end of each iteration.

What are the differences between traditional EVM and agile EVM?

The following section shows main differences:

PMB (performance measurement baseline):

Traditional EVM: The sum of all work package schedule estimates (duration and efforts).
Agile EVM: Total number of story points planned for a release (PRP).

Schedule baseline (often integrated in PMB):

Traditional EVM: Sum of all work Package for each time period calculated for the total duration.
Agile EVM: Total number of planned iterations (PS) multiplied by sprint (or iteration) length.

BAC (budget at complete):

Traditional EVM: The planned budget for the release or project.
Agile EVM: The planned budget for the release.

PPC (planned percent complete):

Traditional EVM: What percentages complete was expected to be at this point in the project?
Agile EVM: The number of current sprint divided by the total number of planned sprints.

APC (actual percent complete):

Traditional EVM: The dollar value of work packages actually completed (AC) divided by total dollar value of the budget at completion (BAC).
Agile EVM: The total number of story points completed (potentially shippable increments) divided by the total number of story points planned.

TCPI (To-Complete Performance Index):

Traditional TCPI: TCPI = Work Remaining / Funds Remaining
Agile TCPI: TCPI = Story Points Remaining / Time-box Remaining (similar to Burn-down charts)

Defect Rate

A defect is an imperfection or deficiency in a project component where that component does not meet its requirements or specifications and needs to be either repaired or replaced. There is a variation in what is actually delivered verses what is expected to be delivered.

The defect detection rate is the number of defects detected per sprint. Assuming that there are defects injected at a constant rate, it is correlated with the velocity. The more story points are delivered, the more defects should be found and fixed as well. Agile teams are normally consistent in the quality of the software they deliver. A drop in velocity combined with a rise in the defect detection rate should trigger an alarm.

Defect Closure rate is the number of defects fixed and closed per sprint. It should be equal to the defect detection rate. If it's not, the number of open defects will rise as you move along to next iterations, leaving the largest part of bug fixing towards the end of the project.

Gap between Total and Closed Defects: This is the difference between the total number of defects and the number of closed defects at any one time. This number should be as low as possible. A low number indicates that the quality of the delivered software so far is good. That implies that there will be few if any surprises once UAT and release preparation starts. And that in turn implies that the velocity and burn rate you have measured are indeed reliable indicators to forecast the remainder of your project. This is the most important metric of all, for if it's low, it means agile team can indeed rely on it.

Approved Iterations

In software development, an application is developed in small sections called iterations. Each iteration is reviewed and critiqued by the software team and potential end-users; insights gained from the critique of an iteration are used to determine the next step in development. Data models or sequence diagrams, which are often used to map out iterations, keep track of what has been tried, approved, or discarded, and eventually serve as a kind of blueprint for the final product.

The challenge in iterative development is to make sure all the iterations are compatible. As each new iteration is approved, developers may employ a technique known as backwards engineering, which is a systematic review and check procedure to make sure each new iteration is compatible with previous ones. The advantage of using iterative development is that the end-user is involved in the development process. Instead of waiting until the application is a final product, when it may not be possible to make changes easily, problems are identified and solved at each stage of development.

The Iteration or Sprint Planning meeting is for team members to plan and agree on the stories or backlog items they are confident they can complete during the sprint and identify the detailed tasks and tests for delivery and acceptance. The iterations must get approved from both the developers as well as stakeholders. During the iteration, if there is remaining time after all features have been delivered, then the team can request that the customer identify additional feature(s) to add to the iteration. If, on the other hand, it is obvious that not all features can be delivered, then the team works with the customer to determine which features could be delayed or perhaps split in order to deliver the most value by the iteration deadline.

Work In Progress

WIP means "Work In Progress". In Kanban, work is limited by a concept called work in progress [WIP]. The team is only allowed to work on a finite number of things at a time. E.g. WIP = 4 means this team can only take 4 things at once.

Work is limited by a concept called work in progress (WIP) limit. The goal of Kanban is flow. Team member sign up for the items using the concept of "pull" the work, where it is most needed to reduce the number of WIP items. WIP limits are used in Kanban, a card-based signaling system.

What does the team do with WIP Limits?

- WIP = 4 means this team can only take 4 things at once. Anything else that needs to be done is put on the back burner and gets prioritized.
- The goal of Kanban is flow.
- Take the most important thing off the list and pull the work when the team is ready.
- Nice way to manage expectations.
- Move the "card" to next status to indicate still WIP or "Done".

SUMMARY

Although just seven tools and techniques are mentioned under this toolkit, these are very important from PMI-ACP exam point of view. The students are encouraged to understand the importance of measurements performed under agile.

Sample Practice Examination on Chapter VI Metrics

Q1: Velocity is one of the agile metrics. What is the definition of team velocity?

    A. The speed at which agile team is working in hours per week
    B. The speed at which user stories are turned into working software
    C. The speed at which increments are integrated into deliverables
    D. The speed at which defects are fixed in one iteration

Q2: The burn-down graph is also used as one of the agile metrics. The team velocity is the _____ of the burn-down graph.

    A. Constant
    B. Same as
    C. Slope
    D. Reverse

Q3: How is the velocity determined in agile environment?

    A. Velocity is imposed on the agile team.
    B. Velocity must remain fixed and constant throughout the delivery.
    C. Velocity gets adjusted automatically.
    D. Velocity is derived from actual data over the period of time.

Q4: The agile project manager must negotiate to get resources at the inception of project, must provide an ideal time of at least 6-7 hours to maintain the team velocity at a constant pace and must ensure that the team is dedicated fully to this project. Which factor may not affect team velocity?

    A. Number of resources
    B. Location of resources
    C. Interruptions
    D. Multi-tasking

Q5: Due to various factors, the team velocity can be slower than expected or faster than expected. That affects the delivery and/or scope. To fulfill one of the agile principles of "welcome changing requirements, even late in the development", you have to be flexible on date or scope. Due to time-boxed concept, agile teams generally prefer being flexible about _____.

    A. Date
    B. Scope
    C. Date or Scope
    D. Date and Scope

Q6: Cycle time in agile is the elapsed time, where the cycle starts with an idea and ends with a finished product. To improve the agile performance, it is encouraged to reduce the cycle time by _____. This is consistent with one of the agile principles.

    A. Working more hours with increasing pace
    B. Reducing the waste
    C. Reducing the story points delivered
    D. Adjusting time-boxed duration

Q7: The agile teams opting for the Kanban approach favor the measure of "Lead Time", over the other better known metrics of "Velocity". Instead of aiming to _____ velocity, improvement initiatives intend to _____ lead time.

    A. Increase, Reduce
    B. Reduce, Increase
    C. Increase, Increase
    D. Reduce, Reduce

Q8: Agile teams are normally consistent in the quality of the software they deliver. A ____ in velocity combined with a ____ in the defect detection rate should trigger an alarm.

    A. Drop, Drop
    B. Rise, Drop
    C. Drop, Rise
    D. Rise, Rise

Q9: The defect detection rate is the number of defects detected per sprint. Defect Closure rate is the number of defects fixed and closed per sprint. It should be equal to the defect detection rate. If it's not, _____

    A. The number of open defects will remain same.
    B. The number of open defects will rise.
    C. The number of open defects will reduce
    D. The number of open defects will remain constant.

Q10: An escaped defect is a defect that was not found by, or one that escaped from, the test team. Instead, the defect was found by _____

A. Developers
B. Scrum Master
C. Product Owner
D. Customer

Answers:

Q1: B. Velocity is one of the agile metrics. The team velocity is defined as the speed at which user stories are turned into working software. The total number of story points that a team can complete in one iteration is called *velocity*.

Q2: C. The burn-down graph is also used as one of the agile metrics. The team velocity is the slope of the burn-down graph.

Q3: D. How is the velocity determined in agile environment? Team decides and estimates velocity. It's *not* imposed on them and team velocity gets adjusted. When a team begins agile development, it takes an educated guess about how much work it can take on in an iteration. After 2 or 3 iterations, this guess becomes more solid. Over time, team velocity is derived from actual data.

Q4: B. These factors can affect team velocity: number of resources, interruption and multi-tasking. It is advisable to have a co-located team but it is allowed to have virtual team so the location of team resources should not affect team velocity.

Q5: B. Due to time-boxed concept, agile teams generally prefer being flexible about scope. Remember time-boxed means no flexibility on dates.

Q6: B. Cycle time in agile is the elapsed time, where the cycle starts with an idea and ends with a finished product. To improve the agile performance, it is encouraged to reduce the cycle time by reducing the waste. This is consistent with the agile principle of "maximize the amount of work not necessary – reduce waste".

Q7: A. The agile teams opting for the Kanban approach favor this measure, over the other better known metrics of velocity. Instead of aiming at increasing velocity, improvement initiatives intend to reduce lead time.

Q8: C. Agile teams are normally consistent in the quality of the software they deliver. A drop in velocity combined with a rise in the defect detection rate should trigger an alarm.

Q9: B. The defect detection rate is the number of defects detected per sprint. Defect Closure rate is the number of defects fixed and closed per sprint. It should be equal to the defect detection rate. If it's not, the number of open defects will rise as you move along to next iterations, leaving the largest part of bug fixing towards the end of the project.

Q10: D. An escaped defect is a defect that was not found by, or one that escaped from, the test team. Instead, the defect was found by customers.

CHAPTER SEVEN

Planning, Monitoring, And Adapting

This chapter covers the following tools and techniques used under "Planning, Monitoring and Adapting" in agile:

> ➤ **Reviews / Retrospective**
> ➤ **Task/Kanban Boards**
> ➤ **Time-boxing**
> ➤ **Iteration Planning**
> ➤ **Release Planning**
> ➤ **Variance and Trend Analysis**
> ➤ **WIP Limits**
> ➤ **Daily Stand Ups**
> ➤ **Burn down Charts**
> ➤ **Burn up Charts**
> ➤ **Cumulative Flow Diagrams**
> ➤ **Backlog grooming/refinement**
> ➤ **Product-feedback Loop**

Planning in Agile

Planning is fundamental to agile project success. In traditional project management, the project execution is plan-driven. In agile project management, the project execution is value-driven; that doesn't mean there is no planning. In fact not only an overall project plan is made, there will be plan for every release, every sprint, and every day. Agile projects involve planning up front and then planning throughout the entire project using both rolling wave planning and progressive elaboration. Plans always change and agile focus on just-in-time planning to accommodate last minute changes and to cope up with real situations.

Planning is part of Dr. Deming's PDCA cycle reflecting the "plan" step. Planning under agile projects may involve determining whether objectives stated under project charter can be achieved, how agile project will be accomplished, and addresses all appropriate agile project management tools, techniques, processes and knowledge areas. Agile project planning encompasses the areas including but not limited to: product roadmap, release planning, iteration planning, product backlogs/user stories, agile estimation, communications/collaboration, agile modeling, resource management, agile EVM, risk management, value-based prioritization etc.

Planning in agile with the roadmap to value has following stages:

> *Stage 1: Product Vision*: This document is created by product owner and describes what the product is, who will use it, why customers will use it, and how it will support company strategy. This is done on annual basis – revise product vision at least once in a year.

> *Stage 2: Product Roadmap*: This document is created by product owner and describes high-level view of product requirements, approximate time frames for deliverables, prioritization, estimation of efforts and gaps. This is done on biannually basis – revise product roadmap at least twice in a year.

> *Stage 3: Release Plan*: This document is created by product owner and describes a high-level timetable for releasing working software. Release plan is created at the beginning of every release. An agile project will have multiple releases with highest priority features with most value to customer appearing first. The releases are done on quarterly basis – revise release plans at least four times in a year.

> *Stage 4: Sprint Plan*: This document is created jointly by product owner, scrum master and development team. Also called as iteration plan, it describes sprint goal, requirements supporting those goals, and how those requirements will be completed in sprint. The sprint plans are done on monthly basis – revise sprint plans at least once in a month, twelve times in a year.

> *Stage 5: Daily Scrum*: This daily scrum meeting is facilitated by the development team to coordinate every day's priorities. All discuss on what was completed yesterday, what will be done today and any roadblocks so that those can be addressed and resolved immediately. The daily scrums are done on daily basis – revisit the project plan at least once in a day by meeting for minimum 15 minutes in 24 hours.

> *Stage 6: Sprint Review*: This monthly scrum sprint review meeting is facilitated by the scrum team at end of every sprint. The team demonstrates the working product or minimally marketable feature or a working increment to stakeholders and seeks a constructive feedback as well as acceptance of what is delivered. The sprint reviews are done on monthly basis – demonstrate at least once every month for minimum an hour.

> *Stage 7: Sprint Retrospective*: This monthly scrum sprint retrospective meeting is facilitated by the scrum team for the scrum team at end of every sprint. The team discusses how sprint went and seeks a constructive feedback from within the team for product and process improvements. At least one area is picked for continuous improvement. The sprint

retrospectives are done on monthly basis – think of improvements at least once every month for minimum an hour.

Planning in agile is iterative process. The teams plan only as much as needed at every stage but perform planning throughout the project. This just-in-time planning prevents planning on low priority requirements up front that may even never be implemented.

Monitoring in Agile

Monitoring is fundamental to agile project success. In traditional project management, the project execution is monitored and controlled. In agile project management, the project monitoring is essentially the inspection for values and processes. In fact not only an overall project is monitored, there will be an inspection for every release, every sprint, and every day.

Monitoring is again part of Dr. Deming's PDCA cycle reflecting the "check" step. Monitoring under agile project may involve dealing with agile metrics/measurements, variances, and burn up and burn down charts, change management, forecasting, continuous improvements, retrospectives, quality control, frequent validation and verifications and many more related activities.

Adapting in Agile

Adapting is fundamental to agile project success. In traditional project management, the project execution is monitored and controlled. In agile project management, adapting is essentially making changes as necessary in the project, product and processes to implement those changes which customer values the most. In fact changes are made not only in overall project but also at every release, every sprint, and every day.

Adapting is the process of customizing the project to agile principles and practices. Adapting may involve process tailoring, continuous integration, adaptive leadership, soft skills negotiations, delivering business value, being ready to accept changes, and many more areas that are subject to changes under traditional plan driven project management.

Reviews / Retrospective

Retrospective is a process used for self-evaluation under agile environment. Although it is treated as an equivalent to a "post mortem" meeting or "lessons learned" meeting at traditional project management, it is better than that. The lessons learned under retrospective meetings are used by the existing agile development team to improve in next iteration. Retrospective doesn't happen at the end of project or at traditional project closure, when the "lessons learned" are meant for the next project and project team. In true sense, the retrospective is used for continuous process improvement and for a more timely improvement impact.

Retrospective is facilitated by an agile team member. Retrospective session contributes to continuous process improvements. A retrospective session is done at the end of each iteration and essentially it is a meeting of team members with a short duration of up to an hour.

Retrospective happens at the end of every iteration. Only agile development team members are invited to participate. Of the topics discussed, one topic is chosen (with team consensus) for improvement in the next iteration. The topic discussions address what went well, what went wrong and how the team can improve in next iteration and following iterations. New topics are chosen every time for subsequent process improvements.

What are the advantages of retrospective?

- Retrospective is in the true sense meant for continuous process improvement. The agile process team votes for one area of process improvement and carries forward/implements in successive iteration(s).
- The improvement story goes under the non-functional Backlog. There is no estimation, and no story points associated with it. The agile development team keeps it in mind and consciously uses it to improve the agile process.
- Frequent retrospectives are excellent ways for teams to analyze, adapt and improve their entire development process performance.
- Sharing these improvement ideas gives the team a chance to bond and support one another, grow closer and self-identifying specific solutions with self-directed team adoption leads to far better performance.

What are the logistics of retrospective?

- Most common retrospective, *the Iteration Retrospective* happens at the end of every Iteration. However the team may schedule weekly or biweekly retrospectives.
- The Retrospective meetings are typically 1-hour duration.
- Retrospective is done by agile development team, and is meant for agile team and is used for process improvement by agile development team.
- The retrospective is NOT used for finger pointing, attacking or blaming anybody. It is used for identifying an area for self-improvement and overall process improvement.
- The agile team can also schedule
  o Release Retrospectives
  o Project Retrospectives
  o Surprise Retrospectives

What are the differences between a Review and Retrospectives Meeting?

- Executive management, other teams, stakeholders, and product owners attend a review meeting versus just the agile team in retrospective meeting.

- A demonstration of feature(s) and/or function(s) is typically included in the review meting for acceptance or backlog reporting/showcase versus a process improvement discussions in the retrospective meeting.
- Review meeting leads to what backlog item(s) to be carried forward in next iteration(s) versus what area was selected for process improvements for next iteration in current retrospective meeting.

What are the differences between Retrospectives and Lessons Learned Meetings?

There are 2 main differences:

- Retrospectives are frequent; these are conducted at end of each iteration and at end of release versus Lessons learned meeting occurring only once at the end of traditional project as part of project closure.
- Retrospective suggests only one improvement area to be considered/implemented in the next iteration versus all the "lessons learned" selected for improvement being valued for use in the next project.

What do you do after Retrospectives?

- Start planning for next iteration.
- Keep the process improvement area in mind throughout next iteration.

Task / Kanban Boards

Kanban means "visual signals". Kanban Boards are the boards where vital project information is displayed in a highly visible way. This facilitates the process of an information radiator. Everyone can see how the work is progressing. Task/Kanban boards are used as an information radiator.

Display information in highly visible way, somewhere in the war room or conference rooms. The concept is adapted from Lean Manufacturing process and as a byproduct of just-in-time (JIT) process. Use boards to display up-to-date current state of the project. The Kanban board shows the items that the teams need to produce next. Color Sticky notes or index cards are pinned on the board representing units of shippable products. As deliverables progresses, the team members remove, move and add cards. It also works as a motivator and reminder to the team. Anyone walking around can see the picture and get status. Agile project progress should be visible.

What is the purpose of Kanban Boards?

- To act as an information radiator for local / co-located teams.

- Distributed teams can use a web camera aiming at the task board or post it on share point facility/ wiki.
- It is equivalent to bill boards / displays at airports showing flights arrived, departed, delayed, or cancelled. The information is readily and visibly displayed on a real time basis so there is no need to ask anyone about current status of project. Similar to a Dow Jones Wall Street Chart Displays.
- Normally they use color coded sticky notes or index cards on the task board to show status of activities.
- Sample Kanban boards show: To Do's, Analysis, Develop, Test, Deploy, Done as columns from left to right and list of ordered activities under each status columns.
- Once a task is completed, it is moved to the next column progressing to the right till its status is "Done" done.
- Kanban boards also help in implementing WIP Limits and motivate agile team members to sign up for tasks exceeding / aggregating under one area (a specific column on Kanban board).

Time-boxing

Time-boxing is a concept in managing time as a fixed block of time that is set aside for an activity / research / discussion / meeting. You stop when allotted time is up, regardless of your progress. Time boxing means fixed duration with pre-defined start and fixed end time.

There is a fixed start, fixed end and fixed duration for any activity and you must stop when your time is up. Just like appearing for 3-hour PMI-ACP certification examination.

What are the advantages of time-boxing?

- This is difficult and valuable.
  - o Difficult because you may be just seconds / minutes away from the solution.
  - o Valuable because you have made as much progress as possible within the time frame.
- Time-boxing meetings can reduce wasted discussions, since the meeting must remain focused in order to end within stipulated time period.
- The Iteration Time-box:
  - o Iterations are exactly one week long and have a strictly defined completion time.
  - o Iteration work ends at a particular time regardless of how much work the team has finished.
  - o Iteration time-boxing doesn't prevent problems. It reveals those problems, giving you an opportunity to correct the situation.
  - o In XP, iteration review demo marks the end of the iteration (schedule the demo at the same time every week).

Iteration Planning

An agile iteration is time-boxed period where customers' top stories get converted into working software. Iteration planning is basically developing the project schedule at the tactical level, whereas release planning is developing the project schedule at the strategic level. Strategic level involves schedule development at high level (features and iterations). Tactical level involves schedule development at lower/detail level (tasks and hours).

There are four things that should happen in each iteration:

- Getting feedback from last iteration's user stories
- Planning next iteration's user stories
- Making sure that next iteration's work will be ready
- Looking for feedback and areas of improvements.

Whatever it takes to produce working, tested software from user stories/backlogs needs to happen during an iteration. Planning to make that happen is Iteration Planning. Whatever it takes to produce working, tested software from user stories/backlogs needs to happen during an iteration. Planning to make that happen is Iteration Planning.

Iteration Planning is the fourth step in agile project planning process consisting of 5 phases: Project Charter, Product Roadmap, Release Planning, Iteration Planning, and Daily Stand-up.

- ➤ Project Charter happens annually – typically once in a year.
- ➤ Product Roadmap happens bi-annually – typically twice in a year, after every 6 months.
- ➤ Release Planning happens quarterly – typically four times in a year, once in every quarter.
- ➤ Iteration Planning happens monthly – typically twelve times in a year, once in a month (can be bi-weekly if required)
- ➤ Stand-Up Meeting happens daily – typically once in a day for 15-minutes, after every 24 hours in working days.

Purpose: Meeting for the team to commit to the completion of a set of the highest ranked product backlog items. Commitment defines Iteration Backlog and is based on the team's velocity (or capacity) and the length of the iteration time-box.

Assumptions:

- ❖ Product backlog items are sized
- ❖ Product backlog stack ranked to reflect priorities of Product Owner
- ❖ There is a general understanding of acceptance criteria for those ranked backlog items.

Commitment from agile development team on the high value and high priority product backlog items to convert each assigned item into a potentially shippable product. Make project progress reports visible at iteration and release levels.

What are the steps in Iteration Planning?

1. The Product owner describes highest ranked product backlog items.
2. The team determines the tasks necessary to complete that product backlog item.
3. Team members volunteer to own the tasks.
4. Task owners estimate the ideal hours they need to finish their tasks.
5. Planning continues while team can commit to delivery without exceeding capacity.

Note: If any individual exceeds their capacity during iteration planning, team collaborates to better distribute the load.

What is typical agenda for Iteration Planning Meeting?

- Opening
- Product Vision and Roadmap
- Development status, state of architecture, results of previous iterations
- Iteration Name and theme
- Velocity in previous iterations / estimated velocity
- Iteration time-box (dates, working days)
- Team capacity
- Issues and concerns
- Review and update definition of Done
- Stories / items from the backlog to consider
- Tasking Out
- New Issues and concerns
- Dependencies and assumptions
- Commit
- Communication and logistics plan
- Parking Lot
- Action Items / Plan
- Retrospect the meeting
- Close – Celebrate a successful planning session

Release Planning

Release Planning is basically developing the project schedule at the Strategic Level, whereas Iteration Planning is developing the project schedule at the Tactical Level.

Release planning is longer-term planning that enables us to answer questions like "When will we be done?" or "Which features can I get by the end of the year?" or "How much will this cost?" Release planning must balance customer value and overall quality against the constraints of scope, schedule, and budget.

Release Planning is the third step in Agile Project Planning Process consisting of 5 phases: Project Charter, Product Roadmap, Release Planning, Iteration Planning, and Daily Stand-up.

- ✓ Project Charter happens annually – typically once in a year.
- ✓ Product Roadmap happens bi-annually – typically twice in a year, after every 6 months.
- ✓ Release Planning happens quarterly – typically four times in a year, once in every quarter / 3-months.
- ✓ Iteration Planning happens monthly – typically twelve times in a year, once in a month.
- ✓ Stand-Up Meeting happens daily – typically once in a day, after every 24 hours in working days.

Purpose: The purpose of Release Planning is to commit to a plan for delivering an increment of product value.

Release Planning is a process to understand the features that will constitute multiple iterations. This is done using top-down planning. Make project progress visible at iteration and release levels.

VARIANCE AND TREND ANALYSIS

Variance analysis is the means by which a group of certain variables (or elements that are subject to change) is broken down into its constituent parts, and the analysis of these parts is, in a way, refined. The goal is to determine the causes of a variance (that is to say, the difference between an expected result and an actual result). A project management team will focus on the variables of scope, cost, and schedule in its variance analysis.

The term "**trend analysis**" refers to the concept of collecting information and attempting to spot a pattern, or *trend*, in the information. In project management trend analysis is a mathematical technique that uses historical results to predict future outcome. This is achieved by tracking variances in cost and schedule performance. In this context, it is a project management quality control tool.

Daily Stand-ups

Another helpful meeting in communication is the daily stand-up. The daily scrum, also referred to as "the daily stand-up" is a brief daily communication and planning forum, in which agile/

scrum teams come together to evaluate the health and progress of the iteration/sprint. The daily stand-up is a time-boxed meeting that occurs at the same time, at the same place, for 15-minutes on a daily basis on all working days.

Since this is a daily routine, all team members must attend the meeting and there will not be any meeting invites or notifications sent to respective team members. This is the best means of face-to-face communication and aimed to resolve multiple problems or issues at hand. The scrum process is characterized by and is recognized mainly due to daily stand-ups and its benefits to agile projects.

As the name suggests, in true sense it's a stand-up meeting and people are typically not allowed to sit or relax since it's a very short, brief, precise quick meeting. Many times the scrum master needs to keep the meeting focused on issues at hand and restrict people diverting to other subjects or getting carried away or taking too much of the meeting time. Also the pigs (in agile terminology) are the ones who can speak and provide their two cents whereas the chickens (in agile terminology) are not supposed to participate in the discussions but only listen to the conversations. If there is any topic that needs more attention or discussions, the scrum master may extend the daily stand-up meeting with team consensus or may request for another separate meeting with few selected people who may be directly involved/impacted.

Daily Stand-up meeting is the fifth and final step in Agile Project Planning Process consisting of 5 phases: Project Charter, Product Roadmap, Release Planning, Iteration Planning, and Daily Stand-up.

> ➤ Project Charter happens annually – typically once in a year.
> ➤ Product Roadmap happens bi-annually – typically twice in a year, after every 6 months.
> ➤ Release Planning happens quarterly – typically four times in a year, once in every quarter / 3-months.
> ➤ Iteration Planning happens monthly – typically twelve times in a year, once in a month.
> ➤ Stand-Up Meeting happens daily – typically once in a day, after every 24 hours in working days.

The target is to keep all team members informed about the tasks at hand. This is not formal "reporting status" kind of meeting.

What is done in daily stand-ups?

- Those team members who are assigned work in the current iteration speak at the meeting.
- Each team member syncs up with each other.
- Each team member voices his or her dependencies or issues.
- Take action to resolve any outstanding issues.

- Daily stand-up is reported by the team, for the team (PM to remove obstacles, help effective team communication, insist team resolves their conflicts).
- The THREE main points for discussion are:
  - What have you done since last meeting?
  - What are you planning to do by next meeting?
  - What impediments (obstacles) are impacting your work progress?
- Let the team decide best location for team stand-up (co-located as well as distributed).
- Invite others to observe and gain understanding.
- Lasts around 15 minutes.
- External issues should be handled outside of the daily stand-up meeting.

Burn down Charts

A burn down chart is a simple, easy to understand graphical representation of "Work Remaining" versus "Time Remaining". It's the graph that shows how quickly we as a team are burning through our customer's user stories, and it assists in predicting when we will be done. The burn down chart is an effective means for teams to make adjustments in order to meet product/project delivery expectations.

Burn down charts play major role in reporting and under agile metrics. Burn-down chart makes all those events visible – such as fluctuating team velocity, adding new stories to the plan, dropping old stories. When something shows up on the burn-down chart, it helps to facilitate conversation with the stakeholders around that thing and also helps to visualize the impact of decisions to be taken / changes to be made. This is the highly visible part of agile planning. We don't hide anything or sugar-coat the facts. We can set realistic expectations with customers and make sure everyone understands those expectations.

What does the Burn down Chart show?

- The burn-down chart is a great vehicle for showing the state of your project. With a glance, you can tell the following:
  - How much work has been done?
  - How much work remains?
  - The team's velocity

Plotting Burn down charts

- On the Y-axis, we track the amount of work remaining (days of efforts or points).
- On the X-axis, we track time (or time remaining) by iteration.
- Record the amount of work remaining each iteration, and plot that on the graph.
- The slope of the line is the team velocity (how much the team completed in each iteration)

- Each column represents the amount of work remaining in the project and indicating we are done when the column burns down to nothing.

Burn up Charts

This is a flipped burn-down chart. By drawing a steady line across the top (Total amount of work + New Stories), any increase in scope is immediately seen, and it's a bit easier to track over the iteration period.

The burn up chart is more convenient for those who use traditional charting techniques.

Burn-up or Burn-down Charts?

- If you like the scope visibility of the "burn-up chart" but prefer the simplicity and concept of "burn-down chart", then combine the two charts to track the total work done in each iteration on the burn-down along with the work remaining.
- Use of either chart supports an easy and visible way to see and set expectations on how much work remains and when you expect to be done.

Cumulative Flow Diagram

A big part of the cumulative flow diagram (CFD) is its ability to visualize how close you are to completion of a large project, and where bottlenecks or waste appears in the process. It's a very powerful and descriptive tool.

CFD is mainly used to identify and reduce waste in the process.

CFD is a concept used in Kanban. For software design, a "cumulative flow diagram" is used to track performance and to visualize where the features / stories are in the workflow across time.

BACKLOG GROOMING / REFINEMENT

The team (or part of the team including the product owner) meets regularly to "groom the product backlog", in a formal or informal meeting which can lead to any of the following:

- removing user stories that no longer appear relevant
- creating new user stories in response to newly discovered needs
- re-assessing the relative priority of stories
- assigning estimates to stories which have yet to receive one

- correcting estimates in light of newly discovered information
- splitting user stories which are high priority but too coarse grained to fit in an upcoming iteration

This refinement is very important to keep the stuff up to date. The refinement is mostly done by the team members, with discussions among team members and decision normally taken by the team itself.

The intent of a "grooming" meeting is to ensure that the backlog remains populated with items that are relevant, detailed and estimated to a degree appropriate with their priority, and in keeping with current understanding of the project or product and its objectives.

An Agile project is also subject to "scope creep", in the form of user stories which do not really yield substantial value but were thought "good ideas at the time", and entered into the backlog before they be forgotten. The grooming weeds out those non-valuable user stories.

PRODUCT FEEDBACK LOOP

Feedback means basically understanding the pros and cons of a product from users' perspective. These can be characteristics, constructive suggestions, criticisms, comments or even encouragements. There are multiple feedback techniques for product. Some of those techniques which are applicable to agile are as follows:

1. Prototyping
2. Simulation
3. Demonstrations
4. Evaluations

Prototyping or software prototyping refers to the activity of creating prototypes of software applications which may produce incomplete versions of the software program being developed.

Paper Prototyping: Instead of presenting only one foremost design, it is recommended that the team rapidly produces multiple prototypes utilizing number of different designs and options. The team achieves this quickly using cheap and inexpensive paper prototype. After that, the team then presents these prototypes by demonstrating various "what-if" scenarios to the customers and seeks constructive feedback from the customers.

The major benefit of prototyping is that the software designer and implementer can get valuable feedback from the users early in the project. The other benefit of the prototype review is that the customers, including end-users, examine the prototype and provide feedback on additions or changes which are valuable to them.

Simulation is the imitation of some real thing, state of affairs, or process. The act of simulating something generally entails representing certain key characteristics or behaviors of a selected physical or abstract system. The main purpose of the simulation is to get the *early feedback* from end users and customers about those key features.

Demonstration or *showcase* is the opportunity to show the work to the world and get some real down-to-earth feedback from the customer. Gather sprint review feedback informally.

Whether the company needs to close a sale, gather end-user feedback, show progress to potential customers, or simply explain how the new product works, it will be needed to demo the software product.

Invite only those people to the demo, whose *feedback* is truly valuable.

- Demonstration shows what the team has been doing so far.
- Demonstration shows how far the team is from final shippable product
- Demonstration shows what can be deployed today if the product owner really had to, since it's done.
- Demonstration is a good way to close out last iteration's work done.
- Demonstration must be driven by the customers so that the team can watch how the customers plan to use the software.

Evaluation is basically giving away a fully developed software copy to prospective customers and allowing them to use it at their leisure. During the evaluation period, keep asking for their feedback. These are generally experts who had used many other competitive products. Normally a questionnaire or point method is followed which is simple but effective in evaluating the pros and cons of the product. Evaluations are used to get some real honest-to-goodness feedback from the customers.

SUMMARY

Although twelve tools and techniques are mentioned under this toolkit, these are very important from PMI-ACP exam point of view. The students are encouraged to understand the importance of planning, monitoring and adapting process under agile.

Sample Practice Examination on Chapter VII Planning, Monitoring and Adapting

Q1: Dr. Deming's PDCA cycle stands for?

A. Plan, Done, Check, Action
B. Plan, Do, Check, Act
C. Plan, Done, Control, Act
D. Plan, Do, Control, Act

Q2: In traditional project management, the project execution is plan-driven. In agile project management, the project execution is _____

A. Sprint driven
B. Customer driven
C. Value driven
D. Investment driven

Q3: Agile projects involve planning up front with details for near term and milestones for far away; and then planning throughout the entire project by adding level of details as they become known, using both ____ and _____.

A. Sprint planning and release planning
B. Mission and vision statements
C. Project charter and product backlogs
D. Rolling wave planning and progressive elaboration

Q4: The Sprint plan is created jointly by product owner, scrum master and development team. Also called as iteration plan and in most likely (as a norm) the sprint plans are done on _____ basis.

A. Weekly
B. Monthly
C. Quarterly
D. Annually

Q5: This daily scrum meeting is facilitated by the development team to coordinate every day's priorities. All discuss on what was completed yesterday, what will be done today and any roadblocks so that those can be addressed and resolved immediately. The daily scrums are done on daily basis – revisit the project plan at least once in a day by meeting for minimum _____ minutes in 24 hours.

A. 10
B. 15
C. 20
D. 30

Q6: This monthly scrum sprint retrospective meeting is facilitated by the scrum team for the scrum team at end of every sprint. The team discusses how sprint went and seeks a constructive feedback from within the team for product and process improvements. At least one area is picked for _____

A. Continuous improvement
B. Review and suggestions
C. Critical thinking
D. Postponement

Q7: In agile project management, the project monitoring is essentially the _____ for values and processes.

A. Checklist
B. Inspection
C. Dashboard
D. Improvement

Q8: Name the process used for self-evaluation under agile environment. It doesn't happen at the end of project or at traditional project closure. In true sense, the process is used for continuous process improvement and for a more timely improvement impact.

A. Lessons Learned
B. Post mortem
C. Critical thinking
D. Retrospective

Q9: Retrospective is primarily done by and is meant for _____, and is used for process improvement.

A. Executive Management
B. Stakeholders
C. Development Team
D. Product Owners

Q10: Kanban Boards are the boards where vital project information is displayed in a highly visible way. Everyone can see how the work is progressing. Task/Kanban boards are used as _____

    A. Staff Status Reporting Tool
    B. Information Radiator
    C. Instructions Bulletin Board
    D. Advertising Medium

Q11: Sample _____ show : To Do's, Analysis, Develop, Test, Deploy, Done as columns from left to right and list of ordered activities under each status columns.

    A. Bill Boards
    B. Kanban Boards
    C. Post-It
    D. Agile Boards

Q12: This is a concept in managing time as a fixed block of time that is set aside for an activity / research / discussion / meeting. You stop when allotted time is up, regardless of your progress.

    A. Time Management
    B. Task Management
    C. Time boxing
    D. Activity Diagram

Q13: Who describes highest ranked product backlog items in the Iteration Planning Meeting, after which the team determines the tasks necessary to complete that product backlog item?

    A. Product Owner
    B. Stakeholders
    C. Scrum Master
    D. Business Analyst

Q14: You are a project manager discussing about completing user stories in upcoming sprint. During the discussions, there were multiple issues which need more details and were kind of "To Be Decided" later. You wanted to keep track of those so you won't forget those later. What are these categorized as?

    A. Unresolved Issues
    B. Parking Lot
    C. Undecided
    D. Ignored

Q15: The term "**trend analysis**" refers to the concept of collecting information and attempting to spot a pattern, or *trend*, in the information. In project management trend analysis is a mathematical technique that uses _____ results to predict _____ results.

    A. Historical, Future
    B. Future, Historical
    C. Current, Future
    D. Historical, Current

Q16: What is called as the difference between an expected result and an actual result?

    A. Standard Deviation
    B. Variance
    C. Sigma
    D. Normal Distribution

Q17: The scrum process is characterized by and is recognized mainly due to daily stand-ups and its benefits to agile projects. The daily stand-up is a meeting that occurs at the same time, at the same place, for 15-minutes on a daily basis on all working days. What is not expected in daily stand-up meetings?

    A. all team members must attend the meeting
    B. it's a time-boxed meeting
    C. meeting invites or notifications will be sent
    D. aimed to resolve multiple issues at hand

Q18: An Agile project in its inception stage, may have user stories which do not really yield substantial value but were thought "good ideas at the time", and entered into the backlog as placeholders before they be forgotten. The grooming weeds out those non-valuable user stories. This may be equivalent in traditional project management as:

    A. Scope Refinement
    B. Scope Creep
    C. Scope Baseline
    D. Scope Burden

Q19: Agile team seeks real down-to-earth and constructive feedback from the customers at various stages of product development. The following feedback techniques are applicable to agile probably with an exception of:

    A. Examination
    B. Simulation

C. Demonstration

D. Evaluation

Q20: The team (or part of the team including the product owner) meets regularly to "groom the product backlog", in a formal or informal meeting which can lead to any of the following except:

A. removing user stories that no longer appear relevant

B. creating new user stories in response to newly discovered needs

C. re-assessing the relative priority of stories

D. keeping user stories that no longer yield substantial value

Answers:

Q1: B. Dr. Deming's PDCA cycle stands for Plan-Do-Check-Act.

Q2: C. In traditional project management, the project execution is plan-driven. In agile project management, the project execution is value-driven; that doesn't mean there is no planning.

Q3: D. Agile projects involve planning up front with details for near term and milestones for far away; and then planning throughout the entire project by adding level of details as they become known, using both rolling wave planning and progressive elaboration. (Read the question carefully, it indicates the answer).

Q4: C. The Sprint plan is created jointly by product owner, scrum master and development team. Also called as iteration plan and in most likely (as a norm) the sprint plans are done on monthly basis – revise sprint plans at least once in a month, twelve times in a year.

Q5: B. This daily scrum meeting is facilitated by the development team to coordinate every day's priorities. All discuss on what was completed yesterday, what will be done today and any roadblocks so that those can be addressed and resolved immediately. The daily scrums are done on daily basis – revisit the project plan at least once in a day by meeting for minimum 15 minutes in 24 hours.

Q6: A. This monthly scrum sprint retrospective meeting is facilitated by the scrum team for the scrum team at end of every sprint. The team discusses how sprint went and seeks a constructive feedback from within the team for product and process improvements. At least one area is picked for continuous improvement.

Q7: B. In agile project management, the project monitoring is essentially the inspection for values and processes. In fact not only an overall project is monitored, there will be an inspection for every release, every sprint, and every day.

Q8: D. Retrospective is the process used for self-evaluation under agile environment. It doesn't happen at the end of project or at traditional project closure. In true sense, the retrospective is used for continuous process improvement and for a more timely improvement impact.

Q9: C. Retrospective is done by agile development team, and is meant for agile team and is used for process improvement by agile development team.

Q10: B. Kanban Boards are the boards where vital project information is displayed in a highly visible way. This facilitates the process of an information radiator. Everyone can see how the work is progressing. Task/Kanban boards are used as information radiator.

Q11: B. Sample Kanban boards show: To Do's, Analysis, Develop, Test, Deploy, Done as columns from left to right and list of ordered activities under each status columns. It is equivalent to bill boards / displays at airports showing flights arrived, departed, delayed, or cancelled. The information is readily and visibly displayed on a real time basis so there is no need to ask anyone about current status of project.

Q12: C. Time-boxing is a concept in managing time as a fixed block of time that is set aside for an activity / research / discussion / meeting. You stop when allotted time is up, regardless of your progress. Time boxing means fixed duration with pre-defined start and fixed end time.

Q13: A. The Product Owner describes highest ranked product backlog items in the Iteration Planning Meeting, after which the team determines the tasks necessary to complete that product backlog item.

Q14: B. You are a project manager discussing about completing user stories in upcoming sprint. During the discussions, there were multiple issues which need more details and were kind of "To Be Decided" later. You wanted to keep track of those so you won't forget those later. These issues are kept in "Parking Lot".

Q15: A. The term **"trend analysis"** refers to the concept of collecting information and attempting to spot a pattern, or *trend*, in the information. In project management trend analysis is a mathematical technique that uses historical results to predict future outcome.

Q16: B. The difference between an expected result and an actual result is known as variance.

Q17: C. Since this is a daily routine, all team members must attend the meeting and there will not be any meeting invites or notifications sent to respective team members. This is the best means of face-to-face communication and aimed to resolve multiple problems or issues at hand.

Q18: B. An Agile project is also subject to "scope creep", in the form of user stories which do not really yield substantial value but were thought "good ideas at the time", and entered into the backlog before they be forgotten. The grooming weeds out those non-valuable user stories.

Q19: A. There are multiple feedback techniques for product. Some of those techniques which are applicable to agile are: Prototyping, Simulation, Demonstrations and Evaluations.

Q20: D. An Agile project is also subject to "scope creep", in the form of user stories which do not really yield substantial value but were thought "good ideas at the time", and entered into the backlog. These should be removed when refining or grooming backlog.

CHAPTER EIGHT

Process Improvement

This chapter covers the following tools and techniques used under "Process Improvement" in agile:

- ❖ **Kaizen**
- ❖ **The Five WHYs**
- ❖ **Retrospectives and Introspective**
- ❖ **Process tailoring / hybrid models**
- ❖ **Value Stream Mapping**
- ❖ **Control Limits**
- ❖ **Pre-mortem (rule setting, failure analysis)**
- ❖ **Fishbone Diagram Analysis**

All these tools and techniques are mainly used for process improvements and to perform root cause analysis (RCA).

KAIZEN

The Sino-Japanese word "kaizen" simply means "change for better". The word refers to any improvement, one-time or continuous, large or small. The word Kaizen in English is typically applied to measures for implementing continuous improvement or even taken to mean a "philosophy of improvements" thereof.

When used in the business sense and applied to the workplace, kaizen refers to activities that continually improve all functions and involve all employees. It also applies to processes that cross organizational boundaries. It has been applied in healthcare, government, banking, and other industries. By improving standardized activities and processes, kaizen aims to eliminate waste, as suggested under lean manufacturing.

Kaizen is a daily process, the purpose of which goes beyond simple productivity improvement. It is also a process that, when done correctly, humanizes the workplace, eliminates overly hard work ("muri"), and teaches people how to learn to spot and eliminate waste in business processes. In all, the process suggests a humanized approach to workers and to increasing productivity: The idea is to nurture the company's people as much as it is to praise and encourage participation in kaizen activities. Successful implementation requires "the participation of workers in the improvement." People at all levels of an organization participate in kaizen, as well as external stakeholders when applicable. Kaizen is most commonly associated with manufacturing operations, but has also been used in non-manufacturing environments.

While kaizen (at Toyota) usually delivers small improvements, the culture of continual aligned small improvements and standardization yields large results in terms of overall improvement in productivity. This philosophy differs from the "command and control" improvement programs. Kaizen methodology includes making changes and monitoring results, then adjusting. Large-scale pre-planning and extensive project scheduling are replaced by smaller experiments, which can be rapidly adapted as new improvements are suggested. In modern usage, it is designed to address a particular issue over the course of a week and is referred to as a "kaizen blitz" or "kaizen event". These are limited in scope, and issues that arise from them are typically used in later blitzes. A person who makes a large contribution in the successful implementation of kaizen during kaizen events is awarded the title of "Zenkai".

The cycle of kaizen activity can be defined as:

- Standardize an operation and activities,
- Measure the operation (find cycle time and amount of in-process inventory).
- Gauge measurements against requirements.
- Innovate to meet requirements and increase productivity.
- Standardize the new, improved operations.
- Continue cycle *ad infinitum*.

THE FIVE WHYS

Another technique used in conjunction with PDCA (Plan-Do-Check-Act) is the Five Whys, which is a form of root cause analysis in which the user asks a series of 5 "why" questions about a failure that has occurred, basing each subsequent question on the answer to the previous. There are normally a series of causes stemming from one root cause, and they can be visualized using fishbone diagrams or tables. The Five Whys can be used as a foundational tool in personal improvement.

5 Whys is an iterative question-asking technique used to explore the cause-and-effect relationships underlying a particular problem. The primary goal of the technique is to determine the root cause of a defect or problem by repeating the question "Why?" Each question forms the basis of the next question. The "5" in the name derives from an empirical observation on the number of iterations typically required to resolve the problem. Thus, even when the method is closely followed, the outcome still depends upon the knowledge and persistence of the people involved.

This is one of the most important aspects in the 5 Why approach - the *real* root cause should point toward a process that is not working well or does not exist. A key phrase to keep in mind in any 5 Why exercise is "people do not fail, processes do". There are two primary techniques used to perform 5 Whys: the fishbone (or Ishikawa) diagram and a tabular format like excel spreadsheet. These tools allow for analysis to be branched in order to provide multiple root causes.

The concept of 5-why is simple:

1. Identify the problem.
2. Ask yourself: why did this happen? Come up with all the causes you can think of.
3. For each of the causes you just identified, ask "why did this happen?" again.
4. Repeat until you've done steps 2 and 3 for five times. You should have identified the root cause by this stage.
5. Find solutions and countermeasures to fix the root cause.

Drawbacks or shortcoming of this method: 5-why is based on personal opinion on what the causes are, and two people performing 5-why analysis on the same problem can come up with widely differing causes and completely different root causes. The issue is slightly negated as long as the person involved in the problem performs the analysis. If they do, then they should have enough expertise to perform an accurate analysis.

RETROSPECTIVES AND INTROSPECTIVE

Retrospective means looking back or dealing with past events or situations. It can also be an exhibition or compilation showing the development of the work of a particular team over a period of time.

Introspection is the process of examining your own thoughts and feelings, to look inside. In most of the time it is done for self-examination, self-observation, self-questioning or for self-reflection.

In software engineering, retrospective is a meeting held by a project team at the end of a project or process (often after an iteration) to discuss what was successful about the project or time period covered by that retrospective, what could be improved, and how to incorporate the successes and improvements in future iterations or projects. Retrospective can be done in many different ways. The *Agile Retrospective Resource Wiki* is a resource for sharing retrospective plans, tips & tricks, tools and ideas to help get the most out of retrospectives.

In agile development, retrospectives play a very important role in iterative and incremental development. At end of every iteration a retrospective is held to look for ways to improve the process for the next iteration.

Each member of the team members answers the following questions:

- What worked well for us?
- What did not work well for us?
- What actions can we take to improve our process going forward?

The Agile retrospective can be thought of as a "lessons learned" meeting. The team reflects on how everything went and then decides what changes they want to make in the next iteration. The retrospective is team-driven, and team members should decide together how the meetings will be run and how decisions will be made about improvements. An atmosphere of honesty and trust is needed in order for every member to feel comfortable sharing their thoughts.

Because Agile stresses the importance of continuous improvement, having a regular Agile retrospective is one of the most important of Agile development practices. The Ninth Agile principle outlined in the Agile manifesto states, "At regular intervals, the team reflects on how to become more effective, then tunes and adjusts its behavior accordingly."

A framework, such as the one suggested below, can be used to provide structure and keep discussion during the retrospective focused. The meeting can be up to one hour.

- ✓ Set the stage - get the team ready to engage in the retrospective, perhaps with a warm-up activity such as Plus, Minus, Interesting (5-10 minutes)
- ✓ Gather data - create a shared picture of what happened during the retrospective (10-15 minutes)
- ✓ Generate insights - discuss what was successful and identify any roadblocks to success (15 minutes)
- ✓ Decide what to do - identify highest priority items to work on and put measurable goals on those items so they can be completed (10-15 minutes)
- ✓ Close the retrospective - reflect on the retrospective and how to improve it, and to appreciate accomplishments of the team and individual interactions (5-10 minutes).

Process Tailoring / hybrid models

There are many processes in the industry today, and they are at varying degrees of maturity and acceptance. Rarely will a process, even a widely accepted one like the RUP (Rational Unified Process), be a perfect fit for an organization. Choose what works for you, take out what doesn't, and tweak the rest.

Select SDLC (Software development lifecycle) for the project and tailor process element accordingly. Pick one (or more) that will help you achieve your goals. Remember that you will still need to tailor your adopted process. For each process element, you can decide to do one of the following:

- Implement the process element as per guidelines
- Waive the process element
- Replace the process element
- Add a new process element

The Software Capability Maturity Model (SW-CMM) is serving as the foundation for a major portion of the process improvement being undertaken in the software industry. CMMI is used as the de-facto guideline for Process Tailoring. Agile conforms to all of KPA (Key Process Areas) under CMMI Level 1 and most of KPAs under CMMI Level 2. It's safe to say that agile projects are very close to CMMI Level 2.

What is Process Tailoring in Software Development?

Tailoring in Software development is the process of extracting a set of processes, tasks and artifacts from the organizations established processes, tasks and artifacts so as to best suit a project to achieve its objectives successfully. If a process makes sense to you, and you believe it will add value to your organization, then adopt it. Otherwise, do not. Do not implement processes just because someone else does. Process tailoring is best done in an iterative manner: tailor some, implement some, and then repeat. You can spend months or even years defining and tailoring the perfect process for your organization, but you won't know how it will work until you try it. You'll save time and effort (and therefore money) in the long run by taking an iterative approach.

Value Stream Mapping

Value stream mapping is a lean manufacturing technique used to analyze and design the flow of materials and information required to bring a product or service to a consumer. Although value stream mapping is often associated with manufacturing, it is also used in logistics, supply chain, service related industries, healthcare, software development, and product development.

The purpose of value stream mapping is to provide optimum value to the customer through a complete value creation process with minimum waste in:

- Design (concept to customer)
- Build (order to delivery)
- Sustain (in-use through life cycle to service)

What is Value?

"Value" is what the customer is buying. Value is a capability provided to a customer, as defined by the customer - which is of the highest quality, at the right time, and at an appropriate price.

Value stream mapping and analysis is a tool that allows you to see waste, and is mainly used to eliminate waste. It provides the analyst a deeper understanding of the system by mapping it out. Value stream mapping is a recognized method used as part of six sigma methodologies.

How is *value stream mapping* implemented?

- Identify the target product, product family, or service.
- Draw current state value stream map, showing the current process steps, delays, and information flows required to deliver the target product or service.
- Draw design flow diagram (inception to launch) for software development.
- Try to use 'standard' symbols for representing entities such as unified modeling language notations.
- Assess the current state value stream map in terms of creating flow improvement by eliminating waste.
- Draw a target future state value stream map.
- Work toward the future state condition.
- Draw the value-adding steps across the center of the map and the non-value-adding steps at right angles to the value stream.
- Separate the value stream activities as one type and the 'waste' activities as another type.
- Call the value streams the processes and the non-value streams the operations.
- Recognize that the non-value-adding steps are often preparatory or tidying up the value-adding step and are closely associated with the person or workstation that executes those value-adding steps.
- Improvements to the overall system is targeted, which can deliver great dividends but it's difficult to make those improvements.

Value stream mapping supports the following agile principle:

"Simplicity - the art of maximizing the amount of work not done - is essential".

CONTROL LIMITS

Agile is not plan-driven; rather it is iterative and adaptive and hence it will change and it's adapt to changes. It still follows Dr. Deming's PDCA cycle (Plan-Do-Check-Act) for continuous improvement and continuous integration. The control limits for Agile projects are derived from the error possibilities which must fit within six standard deviations of a bell-shaped normal curve.

The control limits are established such that less than 3.4 errors in one million opportunities are acceptable. Normal control charts and control limits can be used under Agile projects.

The concepts of control limits for Agile projects are based on:

- Six Sigma
- Normal Theorem of Distribution.
- UCL: Upper Control Limit
- LCL: Lower Control Limit

It is said that a process is under control if the results are within LCL and UCL. Any time the process goes out-of-control, it is suggested to use RCA (Root Cause Analysis) method to investigate and bring back the process under control. This ensures the predictable results every time the process is followed.

The following key concepts must be remembered:

- Control limits for Agile projects link with Deming (or PDCA) cycle and Six Sigma.
- Control limits are introduced as a means to limit variations in product quality.
- Control limits are followed to support Dr. Deming's quality concepts which are based on the point of view for the product:
- Control limits are followed so as to make the product the same way each time and to make it work within limits that are acceptable to the customer.

PRE-MORTEM (RULE SETTING, FAILURE ANALYSIS)

A project post-mortem, also called a project retrospective, is a process for evaluating the success (or failure) of a project's ability to meet business goals.

A typical post-mortem meeting begins with a restatement of the project's scope. Team members and business owners are then asked by a facilitator to share answers to the following questions:

- ➤ What worked well for the team?
- ➤ What did not work well for the team?

The facilitator may solicit quantitative data related to cost management or qualitative data such as perceived quality of the end product. Ideally, the feedback gathered from a project post-mortem will be used to ensure continuous improvement and improve the management of future projects.

Post-mortems are generally conducted at the end of the project process, but are also useful at the end of each stage of a multi-phase project. The term post-mortem literally means "after death."

In medicine, the term is used to describe an examination of a dead body in order to discover the cause of death.

The post-mortem or the agile retrospective is called as the Sprint Retrospective in Scrum. Although there are many ways to conduct a sprint retrospective, a recommendation is to conduct it as a start-stop-continue meeting. This is perhaps the simplest, but often the most effective way to conduct a retrospective. Using this approach each team member is asked to identify specific things that the team should:

- ✓ Start doing
- ✓ Stop doing
- ✓ Continue doing

Failure modes and alternatives

A specific danger of the Agile processes is doing the easy parts and not the hard parts. Let's look at the possible failure modes under 2 most popular agile methodologies:

Failure under SCRUM: A number of are claiming that they are adopting Scrum. But when looked closely they're doing the trivial parts such as daily stand-up meetings and calling someone a Scrum Master. They are missing out on tricky but important ingredients that could actually help them such as making their team cross-functional and reflecting on their practices regularly.

Failure under XP: Similarly, it would be easy to take the trivial parts of XP and not do up-front design and ignore some important elements of the discipline such as on-site customer or constant refactoring.

There could be multiple reasons for this such as:

- Design debt can exceed technical debt
- System can become "ball of mud".
- Failure modes can come from different sources like scrum master, team, product owner and/or the management.

The best approach when failing under Agile is to "FAIL FAST", so the failures can be *corrected*!!

What could be typical failure modes of Agile?

- The agile team does not have retrospectives or the retrospectives are bad. The typical failure happens when suggested actions during the retrospectives get ignored or written off.
- The infrastructure gets worse and architecture becomes unstable in a race to finish features on time. The typical failure happens when distributed teams make this worse.

- There is lack of collaboration in agile planning. The typical failure happens when the whole team is involved during release planning when only key resources are required during planning sessions.
- There are none or too many product owners and both these cases are not advisable. The typical failure happens when the person thinks that agile is yet another hat to wear and that person is already too busy. In such scenarios, they just follow a check list and ask the team to just do agile.
- There are bad scrum masters who use a "command and control" style of project management. They want the team to look faster, yet in reality it slows things down. The typical failure mode happens when there is low morale among team members and decision making capability is taken away from them.
- There is no on-site evangelist. If the teams are distributed, it is recommended that there must be at least one representative on-site at every site. The typical failure happens when it is expected to reap the benefits of agile or benefits of offshore development without an on-site coach at each location.
- There is no solid team. The typical failure happens when there is no empowered team.
- There is tsunami of technical debt. The typical failure happens when the technical debt is not reduced by using techniques such as refactoring and test driven development.
- The management follows the process of only traditional performance appraisals. The typical failure happens when individual heroics get rewarded and others feel that they are not team players.
- The agile team reverts to traditional project management while doing agile project management. The typical failure happens when team thinks that "change is *hard*" and they revert back to old ways of doing business.

Fishbone Diagram Analysis

The fishbone diagram is one of the seven basic tools of quality.

Overview: Root cause analysis is a structured team process that assists in identifying underlying factors or causes of an adverse event or near-miss. Understanding the contributing factors or causes of a system failure can help develop actions that sustain the correction.

A cause and effect diagram, often called a "fishbone" diagram, can help in brainstorming to identify possible causes of a problem and in sorting ideas into useful categories. A fishbone diagram is a visual way to look at cause and effect. It is a more structured approach than some other tools available for brainstorming causes of a problem (e.g., the Five Whys tool). The problem or effect is displayed at the head or mouth of the fish. Possible contributing causes are listed on the smaller "bones" under various cause categories. A fishbone diagram can be helpful in identifying possible causes for a problem that might not otherwise be considered by directing the team to look at the categories and think of alternative causes. Include team members who have personal knowledge of the processes and systems involved in the problem or event to be investigated.

Fishbone Diagram Procedure:

1. Agree on a problem statement (also referred to as the effect). Write it at the center right of the flipchart or whiteboard. Draw a box around it and draw a horizontal arrow running to it. This is written at the mouth of the "fish".
2. Brainstorm the major categories of causes of the problem. If this is difficult use generic headings:
   o Methods
   o Machines (equipment)
   o People (manpower)
   o Materials
   o Measurement
   o Environment
3. Write the categories of causes as branches from the main arrow.
4. Brainstorm all the possible causes of the problem. Ask: "Why does this happen?" As each idea is given, the facilitator writes it as a branch from the appropriate category. Causes can be written in several places if they relate to several categories.
5. Again ask "why does this happen?" about each cause. Write sub–causes branching off the causes. Continue to ask "Why?" and generate deeper levels of causes. Layers of branches indicate causal relationships.
6. When the group runs out of ideas, focus attention to places on the chart where ideas are few.

Depending on the complexity and importance of the problem, you can now investigate the most likely causes further. This may involve setting up investigations, carrying out surveys, and so on. These will be designed to test which of these possible causes is actually contributing to the problem.

SUMMARY

Although eight tools and technique is mentioned under this toolkit, it is important from PMI-ACP exam point of view to understand the process improvement. The students are encouraged to understand the importance of eliminating waste in the processes and adapting to the agile principle of simplicity.

Sample Practice Examination on Chapter VIII Process Improvement

Q1: As an agile coach, just studying carefully the lean manufacturing principles, you suggested that Large-scale pre-planning and extensive project scheduling are to be replaced by smaller experiments, which can be rapidly adapted as new improvements. In your setup, it is designed for implementing continuous improvement or even taken to mean a "philosophy of improvements" and is referred to as _____

  A. Weekly Deal
  B. Kaizen
  C. Command-and-control improvements
  D. Decomposition

Q2: In another technique, the user asks a series of Five Why questions about a failure that has occurred, basing each subsequent question on the answer to the previous. This is a form of _____

  A. Interrogation
  B. Investigation
  C. Observation
  D. Root cause Analysis

Q3: Drawbacks or shortcoming of the Five Why method: Five-why is based on personal opinion on what the causes are, and two people performing Five-why analysis on the same problem can come up with completely _____ root causes.

  A. Identical
  B. Conflicting
  C. Different
  D. No

Q4: Introspection is the process of examining your _____, to look inside. In most of the time it is done for self-examination, self-observation, self-questioning or for self-reflection.

  A. own thoughts and feelings

B. team's thoughts and feelings
C. past events or situations
D. successes and achievements

Q5: In agile development, retrospectives play a very important role in iterative and incremental development. At the end of every iteration a retrospective is held to look for ways to improve the process for the next iteration. Each member of the team members answers the following questions, except:

A. What worked well for us?
B. What did not work well for us?
C. What actions can we take to improve our process going forward?
D. What lessons did we learn?

Q6: According to Scrum guidelines, retrospective is a _____ meeting held by a project team at the end of a project or process (often after an iteration) to discuss what was successful about the project or time period covered by that retrospective, what could be improved, and how to incorporate the successes and improvements in future iterations or projects.

A. Review
B. Planning
C. Process Improvement
D. Productive

Q7: There are many processes in the industry today, and they are at varying degrees of maturity and acceptance. Rarely will a process, even a widely accepted one, be a perfect fit for an organization. Choose what works for you, take out what doesn't, and tweak the rest. What is this called as, under agile?

A. Process Adopting
B. Process Tweaking
C. Process Tailoring
D. Process Selecting

Q8: _____ is a lean manufacturing technique used to analyze and design the flow of materials and information required to bring a product or service to a consumer at an optimum value with minimum waste.

A. Material Inventory Control
B. Statistical Process Flowchart
C. Value Engineering
D. Value Stream Mapping

Q9: Value is a capability provided to a customer, as defined by the customer - which is of the highest quality, at the right time, and at an appropriate price. The value stream activities are of one type and non-value (waste) activities as another type. What will you call the value streams as the _____ and the non-value streams as the _____?

    A. Procedures, counteractive
    B. Inputs, outputs
    C. Processes, operations
    D. Tools, techniques

Q10: Some of the charts are derived from error possibilities that must fit within six standard deviations of a normal curve with LCL and UCL as the _____ limits.

    A. Control
    B. Ceiling
    C. Chart
    D. Customer

Q11: It is said that a process is under control if the results are within LCL and UCL. Any time the process goes out-of-control, it is suggested to use _____ method to investigate and bring back the process under control. This ensures the predictable results every time the process is followed.

    A. Normal Distribution
    B. Root Cause Analysis
    C. Exception Handling
    D. Six Sigma

Q12: The post-mortem or the agile retrospective is called as the Sprint Retrospective in Scrum. Although there are many ways to conduct a sprint retrospective, a recommendation is to conduct it is perhaps the simplest, but often the most effective way to conduct a retrospective. Using this approach each team member is asked to identify specific things that the team should do except:

    A. Start doing
    B. Stop doing
    C. Continue doing
    D. Fast doing

Q13: The best approach when failing under Agile is to _____, so the failures can be *corrected*!!

    A. Fail Fast
    B. Fail Forward
    C. Fail Safe
    D. Fail Slow

Q14: There are few scrum masters who use a _____ style of project management. They want the team to look faster, yet in reality it slows things down. The typical failure mode happens when there is low morale among team members and decision making capability is taken away from them.

   A. Dictatorship
   B. Command-and-control
   C. Non professional
   D. Controlling

Q15: There is one diagram which is used as one of the seven basic quality tools for root cause analysis. It's also known by other names but:

   A. Cause-and-effect diagram
   B. Fishbone Diagram
   C. Deming Diagram
   D. Ishikawa Diagram

Q16: You as an agile coach are helping your team to perform root cause analysis. You asked the team to draw the effect at the center right of whiteboard and draw a circle around it and draw a horizontal arrow running to it. Then you asked every team member to put possible cause and add it as a new branch from the main arrow. When completed, what this diagram will look like?

   A. Deming Wheel
   B. Fishbone Diagram
   C. Flow Chart
   D. Process View Map

Answers:

Q1: B. The Sino-Japanese word "kaizen" simply means "change for better". The word refers to any improvement, one-time or continuous, large or small. The word Kaizen in English is typically applied to measures for implementing continuous improvement or even taken to mean a "philosophy of improvements" thereof.

Q2: D. A technique used in conjunction with PDCA (Plan-Do-Check-Act) is the Five Whys, which is a form of root cause analysis in which the user asks a series of Five "why" questions about a failure that has occurred, basing each subsequent question on the answer to the previous. There are normally a series of causes stemming from one root cause, and they can be visualized using fishbone diagrams or tables.

Q3: C. Drawbacks or shortcoming of the Five Why method: Five-why is based on personal opinion on what the causes are, and two people performing Five-why analysis on the same problem can come up with completely different root causes.

Q4: A. Introspection is the process of examining your own thoughts and feelings, to look inside. In most of the time it is done for self-examination, self-observation, self-questioning or for self-reflection.

Q5: D. Each member of the team members answers the following questions: What worked well for us? What did not work well for us? What actions can we take to improve our process going forward? The Agile retrospective can be thought of as a "lessons learned" meeting, but that's not the question asked in retro.

Q6: B. The Retrospective is done for process improvement by reviewing what went wrong and what could be improved. However at the conclusion, the team decides what to do in future iterations or projects, so at end it becomes a planning meeting.

Q7: C. Process Tailoring in Software development is the process of extracting a set of processes, tasks and artifacts from the organizations established processes, tasks and artifacts so as to best suit a project to achieve its objectives successfully.

Q8: D. *Value stream mapping* is a lean manufacturing technique used to analyze and design the flow of materials and information required to bring a product or service to a consumer. Although value stream mapping is often associated with manufacturing, it is also used in logistics, supply chain, service related industries, healthcare, software development, and product development.

Q9: C. Call the value streams the processes and the non-value streams the operations. Other options don't make any sense.

Q10: A. UCL stands for Upper Control Limit and LCL stands for Lower Control Limit.

Q11: B. It is said that a process is under control if the results are within LCL and UCL. Any time the process goes out-of-control, it is suggested to use RCA (Root Cause Analysis) method to investigate and bring back the process under control. This ensures the predictable results every time the process is followed.

Q12: D. The post-mortem or the agile retrospective is called as the Sprint Retrospective in Scrum. Although there are many ways to conduct a sprint retrospective, a recommendation is to conduct it as a start-stop-continue meeting. This is perhaps the simplest, but often the most effective way to conduct a retrospective. Using this approach each team member is asked to identify specific things that the team should: Start doing, Stop doing, and continue doing. There isn't anything that says about Fast Doing.

Q13: A. The best approach when failing under Agile is to "FAIL FAST", so the failures can be *corrected*!!

Q14: B. There are bad scrum masters who use a "command and control" style of project management. They want the team to look faster, yet in reality it slows things down. The typical failure mode happens when there is low morale among team members and decision making capability is taken away from them.

Q15: C. There is one diagram which is used as one of the seven basic quality tools for root cause analysis. It's also known by other names such as Cause-and-effect diagram, Fishbone Diagram and Ishikawa Diagram.

Q16: B. This will look like a Fishbone Diagram with effect at the mouth of the "fish" and causes as "bones" to the main arrow.

CHAPTER NINE

Product Quality

This chapter covers the following tools and techniques used under "Product Quality" in agile:

> ➤ **Frequent Verification and Validation (V&V)**
> ➤ **DoD – Definition of Done**
> ➤ **Continuous Integration**
> ➤ **Testing, including exploratory and usability**

Agile product quality tools and techniques support the continuous improvement process and advocate the "built-in quality" assurance right from the beginning of the agile development process. Highest quality is built-in the product using certain tools and techniques such as frequent validation and verification, test driven development (TDD) approach, acceptance test driven development (ATDD) and continuous integration etc.

Agile teams address the quality both reactively and proactively. Daily testing and automated testing are means to achieve quality reactively. Examples of proactive quality approaches include face-to-face communication, pair programming, and established coding standards.

Riskier features are created and tested in early sprints. Quality and risk are very closely related. If you take care of the quality right from beginning, the risk of rejection is lesser.

Testing and detecting defects is easier when a smaller amount of work is under test. Fixes are easier and making new builds with fixes is under control when you fix something that was just created verses month old code. This is achieved by continuous integration.

Agile projects incorporate multiple quality feedback loops throughout the project. This ensures quality on otherwise "escaped defects".

Quality Management for agile projects

Three processes are proposed by PMI in 5th Edition of PMBOK, namely Quality Planning, Quality Assurance and Quality Control. These processes can be described as follows for Agile Project Management.

Quality Planning: The customer and team determine appropriate quality policies and standards. The coding/testing standards are usually documented informally. The team decides on what metrics will be helpful in determining quality and also in reporting to management.

Quality Assurance: The entire agile team is responsible and works towards quality assurance, by conducting iteration demos, reviews, retrospectives and process analysis. The team makes sure to include quality personnel as part of the team and involve them in all product development activities. It is well known that quality can be improved only when the processes are improved. Quality assurance is mainly to prevent defects throughout product development and is more process-oriented.

Quality Control: The test team not only detects but prevents the defects thereby trying to achieve the highest quality level in the product at every iteration and at every deliverables. The QA team tests the code under every iteration, automates as many tests as possible to maintain quality controls and increases speed to delivery. QA person also helps customers to understand what the acceptance criteria can be for each feature. QA people play pivotal role in defect tracking as items in the backlog, monitoring product quality by using testing tools and monitoring process quality by using primary tools such as burn-down chart, metrics, brainstorming and root cause analysis.

FREQUENT VERIFICATION AND VALIDATION

Verification: Making sure that we are doing the right things. (Focus is on the fact: do it what customer values most). Examples of verification are Code Review, Requirements Walkthrough, Audit, Check Sheet and quality tools used in Quality Assurance.

Validation: Making sure that we are doing the things right. (Focus is on the fact: do it right the first time). Examples of validation are Unit Testing, Systems Testing, Integration Testing, Inspection, and quality tools used in Quality Control.

Frequent: How frequent is frequent? The agile team performs V&V most frequently, almost on daily basis (in daily stand-up meetings), on weekly basis, on monthly basis (in a typical 4-weeks sprint review meetings), on quarterly basis (in a typical 3-month iteration review meetings), on an annual basis (on product delivery), in retrospective meetings and even in customer demos. Product demos ensure quality for agile projects.

In frequent V&V, the most important thing to remember is that the agile team and customer constantly interact to make sure that the product development and quality is what the customer values most and the team has not progressed in any direction which customer is not aware and the changes are adapted as early as possible and we are not deviating too much from what customer wants.

In agile methodology, testing team members are involved in the project from the early stages and they participate in activities from defining user stories (gathering user requirements) and throughout from inception to deployment. Frequent Validation and Verification (V&V) is used for continuous process improvement.

Unit testing carries topmost priority under agile software development. Agile development team is always aligned to new direction as cohesive team. Early feedback is a key principle followed in agile methodology. On an on-going basis product quality is discussed to support continuous product, process and quality improvements for implementation as early as the next day, next iteration, or next epic.

Testing is daily part of each sprint and is included in each requirement's definition of done. Automated testing tools are used allowing quick and robust testing every day.

What are the advantages of frequent validation and verification?

- The V&V practices in agile and CMMI are mostly the same. The main advantage of V&V is to identify, detect, and fix the defects in early stages thereby reducing the cost of quality and making progress in deploying quality product features on-time thus improving time-to-market.
- Peer reviews, periodical code-reviews, refactoring, unit tests, automatic and manual testing (testing types depending on the implemented software) are all necessary, while some are mandatory, no matter what methodology type is used. V&V enforces most or all of these.
- Agile often employs test driven development to place an increased portion of the testing in the hands of the developer, before it reaches a formal team of testers.
- Agile projects incorporate multiple quality feedback loops throughout the project. Development team receives different types of product feedback in the course of a project and then incorporates this feedback into the product, increasing product quality on regular basis.
- Development team provides quality feedback throughout the day. Product owner gives quality feedback throughout the sprint. Project stakeholders give their quality feedback at end of each sprint. Customer provides their feedback on quality at end of each release. This is the advantage of frequent validation and verification in improving the quality throughout the project and product development.

TDD – Test Driven Development

TDD is a software development technique that literally means "development driven by test cases". TDD evolved from the Extreme Programming (XP) methodology and gives an emphasis on technical excellence and good design. It enforces the developer to think about testing first, even before starting to write first line of code. TDD is one of those quality-specific development techniques incorporated into product creation. Examples of other techniques are pair programming, peer reviews, collective code ownership, and continuous integration. The TDD team would like to provide sustainable development throughout the development life cycle.

TDD helps software developers produce working, high-quality code that's maintainable and, most of all, reliable. Use "the test" to deal with code development complexity.

How does TDD work?

- Red: First write a failing unit test, showing the intent of what the new code is to do.
- Green: Do whatever it takes to pass the above test. If it's successful implementation, add code to source repository. If not, just do enough to get the test pass; the developer develops until the test passes.
- Refactor: Go back and clean up the code. Make it lean, mean and as clear as possible.

What are the benefits of "Test Driven Development"?

- It serves as a good starting point. Instead of struggling to come up with new design from scratch for coding, TDD provides better way and starting point to think about the design, then to think about code.
- It provides a lower total cost of ownership.
- It leads to simpler design and less code.
- It generates reduced complexity and uses the test to deal with complexity.
- It enforces quality to be built in from the start of project.
- It forces you to think analytically.

Few rules of thumb for TDD:

- Rule # 1: Don't write any new code until first a failing test is written.
- Rule # 2: Test everything that could "possibly" break.
- Rule # 3: Always improve by refactoring and do small chunks of refactoring frequently.

Refactoring: Refactoring means paying down the technical debt. Programmer goes back and looks over everything (test code, production code, configuration files, and whatever else was touched to make the test pass) and refactors it all really hard.

Technical Debt: In the process of writing code to make the test pass, there might be certain compromises made by the programmer. These needs to be fixed before they take ugly form of defects, code crashes, memory leaks, performance issues, and in short any kind of roadblock to deliver the minimally marketable feature (MMF). Software Developer is responsible for paying down the technical debt and other team members are supposed to help the developer in that process.

ATDD – Acceptance Test Driven Development

Acceptance test driven development (ATDD) is a practice in which the whole team collaboratively discusses acceptance criteria with examples and then distills them into a set of concrete acceptance tests before development begins.

The product owner is responsible for defining the acceptance criteria for each product backlog item. These are the conditions under which the product owner would be satisfied that the functional and nonfunctional requirements have been met. The product owner may also write acceptance tests corresponding to the acceptance criteria, or he could enlist the assistance of subject matter experts (SMEs) or development team members. In either case, the product owner should ensure that these acceptance criteria (and frequently specific acceptance tests) are created before an item is considered at a sprint-planning meeting. Without them, the team would have an incomplete understanding of the item and would not be ready to include it in a sprint.

It's the best way to ensure that the team has the same shared understanding of what it is they're actually building. It's also the best way to ensure all have a shared definition of done. Acceptance test-driven development (acceptance TDD) is what helps developers build high-quality software that fulfills the business's needs as reliably as TDD helps ensure the software's technical quality. Under ATDD, make sure to focus on the what, not the how.

What is an Acceptance Test?

- Acceptance tests are specifications for the desired behavior and functionality of a system. For each user story an acceptance test relates to how the system handles different conditions and inputs plus reports anticipated outcomes. There are a number of properties that an acceptance test should exhibit.

How does ATDD work?

The acceptance TDD cycle consists of following:

1. Pick a user story
2. Write tests along with the acceptance criteria built into each user story

3. Automate tests including validation steps for each requirement
4. Implement functionality by understanding how to create product that passes user acceptance

This cycle continues throughout the iteration as long as there are more user stories to implement.

What is the benefit of Acceptance Test Driven Development?

- Acceptance TDD helps the team to deliver exactly what the customer wants when they want it, and circumvents implementing the required functionality only half way. It helps in a big way during the User Acceptance Testing.

DoD – Definition of Done

Product quality is ensured by checking completeness and correctness of increments or deliverables or when the backlog item is completely done. Here "done" means it's ready for deployment; nothing more is needed to use that part or feature. "Definition of Done" enforces the following:

- One agile principle of "working software is the primary measure of success" gets implemented.
- Done means the feature is 100 percent completed and indicates that the feature is good to go!
- The definition includes analysis, design, coding, testing and everything else!
- When it is "done", it should be able to go into production without any changes and work properly!
- If the feature can't potentially be shipped, that means it's not done.
- Agile teams may have a different definitions of done at various levels as follows:
  - "Definition of Done" for a feature (which is for story or product backlog item)
  - "Definition of Done" for a sprint (which is for collection of features developed within a sprint)
  - "Definition of Done" for a release (which is potentially shippable increments for a product)

"Done" under agile environment means 100 percent done or fully completed. The user has accepted the feature through user acceptance testing. The feature can go into production right now, and doesn't need any further modifications. Once it's done, the team moves the index card of that user story or feature from WIP into done column on task or Kanban board. Delivering a feature in agile is meant to be "doing everything necessary to produce shippable code".

Definition of Done (DOD)

The agile team defines the DOD. The product owner and development team agree upon the details of the definition. A requirement is considered complete and done only when it's ready for demonstration at the end of a sprint. This is a deliverable and ready to fit in final product, with no more changes needed. This is in fact a potentially shippable increment of product which can be put on the shelf.

Definitions of done normally include (but can have gone through more than these phases):

- ✓ Developed: The development team understood requirements and created the working software as per requirements. They most probably followed Test Driven Development (TDD) approach and/or Acceptance Test Driven Approach (ATDD) to develop the increments.
- ✓ Tested: The agile team created appropriate test cases and tested that the product conforms to the requirements and fit for use. The team also ensured that it complete, correct and defect-free. The team most probably followed pair programming approach and used the best practices of quality assurance. Hopefully most of the testing is done using automated testing tools.
- ✓ Integrated: The agile team used continuous integration to build the product at every stage of development. The team also ensured that the increments work in conjunction with entire final product and related systems as per requirements.
- ✓ Documented: The agile team created sufficient notes to document what was done and how the product was built. Hopefully the team used various meetings such as daily scrum meeting, retrospective meeting, planning meeting, and review meetings. The team mostly used face-to-face communication and created just "barely sufficient" documentation.

The definition of done also includes the "acceptance criterion" and acceptable risks. This changes drastically the risk factor for agile projects allowing the team to focus on most critical activities as sprint deliverables. The team basically builds and delivers a working increment of the product that meets the definition of done in every sprint. The customer sees the value and the team sees that it has a working increment to use now and to build upon later.

Continuous Integration

Continuous Integration is the act of continuously taking changes developers make to their software and integrating them all together continuously throughout the day, cycle, iteration, release, epic etc. It is the practice of creating integrated code builds one or more times each day. As soon as there is even a single line code change, it gets integrated into current build and tested right away. To do this, mostly automated build process is used.

By doing continuous build and integration, it is possible to do incremental integration and also find out any defects / issues right away, since the changes are relatively small and can be traced /tracked / corrected right away. It also ensures that developers are not stepping on each other's toes and the code conflicts can be resolved at an early stage either manually or by automated build tools.

Continuous testing is followed after continuous integration to ensure that the quality is built-in the product. Automated testing tools and regression testing tools are recommended to maintain the quality under agile development. There is a need to merge changes right away. The longer the development goes without integrating changes from other teammates, the harder the merge is whenever done. That's why the continuous integration is performed which can be incremental depending upon the tools used.

The target is to keep production ready code from day one of agile project. When a demo is required, the agile team must be able to do so within few minutes – at the most within an hour. Don't postpone merging code branches, to make final deliverable, to resolve code conflicts and to include library dependencies till last minute or close to Release. Always merge and compile as soon as there is a change in code. This will improve the product quality dramatically and will also make life little easier for release management team.

How to setup Continuous Integration?

Using automated tools and creating automated build process as follows:

- A source code repository
- A check-out and check-in process
- An automated build
- Discipline to work in small chunks

Source Code Repository: is where developers "check-in" their code for archival. It is an integration point to keep a Master Copy of code. Each check-in increments the code's version number for Version Control, which permits merging of branches and provides fallback to previous known working code versions.

Create an Automated Build

- Good automated build compiles the code from the repository, runs the tests, and basically does anything that regularly needs to be done as part of project's build process (like merge, versioning, labeling, warnings, memory leak checks etc)
- Build agents (software) run the build whenever they detect a change in the source code repository.
- Automated Builds
  - ➢ Compile

> ➤ Configure
> ➤ Deploy

- Automated builds can also automate deploying the software into each Development, Test and Production environments based upon build parameters.
- Development can use their own automated build frameworks

Benefits of an Automated Build

- Less human involvement.
- Production ready code available almost all the time.
- Identify build issues for resolution often
- Squash bugs / defects early.
- Lower the cost of making changes to code
- Able to deploy with confidence.
- Make it a non-event (i.e. no big deal)

How to establish a better check-in process?

1. Get latest source from the repository, use check-out.
2. Make changes
3. Run tests
4. Check for any more updates
5. Run tests again
6. Check-in

RESPECT THE BUILD

Dos	Don'ts
✓ Check for Updates	Break the build.
✓ Run all the tests	Check in on top of broken builds.
✓ Check in regularly	Comment out failing unit tests.

Make fixing a broken build a top priority.

Three Simple Truths in Agile Project Mgmt:

1. It is impossible to gather all the requirements at the beginning of a project.
2. Whatever requirements gathered, are guaranteed to change.
3. There will always be more to do than time and money will allow.

Once accepted, teams can then think and innovate with a level of focus and clarity in agile.

What is the difference between continuous integration and continuous improvement?

Continuous integration is related to software code and artifacts and documents, whereby the code is always kept in production-ready state by using automated build process.

Continuous improvement is process related and it attempts to build high quality at every stage and step of agile development by using frequent validation and verification as well as process tailoring, based on CMMI as the basic process.

TESTING, INCLUDING EXPLORATORY AND USABILITY

Plan-driven, sequential processes focus on using (or exploiting) what is currently known and predicting what isn't known. Scrum favors a more adaptive, trial-and-error approach based on appropriate use of exploration. The term "exploratory testing" has been popularized by a community of testers who follow context-driven testing.

Exploratory testing is characterized by the following aspects:

- ✓ It emphasizes the tester's autonomy, skill and creativity, much as other Agile practices emphasize these qualities in developers;
- ✓ It recommends performing various test-related activities (such as test design, test execution, and interpretation of results) in an interleaved manner, throughout the project, rather than in a fixed sequence and at a particular "phase";
- ✓ It emphasizes the mutually supportive nature of these techniques, and the need for out-of-box testing approaches rather than a formal "test plan".

Exploration refers to times when we choose to gain knowledge by doing some activity, such as building a prototype, creating a proof of concept, performing a study, or conducting an experiment. In other words, when faced with uncertainty, we tend to testing by exploring. Many times, when the requirements are not known or too many changes have happened or the features are changed to value the customer then an ad-hoc testing is performed. This may be outside the known test cases or test suites and not going on beaten regular known path but to test alternatives which are out-of-box scenarios.

Agile teams tend to shift and redraw the role boundaries between "developer" and "tester", mostly as a result of the heavy use of automated unit and functional tests by developers - an extreme form of scripted testing.

These activities are not sufficient to ensure quality, and Agile teams can find valuable assets in team members who have well-developed testing skills. These skills will be deployed more effectively in the exploratory style on an Agile team, as this style is more consistent with an Agile approach than the "scripted testing" style.

Usability Testing: Another important aspect of testing is to test if the product is "fit for use". This is where the usability is tested. The testing is performed to evaluate ease of use, ease of navigation, logical sequencing of features and overall how useful the product or feature is.

Usability testing is a long-established, empirical and exploratory technique to answer questions such as "how would an end user respond to our software under realistic conditions?"

It consists of observing a representative end user interacting with the product, given a goal to reach but no specific instructions for using the product.

Members of the team (possibly including usability specialists) observe the user's actions without intervening, recording what transpires (either informally, e.g. taking notes, or more comprehensively, using video, eye-tracking, screen captures or specialized software). Post-test analysis will focus on any difficulties encountered by the user, illustrating differences between the team's assumptions and actual behavior.

SUMMARY

Although just four tools and techniques are mentioned under this toolkit, these are very important from PMI-ACP exam point of view. The students are encouraged to understand the importance of product quality to be achieved under agile.

Sample Practice Examination on Chapter IX Product Quality

Q1: As per PMBOK fifth edition, quality assurance is _____ oriented and quality control is ____ oriented.

 A. Product, Process
 B. Process, Product
 C. Tools, Techniques
 D. Techniques, Tools

Q2: The agile team is writing the test cases first and then challenging the development team to write the code such that it will pass those test cases. What is this approach known as?

 A. Rapid Application Development
 B. Validation and Verification
 C. Test Driven Development
 D. Exploratory Testing

Q3: Testing and detecting defects is easier when a smaller amount of work is under test. Fixes are easier and making new builds with fixes is under control when you fix something that was just created verses month old code. This is achieved by _____.

 A. Rapid Development
 B. Continuous Integration
 C. Iterative Integration
 D. Continuous Improvement

Q4: Some of the well-known principles and facts about product quality are true except this one:

 A. Quality is everyone's responsibility
 B. Quality is built-in.
 C. Prevention over inspection
 D. Cost of quality is zero.

Q5: The agile team is performing frequent verification and validation. In validation, the main focus is on the fact to do it right the first time. What is the best description of validation?

A. Making sure that we are doing the right things.
B. Making sure that we are doing the things right.
C. Making sure that we are doing the best things.
D. Making sure that we are doing the things best.

Q6: Under Test Driven Development (TDD), the team has written failing unit tests, showing the intent of what the new code is supposed to do. The development team, due to multiple factors, is able to do just enough to get the test pass. The team knows that they created _____ and will clean up the code later.

A. Defects
B. Technical Debt
C. Mess
D. Feature discrepancy

Q7: The agile team defines the DOD. From an agile perspective DOD means:

A. Delivery On Demand
B. Definition Of Done
C. Department of Defense
D. Done On Development

Q8: Continuous Integration is the act of continuously taking changes developers make to their software and integrating them all together continuously throughout the day, cycle, iteration, release, epic etc. There is a need to merge changes right away. The longer the development goes without integrating changes from other team members; the _____ it gets to merge whenever done.

A. Easier
B. Harder
C. Faster
D. Slower

Q9: As an agile team member, when faced with uncertainty, they tend to do testing by exploring. An ad-hoc testing is normally performed under following scenarios, except when:

A. Requirements are not known
B. Too many changes have happened
C. Formal test scripting is followed
D. Features are changed to value the customer

*Q10: What kind of testing is performed to evaluate ease of use and to answer questions such as "how would an end user respond to our software under realistic conditions?"

    A. End User Testing
    B. Usability Testing
    C. Exploratory Testing
    D. Mock Testing

Answers:

Q1: B. As per PMBOK fifth edition, quality assurance is process oriented and quality control is product oriented. However the quality of product can be improved only if the processes are improved.

Q2: C. The agile team is writing the test cases first and then challenging the development team to write the code such that it will pass those test cases. This approach is known as Test Driven Development (TDD).

Q3: D. Testing and detecting defects is easier when a smaller amount of work is under test. Fixes are easier and making new builds with fixes is under control when you fix something that was just created verses month old code. This is achieved by continuous integration.

Q4: D. Some well-known principles and facts about product quality are that: Quality is everyone's responsibility, Quality is built-in and Prevention over inspection is the best practice.

Q5: B. Validation: Making sure that we are doing the things right. (Focus is on the fact: do it right the first time). Examples of validation are Unit Testing, Systems Testing, Integration Testing, Inspection, and quality tools used in Quality Control.

Q6: B. Under Test Driven Development (TDD), the team has written failing unit tests, showing the intent of what the new code is supposed to do. The development team, due to multiple factors, is able to do just enough to get the test pass. The team knows that they created technical debt and will clean up the code later.

Q7: B. The agile team defines the DOD. From an agile perspective DOD means Definition of Done. The product owner and development team agree upon the details of the definition.

Q8: B. Continuous Integration is the act of continuously taking changes developers make to their software and integrating them all together continuously throughout the day, cycle, iteration, release, epic etc. There is a need to merge changes right away. The longer the development goes without integrating changes from other team members; the harder it gets to merge whenever done.

Q9: C. In other words, when faced with uncertainty, we tend to testing by exploring. Many times, when the requirements are not known or too many changes have happened or the features are changed to value the customer then an ad-hoc testing is performed. This may be outside the known test cases or test suites and not going on beaten regular known path but to test alternatives which are out-of-box scenarios.

Q10: B. Usability testing is a long-established, empirical and exploratory technique to answer questions such as "how would an end user respond to our software under realistic conditions?"

CHAPTER TEN

Risk Management

This chapter covers the following tools and techniques used under "Risk Management" in agile:

* ❖ **Risk Adjusted Backlog**
* ❖ **Risk Burn-down Graphs**
* ❖ **Risk-based Spike**
* ❖ **Architectural Spike**

Risk refers to those factors that contribute to a project's success or failure. Risk is an intrinsic part of software development; no product can come to life risk-free. Correlated with risk is uncertainty. The more uncertainty there is, the riskier the project is. The less we know about what to develop and how to do it, the more uncertainty is present. Knowledge, uncertainty, and risk are therefore interlinked.

Riskier features are created and tested in early sprints. Risk factor is high at the beginning of the project and is lowered gradually as the project progresses. Agile projects are three times more likely to succeed than traditional projects. It is imperative that the risk register be made available for the team so that it can be managed and monitored collaboratively. At every sprint meeting, the risk register must be reviewed and updated with any new information obtained over the sprint. This way risk management becomes an integral part of Agile.

Risk Adjusted Backlog

The product backlog is used as a tool for managing changes within the project. After product backlog is created, the factors that are used in prioritizing the product backlog are: value, knowledge, uncertainty, and risk. Risk is an essential characteristic of product innovation. Every decision regarding a project - whether made explicitly or implicitly - has risk associated with it. The team can reprioritize requirements on regular basis because they can add changes and also make adjustments to the product backlog. This helps dramatically to turn the traditional risk associated with scope changes into building a better valuable product.

Having the customer prioritize the master story list or product backlog from a business perspective ensures the biggest bang for their buck. Then ask the agile team to prioritize the list to identify items with most technical risk. Tackling those stories early that are important to the customer, will bring value and also prove the software architecture. By connecting the dots early and going end-to-end, one can eliminate a lot of risk while gaining knowledge about building the system. This becomes the risk adjusted backlog.

The backlog may need to be adjusted not only on threats but based on opportunities (positive risk) also. In the exam, remember that risk is tied to value. If a project or item is of high value but also carries high risk then that needs risk adjustment in the backlog.

Why risky items in the backlog should be at high-priority?

- Risk and uncertainty influence product success therefore uncertain and risky items should be high-priority. This accelerates the generation of new knowledge, drives out uncertainty, and reduces risk.
- Risk-adjusted backlog approach tries to identify and mitigate the risk at an earlier stage of development. Tackling uncertain, risky items early creates a risk-driven approach that may enforce early failure.
- Failing early allows the Scrum team to change course while there is still the opportunity, for instance, to modify the architecture and technology selection, or to adjust the team composition.
- The best approach to deal with risk-adjusted backlog under agile is "fail fast" – the team and management would like to know earlier about the failures rather too late. The management can even take decisions to cancel the project before hitting the point of no-return.
- It can be difficult to accept a risk-driven, fail-early approach for individuals and organizations that are used to traditional processes, where problems and impediments surface late in the game and are often perceived as bad news rather than an opportunity to learn and improve.

Risk Burn-Down Graphs

The technique used in managing risk on agile projects is "risk burn down graphs or charts". A great deal of explicit risk management becomes unnecessary when a project uses an agile approach.

The short iterations, single-minded focus on delivering working software, heavy emphasis on automated tests, and frequent customer deliveries help teams avoid the biggest risk most projects face—that of eventually delivering nothing. So, many agile projects don't follow any form of explicit risk management.

How do you create "Risk Burn-down Graphs"?

- Before you create a risk burn down chart, you need to collect
  - List of project's top risks
  - Probability of the risk occurring
  - Size/extent of the loss that would occur if it happened.
- Draw Risk Burn Down Table.
- It is recommended creating a risk census during the first sprint/iteration planning meeting and then updating it quickly during subsequent planning meetings as new risks are identified or as the probabilities or sizes of known risks change.
- The risk burn down chart is then created by plotting the sum of the risk exposure values from the census.
- General recommendation is to sum only the top ten risks even if the team has identified more. Do this even if the top ten change over the course of the project.
- The risk burn down chart is updated on regular basis.

The goal of the risk burn-down graphs is to graphically display how the total risk value changes over time. In theory, the risk total should drop over the course of the project because of various reasons. As with a regular release burn down chart, we should see a linear drop in risk over the course of the project.

In essence, the burn-down chart represents the status of the risk across the iterations. From a project management perspective, this is an excellent indicator of how the risks are managed and controlled.

Risk Based Spike

A spike is an experiment that allows developers to learn just enough about something unknown in a user story, e.g. a new technology, to be able to estimate that user story. A spike must be time-boxed. This defines the maximum time that will be spent learning and fixes the estimate for the spike. William McKnight of 3M once said "Give it a try - and quick". Apply this advice when using a spike.

Risk-based Spike is about exploring the known unknown and probably throwing away everything that was researched and any prototypes developed. Since everything is planned up front in agile, there may be situations where the team reaches a path that has not been determined. If a question arises about which path to follow on, the agile team may execute a "spike" or rapid experiment to determine the best way. In doing so, the risk can be the main factor rather than time-boxed. This allows the team to associate risk factor with the spike by performing quantitative and qualitative risk analysis. This also provides guidelines on whether it is worth to experiment or not.

Spikes are a really good way for teams to figure out stuff that they don't know and need to know in order to understand the complexity so that it can be properly estimated, or quoted on or simply to find out if something is technically possible or not.

Why should you remember to do in a Risk-based Spike?

- A Spike is an exceptional way of working when we feel we don't have enough information to give the customer realistic expectations. The goal of the Spike is to establish those expectations.
- In **agile software** development, a **spike** is a story that cannot be estimated until a development team runs a time-boxed investigation.
- A Spike Solution:
  1) is an experimental solution that cuts through all the "layers".
  2) is necessarily time-boxed.
  3) is always intended to be thrown away.
- 'Spikes' are **time boxed periods of research and development** used in Agile Software Development environments to research a concept and/or create a simple prototype.
- Spikes will usually **take place in between sprints** and are often introduced before the delivery of large Epics or User Stories in order to:
  o Secure budget
  o Expand knowledge
  o Proof of concept
- Risk Categorizations:
  o Business – customer value, priority, and/or satisfaction
  o Technical – uncertainties of solution path, skills, or hardware platform
  o Logistical – schedule, funding, staffing
  o Risks may be attributed to Political, Environmental, Societal, Technological, Legal or Economic ("PESTLE") factors.
- Follow the usual Risk Process Sequence:
  o Identify
  o Access
  o Respond
  o Review

Architectural Spike

An architectural spike is an experiment that allows developers to learn just enough about something unknown in the architecture of software being developed. An architectural spike must also be time-boxed. This defines the maximum time that will be spent learning and fixes the estimate for the architectural spike.

- Architectural Spikes: A Spike in Extreme Programming (XP) terms is an attempt to reduce the risk associated with an unknown area of the system, technology or application domain. Research and analysis of the architecture to use should be carried out and fed into release planning meeting.
- Non-architectural Spikes: Other spikes are used during project-planning phase to determine unresolved issues.

Every product has architecture therefore frame all the stories with architecture and make it cohesive. At end of architectural spike, share the estimate to invest and propose benefits at milestones.

Failing Fast

This concept is mainly related to the common business objective of getting to know the bad news earlier than later in the software development life cycle. This may also help to reduce the "missed defects" which cost 10 times more with every phase it is missed to fix. The agile development teams would like to identify critical problems and possible failures within first few sprints. Testing within sprints enforces the idea of *failing fast*. The sunk cost and risk is heavy after a long effort for requirements, design, and development, and then finding problems that will prevent further progress of the project.

This concept can also be extended to finding whether the product will work in the marketplace at early stage. The project may even be cancelled early if the indications are that the customer won't buy or use the product. It may also help to get back on track with what customer wants before it is too late.

Failing fast doesn't necessarily mean cancelling or calling off the phase or project. If any catastrophic issues are found at early stages, the agile team has the time and budget to fix it or adapt to different approach to create the product. The definition of done plus the idea of failing fast along with agile foundation principles will help to lower the risk as the project progresses over time span.

SUMMARY

Although just four tools and techniques are mentioned under this toolkit, these are very important from PMI-ACP exam point of view. The students are encouraged to understand the importance of risk management performed under agile.

Two very important factors to reduce risks in agile projects are the concept about "definition of done" and the idea of "failing fast". Keep these in mind during examination.

Sample Practice Examination on Chapter X Risk Management

Q1: Risk refers to those factors that contribute to a project's success or failure. Risk is an intrinsic part of software development; no product can come to life risk-free. Correlated with risk is uncertainty. The more uncertainty there is, the _____ the project is.

    A. More riskier
    B. Less riskier
    C. Riskier
    D. More challenging

Q2: Risk factor is _____ at the beginning of the project and gets _____ gradually as the project progresses.

    A. High, lowered
    B. Low, upwards
    C. High, higher
    D. Low, lower

Q3: Having the _____ prioritize the master story list or product backlog from a business perspective ensures the biggest bang for their buck.

    A. Product Owner
    B. Scrum Master
    C. Customer
    D. Project Manager

Q4: Risk refers to those factors that contribute to a project's success or failure. Risk is an intrinsic part of software development; no product can come to life risk-free. All of the following are characteristics of risks except:

    A. Risk is always in the future.
    B. If a risk occurs, it will have an effect on at least one project objective

    C. Risk can't be avoided

    D. Risk is an uncertain event or condition.

Q5: Risk and uncertainty influence product success therefore uncertain and risky items should be high-priority. This accelerates the generation of new knowledge, drives out uncertainty, and reduces risk. Risk-adjusted backlog approach tries to identify and mitigate the risks at _____ stage(s) of development. This creates a risk-driven approach that may enforce early failure by tackling uncertain and risky items.

    A. Earlier

    B. Later

    C. All

    D. Crucial

Q6: The goal of the risk burn-down graphs is to graphically display how the total risk value changes over time. In theory, the risk total should _____ over the course of the project because of various reasons.

    A. Escalate

    B. Drop

    C. Be Constant

    D. Be ignored

Q7: Since everything is planned up front in agile, there may be situations where the team reaches a path that has not been determined. If a question arises about which path to follow on, the agile team may execute a _____, rapid experiment to determine the best way. In doing so, the risk can be the main factor rather than time-boxed.

    A. Decision Tree

    B. Flowchart

    C. Spike

    D. Planning Poker

Q8: A Spike in Extreme Programming (XP) terms is an attempt to reduce the risk associated with an unknown area of the system, technology or application domain. What is this Spike categorized as?

    A. Architectural

    B. Design

    C. Development

    D. Testing

Q9: _____ doesn't necessarily mean cancelling or calling off the phase or project. If any catastrophic issues are found at early stages, the agile team has the time and budget to fix it or adapt to different approach to create the product.

    A. Testing Fast
    B. Failing Fast
    C. Changing Fast
    D. Adapting Fast

Q10: Your agile team is in meeting and discussing heavily about how to adjust the backlogs to identify the risks and also counting on the strengths and weaknesses of the team to offset threats and opportunities accordingly. What technique are they using?

    A. Expert Judgement
    B. PERT Analysis
    C. SWOT Analysis
    D. Brainstorming

Answers:

Q1: C. Risk refers to those factors that contribute to a project's success or failure. Risk is an intrinsic part of software development; no product can come to life risk-free. Correlated with risk is uncertainty. The more uncertainty there is, the riskier the project is.

Q2: A. Risk factor is high at the beginning of the project and is lowered gradually as the project progresses.

Q3: C: Having the customer prioritize the master story list or product backlog from a business perspective ensures the biggest bang for their buck.

Q4: C. The objective of risk management is to avoid or mitigate the risk; so risk can be avoided.

Q5: A. Risk-adjusted backlog approach tries to identify and mitigate the risks at earlier stage(s) of development. This creates a risk-driven approach that may enforce early failure by tackling uncertain and risky items.

Q6: B. The goal of the risk burn-down graphs is to graphically display how the total risk value changes over time. In theory, the risk total should drop over the course of the project because of various reasons. As with a regular release burn down chart, we should see a linear drop in risk over the course of the project.

Q7: C. Since everything is planned up front in agile, there may be situations where the team reaches a path that has not been determined. If a question arises about which path to follow on, the agile team may execute a "spike" or rapid experiment to determine the best way. In doing so, the risk can be the main factor rather than time-boxed.

Q8: A. Architectural Spikes: A Spike in Extreme Programming (XP) terms is an attempt to reduce the risk associated with an unknown area of the system, technology or application domain. Research and analysis of the architecture to use should be carried out and fed into release planning meeting.

Q9: B. Failing fast doesn't necessarily mean cancelling or calling off the phase or project. If any catastrophic issues are found at early stages, the agile team has the time and budget to fix it or adapt to different approach to create the product.

Q10: C. SWOT stands for strengths, weaknesses, opportunities and threats.

CHAPTER ELEVEN

Value-Based Prioritization

This chapter covers the following tools and techniques used under "Value-based Prioritization" in agile:

- ➤ **ROI / NPV / IRR**
- ➤ **Compliance**
- ➤ **Customer-valued prioritization**
- ➤ **Requirements Reviews**
- ➤ **Minimal Viable Product (MVP)**
- ➤ **Minimal Marketable Feature (MMF)**
- ➤ **Relative Prioritization / Ranking**
- ➤ **MoSCoW**
- ➤ **Kano Analysis**

Prioritization is the decision making process where the customer selects the product backlog items or user stories to be implemented and this selection is generally based on the values seen by the customer.

ROI/NPV/IRR

The first and foremost parameter in value-based prioritization is monetary benefit, which can be judged using ROI or NPV or IRR methods. All three methods are discussed below:

ROI means "Return on Investment".

Agile projects provide a superior return on investment compared to other software projects where "the business is forced to wait for the completion of the entire project before it can begin deriving a benefit from that investment."

Superior ROI is the first reason for using agile development. Get more "done" is expressed as ROI in agile.

What are the benefits of using agile to increase ROI?

- The benefits of using agile methods range from 10 percent to 100 percent for increased cost-effectiveness, productivity, quality, cycle-time reduction, and customer satisfaction. The use of agile methods as a new product development approach does result in increased ROI.
- On average, studies of agile methods reported 29 percent better cost, 91 percent better schedule, 97 percent better productivity, 50 percent better quality, 400 percent better satisfaction, and 470 percent better ROI than CMMI.
- The latest trend is to mix-and-match scrum and XP to tap into practices like *pair programming* (PP) and test-driven development (TDD) to increase productivity and quality." One agile method alone is not the recipe for success to improve ROI, and like a lot of things, it becomes essential to look under the covers to discover what is really working.

NPV means "Net Present Value"

Present value is today's value of an amount of money in the future. Generally, there is a preference to get money rather sooner than later. This is due to various reasons like political instability, inflation, currency exchange, international trade, global influences, cyclic adjustments, trends etc.

Net present value is used to calculate the total of all cash flows (in and out) that can be directly linked to the agile project. If it is positive, then it is good. Otherwise, the management will reconsider the investment.

Example of NPV:

The initial cost of the project is 20,000 dollars in year zero. It is estimated that the project will generate cash inflows in the years 1-3 of 10,000 dollars each.

Assuming a discounting factor of 10 percent (which is 0.10):

Year 0: PV = -20,000 dollars

Year 1: PV = 10,000 dollars / (1+0.1) = 9,091 dollars

Year 2: PV = 10,000 dollars / (1+0.1)*(1+0.1) = 8,264 dollars

Year 3: PV = 10,000 dollars / (1+0.1)*(1+0.1)*(1+0.1) = 7,513 dollars

The resulting "Net Present Value" is the sum of the present values above:

NPV = -20,000 dollars + 9,091 dollars+ 8,264 dollars + 7,513 dollars = 4868 dollars

The NPV here is positive and therefore favorable.

IRR means "Internal Rate of Return".

Other non-financial and financial investment appraisal techniques are available such as payback and IRR.

Payback period = costs / annual cash flow

Internal rate of return (IRR) or discounted cash flow rate of return is used when comparing disparate investment options to arrive at a common base.

IRR is a good measure of the quality of the investment. NPV and IRR are some handy tools for evaluating and comparing projects.

Compliance

The prioritization can be forced to be based on the compliance due to the nature of business. In general, **compliance** means conforming to a rule, such as a specification, policy, standard or law. Normally it takes lot of paperwork to demonstrate the compliance and on the contrary agile is proponent of "working software over heaps of documentation". However there can be a state of "agile compliance", where businesses can make quick moves without compromising on compliance efforts.

It is strongly suggested to map agility requirements to compliance governance policy. The team or members generally discover the optimal level of compliance without compromising business agility. It may be a challenge to find the correct path to secure, agile compliance in the organization, but it is doable.

How best can an agile project deal with compliance?

- Reach out to the compliance group members at the inception of an agile project.
- Learn about existing compliance processes and risks.
- Find an interested compliance group member with whom the team can work over time, an "agile compliance champion" perhaps.
- Coach the group over time to be prepared for an audit.
- Use some sort of agile compliance management systems (CMS) that help push compliance tasks to the operational level, enabling staff to fulfill their compliance responsibilities in the course of their regular jobs and helping assure that those tasks are completed.

- Prepare "barely sufficient" documents at the minimal for the compliance and demonstrate that those guidelines outlined in the compliance documents are followed throughout the process of agile software development.

Compliance (organization)

Compliance means conforming to a rule, such as a specification, policy, standard or law.

Agile software development may be required to be conforming to:

- CMMI (Capability Maturity Model Integration specified by SEI)
- ISO (International Organization for Standards)
- IEEE (Institute of Electrical and Electronics Engineers)
- RUP/UP/Open UP (Rational Unified Process / Unified Process)
- SOX (Sarbanes Oxley)

Customer-valued prioritization

The customer or product owner can provide the business priorities, and then the team and the customer can work together to sort out the user stories that get completed in each iteration. This step aligns the team on the priorities and contributes to team buy-in. Some features may need to be delivered together to provide value to the customer.

Any team member can customize the prioritization as part of agile team to meet company's unique needs. One should start with customer value and then consider other areas that are of value in the development environment. These areas can include market share, usability, feature expenses, money, investor value, and innovation etc.

Why should one follow customer-valued prioritization?

- Prioritizing features helps the team deliver value to the customer sooner.
- Prioritizing features lets the team deliver the critical features, even before full project gets completed.
- Determining prioritization allows team to consider other factors such as risk, frequency of use, and dependencies to create final customer-valued prioritized backlog.

Requirements Reviews

There are usually more requirements than feasible given budget and schedule constraints. Thus it's important to select the most valuable ones for implementation in order to ensure the delivery of a high value system. Simple prioritization approaches like 1- 10 ranking or MoSCoW (must, could, should and want-to haves) are unable to capture the true value of the requirements. There are numerous ties (same ranking or importance or value) requiring one to repeat the process for the tied items, which may be time consuming for agile teams. These techniques assume that the stakeholders understand the intrinsic value of requirements and can correctly score them on a 1-10 scale or add them to the appropriate priority bucket in case of MoSCoW.

There are different prioritization frameworks that could be used to perform value-based requirements prioritization (VBRP). A multi-criteria decision analysis (MCDA) framework can be used for prioritizing test-cases, scoping to select the most valuable requirements for a release or product roadmap, value focused resource allocation and value-oriented product customization.

Business analysts in an agile team can use VBRP to prioritize the requirements and the testing team will prioritize test-cases with respect to the corresponding requirements. The test-case priorities are influenced by that of the corresponding requirement providing a better metric of priority or value. VBRP can also be used for resource planning and allocation to channelize the effort on the most valuable requirements in case of a fixed-bid and fixed-schedule projects. The planning, design and implementation activities for deliverables are all based around the most valuable items.

MVP – Minimal Viable Product

In product development, the **minimum viable product** (**MVP**) is the product with the highest return on investment versus risk. Minimum viable product may also be referred to as minimum feature set. A minimum viable product may be a prototype, an entire product, or a sub-set of product (such as a feature).

A minimum viable product has just those core features that allow the product to be deployed, and no more. The product is typically deployed to limited selective customers, such as early adopters that are thought to be more forgiving, more likely to give feedback, and able to grasp a product vision from an early prototype or marketing information. It is a strategy targeted at avoiding building products that customers do not want, that seeks to maximize the information learned about the customer per dollar spent. *"The minimum viable product is that version of a new product which allows a team to collect the maximum amount of validated learning about customers with the least effort."* It requires judgment to figure out, for any given context, what MVP makes sense.

An MVP is not a minimal product; it is a strategy and process directed toward making and selling a product to customers. It is an iterative process of idea generation, prototyping, presentation, data collection, analysis and learning. One seeks to minimize the total time spent on iteration. The process is iterated until a desirable product/market fit is obtained, or until the product is deemed to be non-viable. Results from a minimum viable product test aim to indicate if the product should ever be built to begin with. Testing will evaluate if the initial problem or goal has been solved in a manner which makes sense to move forward.

The purpose of MVP is multi-fold as follows:

- Be able to test a product hypothesis with minimal resources
- Accelerate learning
- Reduce wasted engineering hours
- Get the product to early customers as soon as possible
- Base for other products

MMF – Minimal Marketable Feature

A Minimal Marketable Feature (MMF) is a feature that is **minimal**, because if it was any smaller, it would not be deliverable. A MMF is a feature that is **marketable**, because when it is released as part of a product, people would use (or buy) the feature. A MMF is a **feature** that is different than a typical user story in scrum or extreme programming, because it is chosen for implementation after value based prioritization. However, value can be measured in many ways, such as revenue generation, cost savings, competitive differentiation, brand-name projection, and enhanced customer loyalty.

As the name implies, a MMF is characterized by the three attributes: **minimum, marketable, and feature.** The most significant characteristic of a MMF is the fact that it represents a distinct and *deliverable feature* of the system. A MMF must also provide significant value to the customer. Many in the lean world are now using minimum viable product (MVP), minimum viable feature (MVF) or minimum marketable release (MMR) instead of MMF.

Relative Prioritization / Ranking

Traditionally the technique of relative prioritization or ranking has been used in deciding the value. One such method that can be used for relative prioritization is known as CARVER. This can be matrix based or ranking based representation of relative prioritization for values.

CARVER stands for Criticality, Accessibility, Return (or Recuperability), Vulnerability, Effect, and Recognizability.

Relative prioritization or ranking is used to determine which projects and features are more important than others. A ranking method (assigning numeric value) can be used to compare between projects and features. One can create a CARVER matrix to prioritize certain projects. Keep in mind that the rankings created may vary and are all relative to the primary objective, mission, or purpose.

What is CARVER?

- **Criticality**: How critical is the project/feature? A low criticality project might be nice to do, but it's probably not going to make that much difference.
- **Accessibility.** Does the team have the means to tackle this project or feature immediately, or does it have prerequisites? Are there any constraints?
- **Return.** How great is the expected return on commitment of resources? Is it worth the efforts?
- **Vulnerability.** How vulnerable are the features in this project that is being considered? An inexpensive feature/project is more vulnerable than an expensive one.
- **Effect.** If the feature gets successfully completed, what effect will it have on the project, on the company and on the team? The agile teams want to be proud to deploy the selected feature(s).
- **Recognizability.** Is the project/feature crystal clear or totally fuzzy? How easy is it to recognize the steps necessary to complete the feature? Have this type of project done before, or will have to figure out the steps? Clear goals with clear steps will score higher on recognizability than foggy goals with unclear steps.

MoSCoW

This prioritization method was developed by Dai Clegg and first used extensively with the Dynamic Systems Development Method (DSDM). Prioritization can be applied to requirements, tasks, products, use cases, user stories, acceptance criteria and test cases.

MoSCoW (must, should, could, and want-to haves) is a technique for helping to understand priorities.

The **MoSCoW method** is a prioritization technique used in management, business analysis, project management, and software development to reach a common understanding with stakeholders on the importance they place on the delivery of each requirement - also known as *MoSCoW prioritization* or *MoSCoW analysis*. MoSCoW is often used with time boxing, where a deadline is fixed so that the focus can be on the most important requirements, and as such is a technique commonly used in agile software development approaches such as rapid application development (RAD) and DSDM.

The term *MoSCoW* itself is an acronym derived from the first letter of each of four prioritization categories (*Must have, Should have, Could have*, and *Would like but won't get*).

Prioritization of MoSCoW requirements

All requirements are important, but they are prioritized to deliver the greatest and most immediate business benefits early. Developers will initially try to deliver all the *Must have, Should have* and *Could have* requirements but the *Should* and *Could* requirements will be the first to go if the delivery timescale looks threatened.

The plain English meaning of the prioritization categories has value in getting customers to better understand the impact of setting a priority, compared to alternatives like *High, Medium* and *Low.*

The categories are typically understood as:

Must have

These provide the Minimum Usable Subset (MUS) of requirements which the project guarantees to deliver. Requirements labeled as *MUST* are critical to the current delivery time-box in order for it to be a success. If even one *MUST* requirement is not included, the project delivery should be considered a failure. Requirements can be downgraded from *MUST,* by agreement with all relevant stakeholders; for example, when new requirements are deemed more important than current *MUST.* Ask the question, "What happens if this requirement is not met?" If the answer is "cancel the project – there is no point in implementing a solution that does not meet this requirement" then it is a Must Have requirement. If there is some way round it, even if it is a manual workaround, then it will be a Should Have or a Could Have requirement. Downgrading a requirement to a Should Have or Could Have does not mean it won't be delivered, simply that delivery is not guaranteed.

Should have

Requirements labeled as *SHOULD* are important but not necessary for delivery in the current delivery time-box. While *SHOULD* requirements can be as important as *MUST,* they are often not as time-critical or not vital or there may be another way to satisfy the requirement, so that it can be held back until a future delivery time-box.

Could have

Requirements labeled as *COULD* are desirable but not necessary, and could improve user experience or customer satisfaction for little development cost. These will typically be included if time and resources permit. These are wanted but less important, since there will be less impact if left out (compared with a Should Have requirement).

Won't have

Requirements labeled as *WON'T* have been agreed by stakeholders as the least-critical, lowest-payback items or not appropriate at that time. As a result, *WON'T* requirements are not planned into the schedule for the delivery time-box. *WON'T* requirements are either dropped or reconsidered for inclusion in later time-boxes. (Note: occasionally the term *Would like* is substituted, to give a clearer understanding of this choice).

The general recommendation is no more than 60% effort for Must Haves for a project, with 40% Should Have and Could Have.

Kano Analysis

Kano Model was proposed in 1984 by Dr. Noriaki Kano, based on his study of Herzberg's "Motivation – Hygiene" theory. Kano is a technique for classifying customer needs and determining appropriate levels of innovation for products and services. Kano Analysis is a new product requirements tool and is being used in agile methodologies for prioritizing requirements.

Kano is based on three core tenets:

- Value attracts customers.
- Quality keeps customers and builds loyalty
- Innovation is necessary to differentiate and compete in the market

The Kano model distinguishes between three types of customer requirements – Must-Be requirements, One-Dimensional requirements and Attractive requirements. Agile team pulls out the latent requirements which are unknown until revealed by someone else. Kano and agile are all about user value. Agile focuses on projects where user satisfaction is primary. The product evolves from user experience and adoption. Change is indeed encouraged and value is "pulled" into the market, not pushed. Remember that satisfying the customer is more important than following a plan.

Kano and Agile together bring reality to vision. Kano analysis kicks off envisioning and exploring. There are several methods of analysis. On Kano Chart, there are four quadrants, where customer satisfaction is on y-axis and Product Functionality is on x-axis. On the Kano Chart, the upper right quadrant is the place to be, where it's customer delight. The customer is fully satisfied with all product functionality being delivered with best value, since it exceeds all customer requirements with performance features.

SUMMARY

All these nine tools and techniques mentioned under this toolkit are very important from PMI-ACP exam point of view. The students are encouraged to understand the importance of value-based prioritization performed under agile.

Sample Practice Examination on Chapter XI Value Based Prioritization

Q1: The following are methods in value-based prioritization for agile projects, based on monetary benefits, except:

    A. ROI – Return on Investment
    B. EVM – Earned Value Method
    C. NPV – Net Present Value
    D. IRR – Internal Rate of Return

Q2: Present value is today's value of an amount of money in the future. Generally, there is a preference to get money rather ____ than _____. This is due to various reasons like political instability, inflation, currency exchange, international trade, global influences, cyclic adjustments, trends etc.

    A. Sooner, Later
    B. Later, Sooner
    C. Now, Never
    D. Steady, Now

Q3: In general, **compliance** means conforming to a rule, such as a specification, policy, standard or law. Normally it takes lot of paperwork to demonstrate the compliance and on the contrary agile is proponent of:

    A. Continuous attention to technical excellence
    B. Simplicity – minimize the waste
    C. Working software over documentation
    D. Welcome changing requirements even late in development.

Q4: There are many value-based prioritization options that an agile team will need to do. The product owner can provide the business priorities, and then the team and the customer can work together to sort out the user stories that get completed in each iteration. Out of all the following areas, which best reflects the above:

   A. Market Value
   B. Investor Value
   C. Feature Value
   D. Customer Value

Q5: There are usually more requirements than feasible given budget and schedule constraints. As an agile team, you have the challenge to select those in order to ensure the delivery of prioritized requirements. What will be your best approach?

   A. Deliver all requirements spread over sprints
   B. Perform value-based requirements prioritization
   C. Select only those the customer wants and wishes
   D. Select those requirements based upon available resources

Q6: A _____ is that version of a new product which allows a team to collect the maximum amount of validated learning about customers with the least effort. It has just those core features that allow the product to be deployed, and no more. The product is typically deployed to limited selective customers, such as early adopters that are thought to be more forgiving, more likely to give feedback, and able to grasp a product vision from an early prototype or marketing information.

   A. Minimal Marketable Feature
   B. Minimal Viable Product
   C. Evaluation Copy
   D. Minimal Shippable Product

Q7: As the name implies, a MMF is characterized by the three attributes, except:

   A. Maximum
   B. Minimum
   C. Marketable
   D. Feature

Q8: Traditionally the technique of relative prioritization or ranking has been used in deciding the value of the features in a project. A ranking method (assigning numeric value) can be used to compare between projects and features. What is the NOT true of ranking method?

   A. Ranking on a scale is relatively easy and simple method.
   B. Rankings are relative to the primary objective, mission, or purpose
   C. Rankings created by stakeholders are always same all the time
   D. Ranking method is usually assigning a numeric value between 1-10

Q9: The _____ is a prioritization technique used in management, business analysis, project management, and software development to reach a common understanding with stakeholders on the importance they place on the delivery of each requirement.

    A. Stakeholder Analysis
    B. Requirements Traceability Matrix
    C. MoSCoW method
    D. Maximum Value Deliverables

Q10: The agile team is performing MoSCow analysis since all requirements are important, but they are prioritized to deliver the greatest and most immediate business benefits early. On a feature, a member asked the question: "What happens if this requirement is not met?" If the answer is "cancel the project – there is no point in implementing a solution that does not meet this requirement" then it is a _____requirement.

    A. Must Have
    B. Should Have
    C. Could Have
    D. Won't Have

Q11: Requirements labeled as _____ are desirable but not necessary, and may improve user experience or customer satisfaction for little development cost. These will typically be included if time and resources permit. These are wanted but less important, since there will be less impact if left out.

    A. Must Have
    B. Should Have
    C. Could Have
    D. Won't Have

Q12: Kano is a technique for classifying customer needs and determining appropriate levels of innovation for products and services. Kano Analysis is a new product requirements tool and is being used in agile methodologies for prioritizing requirements. The Kano model distinguishes between three types of customer requirements, except:

    A. Must-Be requirements
    B. Should-Be requirements
    C. One-Dimensional requirements
    D. Attractive requirements

Q13: On Kano Chart, there are four quadrants, where customer satisfaction is on y-axis and Product Functionality is on x-axis. On the Kano Chart, the _____ is the place to be, where it's customer delight. The customer is fully satisfied with all product functionality being delivered with best value, since it exceeds all customer requirements with performance features.

A. lower right quadrant
B. upper right quadrant
C. lower left quadrant
D. upper left quadrant

Q14: Net present value (NPV) is used to calculate the total of all cash flows (in and out) that can be directly linked to the agile project. If it is _____, then it is good. Otherwise, the management will reconsider the investment.

A. Zero
B. Positive
C. Negative
D. One

Answers:

Q1: B. The EVM or Earned Value Management is a technique used in cost management to evaluate cost performance and do forecasting about cost and schedule. All three others ROI, NPV and IRR methods are used in value-based prioritization for agile projects, based on monetary benefits.

Q2: A. Present value is today's value of an amount of money in the future. Generally, there is a preference to get money rather sooner than later. This is due to various reasons like political instability, inflation, currency exchange, international trade, global influences, cyclic adjustments, trends etc.

Q3: C. In general, **compliance** means conforming to a rule, such as a specification, policy, standard or law. Normally it takes lot of paperwork to demonstrate the compliance and on the contrary agile is proponent of "working software over heaps of documentation". Others are valid agile principles but not best answers here.

Q4: D. The customer or product owner can provide the business priorities, and then the team and the customer can work together to sort out the user stories that get completed in each iteration. One should start with customer value and then consider other areas that are of value in the development environment. These areas can include market share, usability, feature expenses, money, investor value, and innovation etc.

Q5: B. There are usually more requirements than feasible given budget and schedule constraints. Thus it's important to select the most valuable ones for implementation in order to ensure the delivery of a high value system. There are different prioritization frameworks that could be used to perform value-based requirements prioritization (VBRP).

Q6: B. MVP or Minimal Viable Product has just those core features that allow the product to be deployed, and no more. The product is typically deployed to limited selective customers, such as early adopters that are thought to be more forgiving, more likely to give feedback, and able to grasp a product vision from an early prototype or marketing information.

Q7: A. As the name implies, a MMF is characterized by the three attributes: *minimum, marketable, and feature*. Maximum word here is misleading, be careful.

Q8: C. Traditionally the technique of relative prioritization or ranking has been used in deciding the value of the features in a project. A ranking method (assigning numeric value) can be used to compare between projects and features. Keep in mind that the rankings created may vary and are all relative to the primary objective, mission, or purpose.

Q9: C. The **MoSCoW method** is a prioritization technique used in management, business analysis, project management, and software development to reach a common understanding with stakeholders on the importance they place on the delivery of each requirement.

Q10: A. The agile team is performing MoSCow analysis since all requirements are important, but they are prioritized to deliver the greatest and most immediate business benefits early. On a feature, a member asked the question: "What happens if this requirement is not met?" If the answer is "cancel the project – there is no point in implementing a solution that does not meet this requirement" then it is a Must-Have requirement.

Q11: B. Requirements labeled as *COULD* are desirable but not necessary, and could improve user experience or customer satisfaction for little development cost. These will typically be included if time and resources permit. These are wanted but less important, since there will be less impact if left out (compared with a Should Have requirement).

Q12: B. Kano is a technique for classifying customer needs and determining appropriate levels of innovation for products and services. Kano Analysis is a new product requirements tool and is being used in agile methodologies for prioritizing requirements. The Kano model distinguishes between three types of customer requirements - Must-Be requirements, One-Dimensional requirements and Attractive requirements.

Q13: B. On Kano Chart, there are four quadrants, where customer satisfaction is on y-axis and Product Functionality is on x-axis. On the Kano Chart, the upper right quadrant is the place to be, where it's customer delight. The customer is fully satisfied with all product functionality being delivered with best value, since it exceeds all customer requirements with performance features.

Q14: B. Net present value is used to calculate the total of all cash flows (in and out) that can be directly linked to the agile project. If it is positive, then it is good. Otherwise, the management will reconsider the investment.

PART III

Overview: PMI-ACP Knowledge and Skills

CHAPTER TWELVE

Level I Knowledge And Skills

The Agile practitioner examination includes 33 knowledge and skills areas. This chapter covers the 11 knowledge and skills classified at Level 1. Be aware that ALL 33 knowledge and skills are included in PMI-ACP exam with equal importance. The 33 K&S are distributed over 3 chapters for simplicity.

- ➢ **Agile contracting methods**
- ➢ **Agile discovery**
- ➢ **Agile Frameworks and terminology**
- ➢ **Agile hybrid models**
- ➢ **Agile Manifesto values and principles**
- ➢ **Agile methods and approaches**
- ➢ **Agile project accounting principles**
- ➢ **Agile project chartering**
- ➢ **Agile sizing and estimation**
- ➢ **Agile values and principles**
- ➢ **Building agile teams**

There are 11 knowledge and skills listed under this level I. Realistically speaking, expect at the least 1 or 2 questions about each item from the above list. There will be 60 questions based on 33 K & S.

Agile Contracting methods

Traditional contracting methods can fall into three categories:

- • Fixed-price contracts: involve setting a fixed total price for a defined product, service, or result.

- o Firm Fixed Price Contracts (FFP).
- o Fixed Price Incentive Fee Contracts (FPIF).
- o Fixed Price with Economic Price Adjustment Contracts (FP-EPA)
- Cost-reimbursable contracts: involve payments for actual cost incurred plus a seller profit fee.
  - o Cost Plus Fixed Fee Contracts (CPFF)
  - o Cost Plus Incentive Fee Contracts (CPIF)
  - o Cost Plus Award Fee Contracts (CPAF)
- Time and Material Contracts (T&M): are a hybrid type of contractual arrangement that contain aspects of both cost-reimbursable (CP) and fixed-price (FP) contracts.
  Agile contracting methods can fall into one of the following categories (not all are listed):
- Fixed-price, fixed-scope (and fixed-time/fixed-schedule)
- Fixed-price, fixed-scope (and possibly fixed-time) but collaborate with the customers to alter scope
- Time and materials
- Hybrid of T&M and fixed price
- Not-to-exceed with fixed-fee (NTE/FF)
- Fixed price per function point or story point
- Incremental delivery with payment on incremental acceptance

Most of the customers demand fixed bid contracts with fixed time, cost and scope variables. Since software development firms and their customers need legal contracts, this leaves the Agile practitioners to handle the apparent contradiction between the customers' desire for "certainty" with their own commitment to Agile values such as *responding to change*. Agile contracting methods are not very well defined because it is difficult to describe/outline challenges in contracting when agile methods are used under contractual software development environments. Key success factors include developing a responsive contract modification process that allows for quick change management and identifying non-tangible scope deliverables beyond the software components.

What are the possible solutions to the challenges under Agile contracting methods?

- <u>Requirements vs. Product Backlog</u>: Instead of using the "requirements" for bidding, use "product backlog" or "user stories" to complete request for proposal (RFP). There may not be requirements defined under conventional contract documents. Instead the product backlogs are used, which are subject to change driven by risk, priority and customer value. One of the Agile Manifesto supports customer collaboration over contract negotiation. Under these circumstances the customer collaboration is also needed in writing, modifying and fulfilling contracts. New revised contracting methods may come up under Agile contracting.
- <u>Final Delivery vs. Incremental Delivery</u>: Instead of focusing on only "final delivery", pursue the concept of "incremental delivery". Normally the contract or project is closed upon user acceptance of final delivery. Under Agile, it is strongly recommended to provide

incremental delivery. The Agile contracting methods need to take this into consideration that there will be incremental deliveries in the project and the payments may be based upon partial deliverables acceptable by customers.

- <u>Final Acceptance vs. Demo & Feedback</u>: Instead of insisting on "final acceptance", give the demonstration and ask for feedback. Under Agile, the customer will be invited at end of each iteration or release during retrospective meetings and will be requested to drive the demo and provide feedback. This may constitute partial acceptance of product and the Agile contracting methods may evolve based on partial incremental deliverables.

- The best solution for challenges under Agile contracting methods is to have a well-defined planning and acceptance process for each iteration.

Agile Discovery

The core values of Agile methodologies for software development were expressed in the "Manifesto for Agile Software Development". It introduced several principles, two of which can be considered very important also for the agile discovery. Here are these two principles:

1. Individuals and interactions over processes and tools
2. Responding to changes over following a plan.

Some values and practices of agile software development are also useful in support of discovery process. The Agile practitioners dream of an agile discovery environment that would bring significant improvements to the work.

Agile frameworks and terminology

There are many agile frameworks and different terminology terms are used in these agile frameworks. It is important to understand these terms and how these are used in communicating among agile community.

SCRUM is one of the most popular agile frameworks. Other agile frameworks are Extreme Programming (XP), Lean, Agile Modeling (AM), Agile Unified Process (AUP), Dynamic Systems Development Method (DSDM), Feature Driven Development (FDD), and Crystal etc.

An Overview of SCRUM

SCRUM is the most popular and widely used agile framework in software development. Scrum is an iterative and incremental approach for completing complex projects. Scrum is an agile process that allows the team to focus on delivering the highest business value in the shortest time. Scrum has at its core the *sprint* – a term used for iteration. Scrum teams use specific roles, artifacts, and ceremonies.

The three specific roles used in scrum are – Product Owner, Scrum Master and Scrum Team Member.

The four specific ceremonies conducted under scrum are – Sprint Planning, Sprint Review, Sprint Retrospective and Daily Scrum Meeting.

The three specific artifacts used in scrum are – Product Backlog, Sprint Backlog and Burn-down Charts.

In typical SCRUM, a *product owner* captures requirements and creates a prioritized wish list called a *product backlog*. The *scrum team* has a certain amount of time, a *sprint*, to complete its work - usually two to four weeks, but meets each day to assess its progress (*daily scrum meeting*). Along the way, the *scrum master* keeps the team focused on its goal. At the end of the sprint, the work should be *potentially shippable*, as in ready to hand over to a customer, or to put on a store shelf, or to show to a stakeholder. The sprint begins with *sprint planning* meeting and ends with a *sprint review* and *retrospective*.

The main principles of Scrum include:

- ✓ **Time-boxing.** Everything is time boxed. The team wants to plan when they get the feedback on what they are doing and how they are doing. The feedback makes the team to understand better and with better understanding, the focus is stronger and delivery becomes more value driven.
- ✓ **Self-managing Teams.** These teams generate lot of energy because they work closely together and also become responsible for organizing themselves. These teams make them very productive and self-managed thereby delivering high business added value products to the customer.
- ✓ **Potentially Shippable Increments.** Working pieces of the application are the only possible measurements for true status of the project. Every team member works towards achieving the acceptance of the product increment created during sprint. The team is satisfied with creating the potentially shippable increments which are conforming to the definition of done set by team and accepted by customer by acknowledging that it is bringing the business value.

Within each sprint, the scrum team develops and tests a functional part of the product (coming from product and sprint backlog) until the product owner accepts it and the functionality becomes a potentially shippable product increment. When one sprint finishes, the next one starts. Scrum teams deliver product features in increments at end of each sprint. A product release occurs at end of sprint or after several sprints. The sprint, as well as the processes within it, repeats over and over. This makes it iterative as well as incremental process.

An Overview of Extreme Programming

Extreme Programming (XP) has emerged as one of more popular agile methods, specific to software. XP is a disciplined approach to delivering high-quality software quickly and continuously. Extreme programming takes the best practices of software development to an extreme level.

The main principles of XP include:

- ✓ **High customer involvement.** Communication between customer and programmer is direct. The programmer needs to know the business requirements to design the optimum technical solution. High customer involvement is needed.
- ✓ **Coding as core activity.** Code delivers not only solutions and features, but also helps to explore problems. Coding is the most essential and core activity in delivering value to the customer.
- ✓ **Continuous testing.** Lots of testing done on continuous basis helps to identify defects at early stages. Defects can be fixed right away before they go any further. Developers don't start coding unless acceptance criteria for the requirements and unit tests for the design are not worked out. Best practices of Test Driven Development (TDD) and Acceptance Test Driven Development (ATDD) are followed throughout the development process.
- ✓ **Continuous planning.** Keep the design simple, so that cost to change the code is lower. The team improves design continuously by refactoring code - removing duplications and reusing common code. The team follows key practices of XP in areas of sustainable pace, pair programming, and rapid feedback.
- ✓ **Deliver working software.** Close teamwork to deliver working software at very frequent intervals, typically every 1-3 weeks. Continuous integration and automation helps to deliver working software consistently over shorter period of time – small releases.

The original XP recipe is based on *four simple values* – simplicity, communication, feedback, and courage.

XP is also based on *twelve key practices*: Planning Game, Small Releases, Customer Acceptance Tests, Simple Design, Pair Programming, Test-Driven Development, Refactoring, Continuous Integration, Collective Code Ownership, Coding Standards, System Metaphor and Sustainable Pace.

XP is "extreme" because XP intentionally pushes the software development best practices to its extreme, which has resulted in a strong track record of XP improving software development efficiency and its success.

- ❖ If code reviews are good, <u>review code all the time</u> (pair programming)
- ❖ If testing is good, everybody will <u>test all the time</u>

❖ If simplicity is good, keep the system in the simplest design that supports its current functionality. (<u>simplest thing that works</u>)

❖ If design is good, everybody will design daily (<u>refactoring</u>)

❖ If architecture is important, everybody will work at defining and refining the architecture (<u>metaphor</u>)

❖ If integration testing is important, build and <u>integrate test several times a day</u> (continuous integration)

❖ If short iterations are good, <u>make iterations really, really short</u> (hours rather than weeks)

An Overview of Lean

Lean has its origins in manufacturing. Lean Software Development focuses on structure and owes much of its principles and practices to the Lean Manufacturing movement and the practices of companies like Toyota. In Lean manufacturing, Toyota created a just-in-time process where the concept of Kanban boards was adopted to control production. The focus of lean is business value and minimizing activities outside of product development.

Lean software development focuses the team on delivering value to the customer, and on the efficiency of the "Value Stream," the mechanisms that deliver that value.

The main principles of Lean include:

✓ **Eliminating Waste.** Waste includes creating features not needed, building wrong things and thrashing. Don't create lots of things that are partially done or non-functional. Whatever is produced must have value and must be working fully and ready for use.

✓ **Amplifying Learning.** Learning enables continuous improvements and predictability. Provide environment that promotes individual as well as team learning. Master various skills and mentor others.

✓ **Deciding as Late as Possible.** Make decisions at the right time and at the last responsible minute when all options with risks are known.

✓ **Delivering as Fast as Possible.** Work at once on vital few which carry values so that those features will get delivered. Manage workflow, rather than schedules.

✓ **Empowering the Team.** Engage everyone. Take pride on what you do and what the team is doing. Work in teams working autonomously. Motivate the development team with actions.

✓ **Building Integrity In.** Build quality in. Correct defects immediately before final inspection. Use automation and best practices like Test Driven Development (TDD). Break dependencies so that any feature can be developed at any time.

✓ **Seeing the Whole.** Optimize the whole. Solve problems, not just symptoms. Deliver working solution. Think long-term when creating products and solutions.

Lean eliminates waste by selecting only the truly valuable features for a system, prioritizing those selected, and delivering them in small batches. It emphasizes the speed and efficiency of development workflow, and relies on rapid and reliable feedback between programmers and customers.

Kanban: Kanban as applied to software development is a pull-based planning and execution method. Rather than planning work items up front and pushing them into the work queue of a team, the team signals when they are ready for more work and pull it into their queue. Kanban focuses on maximizing the throughput of a team. One of the ways it achieves this goal is through the application of Work-in-Process (WIP) limits in each of the states of a work item. Under a Kanban (or Lean) approach, queues or inventories of work in any state are seen as waste. The WIP limits enable a team to focus on the optimal flow of work items through the system, minimizing any associated waste. Kanban allows teams to achieve process optimizations while respecting and maintaining a sustainable pace.

An Overview of Other Agile Methodologies

Crystal: The Crystal methodology is one of the most lightweight, adaptable approaches to software development. Crystal is actually comprised of a family of methodologies (Crystal Clear, Crystal Yellow, Crystal Orange, etc.) whose unique characteristics are driven by several factors such as team size, system criticality, and project priorities. This Crystal family addresses the realization that each project may require a slightly tailored set of policies, practices, and processes in order to meet the project's unique characteristics.

DSDM: DSDM grew out of the need to provide an industry standard project delivery framework for what was referred to as Rapid Application Development (RAD) at the time. DSDM methodology has evolved and matured to provide a comprehensive foundation for planning, managing, executing, and scaling agile and iterative software development projects. DSDM is based on nine key principles that primarily revolve around business needs/value, active user involvement, empowered teams, frequent delivery, integrated testing, and stakeholder collaboration. DSDM specifically calls out "fitness for business purpose" as the primary criteria for delivery and acceptance of a system, focusing on the useful 80% of the system that can be deployed in 20% of the time.

FDD: FDD is a model-driven, short-iteration process. It begins with establishing an overall model shape. Then it continues with a series of two-week "design by feature, build by feature" iterations. The features are small, "useful in the eyes of the client" results. FDD designs the rest of the development process around feature delivery using the following eight practices: Domain Object Modeling, Developing by Feature, Component /Class Ownership, Feature Teams, Inspections, Configuration Management, Regular Builds, Visibility of Progress and Results.

Agile hybrid models

Typically there are three types of project life cycles:

1. Predictive Life Cycles: These (also known as fully plan-driven) are ones in which the project scope, and the time and cost required to deliver that scope, are determined as early in the project life cycle as practically possible. These projects proceed through a series of sequential phases and the work performed in each phase is distinct. This can be broadly described as "Waterfall style" of software development life cycle.

2. Iterative and Incremental Life Cycles: These are the ones in which project phases (also called iterations) intentionally repeat one or more project activities as the project team's understanding of the product increases. Iterations develop the product through a series of repeated cycles, while increments successively add to the functionality of the product. These life cycles develop the product both iteratively and incrementally. This can be broadly described as "Unified Process" (UP or Open-UP) style of software development life cycle.

3. Adaptive Life Cycles: These (also known as change-driven or agile methods) are intended to respond to high levels of change and ongoing stakeholder involvement. Adaptive methods are also iterative and incremental, but differ in that iterations are very rapid (usually of 2 to 4 weeks) and are fixed in time and cost. Adaptive projects generally perform several processes in each iteration. This can be broadly described as "Agile style" of software development life cycle.

Instead of arguing which style is better, a much more productive discussion would be when to use agile and when not to use it, rather than compare it to a method that never made much sense to start with. A truly well-rounded practitioner knows that it is not the 'approach' that is important, but the ability to deliver what the business needs – whatever that deliverable is and whatever the environment.

Waterfall is not the only alternative to agile and at the same time, "pure agile" is not appropriate for all projects. Agile projects share certain characteristics (a backlog of work, self-organizing teams, rapid, incremental delivery of new functionality to users) that aren't necessarily value-adding for all projects and under all circumstances. Agile is not a silver bullet. Since you have many options, please consider using them.

This is where an agile hybrid model is proposed and should be implemented by agile practitioner based on the environment in which it will be applied. Many organizations are successfully using hybrid models that incorporate elements of agile and non-agile techniques with the goal of quickly introducing new features while ensuring proper system documentation and utilizing traditional business analysis techniques to help keep a project on track and reduce risks, uncertainty, and requirements churn. This mixing and matching of software process elements from agile and non-agile (more formal) approaches is a much more practical way of using these methods.

Agile Manifesto values and principles

The four items under agile manifesto are:

- **Individuals and interactions** over processes and tools
- **Working software** over comprehensive documentation
- **Customer collaboration** over contract negotiation
- **Responding to change** over following a plan

Note: While there is value in the items on right, *we value the items on left more.*

The twelve principles under agile are:

- ❖ Our highest priority is *to satisfy the customer* through *early and continuous delivery of valuable software.*
- ❖ *Welcome changing requirements*, even late in development. Agile processes harness change for the customer's competitive advantage.
- ❖ *Deliver working software frequently*, from a couple of weeks to a couple of months, with a preference to the shorter timescale.
- ❖ Business people and developers *must work together daily* throughout the project.
- ❖ Build projects around *motivated individuals*. Give them the environment and support they need, and trust them to get the job done.
- ❖ The most efficient and effective method of conveying information to and within a development team is *face-to-face conversation.*
- ❖ *Working software* is the primary measure of progress.
- ❖ Agile processes promote sustainable development. The sponsors, developers, and users should be able to *maintain a constant pace* indefinitely.
- ❖ *Continuous attention* to technical excellence and good design enhances agility.
- ❖ *Simplicity* - the art of maximizing the amount of work not done - is essential.
- ❖ The best architectures, requirements, and designs *emerge from self-organizing teams.*
- ❖ At regular intervals, the team reflects on *how to become more effective*, then tunes and adjusts its behavior accordingly.

These four manifesto and twelve principles are very important to PMI-ACP certification examination and every candidate must REMEMBER these word-by-word, line-by-line.

Please make sure that you understand the words and meanings used in all four manifesto and twelve principles.

Agile method and approaches

At most care must be taken when applying new agile practices under existing organizational procedures, methods and processes. There can be resistance as well as welcome from known and unknown peoples and groups. Training and mentoring are the best suggested methods to adapt to Agile practices.

Please remember the following key factors when applying new agile principles:

- *Agile methods are adaptive rather than predictive.*
- *Agile methods are people-oriented rather than process-oriented.*
- Agile methods are in different flavors rather than just vanilla as seen below:
    - Agile Manifesto
    - XP (Extreme Programming)
    - SCRUM
    - Crystal
    - Test Driven Development (TDD)
    - Lean Development

Variations in Agile methods and approaches

At very high level, there are:

- ➢ Four Agile Manifesto
- ➢ Twelve Agile Principles and
- ➢ Multiple Agile Methods such as:
    - o XP
    - o SCRUM
    - o DSDM
    - o Crystal etc.

However:

- No one method is CORRECT.
- No one method is APPROPRIATE
- No one method is BEST.
- No one method SUITABLE

All methods have variations, their own pluses & minuses, and own pros and cons.

The best approach for agile teams is to "mix & match" as they progress.

Agile project accounting principles

Agile project accounting principles are just like any other normal organizational project accounting principles. Organizations revolve around the numbers – ROI, risk/reward, investment/return, burn-rate, etc.

Burn rate - Agile teams' burn rate is calculated with reference to an individual sprint. Consider 5 team members have an average billing rate of 50 dollars/hour and work in 2-week sprints, then the burn rate for the team is 50 x 5 x 40 x 2 = 20,000.00 dollars/sprint

Earned Value Management systems (EVM) need to be significantly re-thought in terms of agile concepts. Similarly the portfolio management systems need detail attention. Currently Agile project accounting principles are limited to

- IRR (Internal Rate of Return) and
- Valuation of iteration / features delivered.

Agile project chartering

A **project charter**, **project definition** or **project statement** is a statement of the scope, objectives and participants in a project. It provides a preliminary delineation of roles and responsibilities, outlines the project objectives, identifies the main stakeholders, and defines the authority of the project manager. It serves as a reference of authority for the future of the project. The terms of reference are usually part of the project charter.

The project charter is a formal document used to justify, explain, define, and ultimately authorize a project. The purpose of the project charter is to document:

- Reasons for undertaking the project
- Objectives and constraints of the project
- Directions concerning the solution
- Identities of the main stakeholders
- In scope and out-of-scope items
- High level risk management plan
- Communication plan
- Target project benefits
- High level budget and spending authority

A useful project charter contains three key elements:

1. **Vision**: The vision defines the "why" of the project. This is reason for project's existence.

2. **Mission**: This is the "what" of the project and it states what will be done in the project to achieve its purpose.
3. **Success criteria**: The success criteria are management tests that describe effects.

The elements of project charter under agile projects should continue along traditional route of preparing paperwork to get approval but should be barely sufficient and follow progressive elaboration.

Agile sizing and estimation

Please see the detail description under Chapter Three, Agile Estimation.

Agile values and principles

Please see the detail descriptions under Chapter One, All about Agile.

Building agile teams

An agile team is an empowered and high performance team. Therefore building an efficient agile team involves both, building an empowered team as well as building a high performance team.

Building empowered teams

What is Empowerment? Empowerment is the act of vesting substantial responsibility in the people nearest to the problems to be solved. The person doing the job knows far better than anyone else, the best way of doing the job, and is also the best fitted to improve it.

What is a team? A team is a small number of people with complementary skills who are committed to a common purpose, performance goals and approach for which they hold themselves mutually accountable. An empowered team is capable to make the necessary changes and decisions to the processes and products to add values incrementally and deliver valuable software to the customer ultimately.

What brings empowerment in a team? When mutual accountability is practiced within a team, there is high commitment and trust among the team members. Team members take ownership of their work products. Mutual accountability and ownership lead to empowerment and enable higher levels of productivity, quality and achievement of goals.

Team success is dependent on a healthy interaction of employees with customers, while supported by management. TEAM here stands for:

- **T**ogether
- **E**veryone
- **A**chieves
- **M**ore

What are the ten characteristics of empowerment?

- Significance – meaning
- Learning – competence
- Trust
- Reward system – acknowledgement
- Cultural pride
- Future – career trajectory
- Development – reflective backtalk
- Alignment
- Attunement
- Fun

High performance teaming (HPT): Organization that have embraced empowerment principles and accomplish their goals with high performance teams, demonstrate these eight key characteristics:

- ❖ Sense of purpose
- ❖ Open communication
- ❖ Trust and mutual respect
- ❖ Shared leadership
- ❖ Effective working procedures
- ❖ Building on differences
- ❖ Flexibility
- ❖ Adaptability
- ❖ Continuous learning

It becomes easier for agile project manager to build an empowered team when the team is co-located and is of small size, due to continuous face-to-face interaction and communication. It is also promoted under servant leadership style.

Building high-performance teams

Building high-performance team is a two-step process, first establish the team, and then maximize the team's performance. For that the team will need excellent team communication and accelerated team action and execution.

- **Establishing the team**: This task may include establishing a team vision, mission and values; establishing team norms and guidelines; setting team performance goals and objectives; and clarifying team roles.
- **Maximizing team performance**: This task may include making choices; taking accountability; supporting others; acting with integrity; building commitment; and building trust etc.
- **Building team communication**: This task may include communicating openly & honestly; giving team feedback & coaching; listening; acknowledging others, resolving conflicts; and learning from others.
- **Accelerating team action and execution**: This task may include team action planning and conducting effective team meetings etc.

These are the characteristics of HPT (High Performance Teams):

- Common purpose.
- Clear roles
- Accepted leadership
- Effective processes
- Solid relationships
- Excellent communications

SUMMARY

All these 11 knowledge and skills areas covered under level I are important, and they carry equal weight in the exam. The student is advised to study these thoroughly and to spend enough time and efforts on this level I areas to get through the PMI ACP exam.

Sample Practice Examination on Chapter XII Level I Knowledge & Skills

Q1: Agile contracting methods are not very well defined because: (choose the best)

    A. Agile doesn't support contracting

    B. The regulatory and business compliance governance is against agile principles.

    C. It is difficult to describe/outline challenges in contracting when agile methods are used

    D. Standard contracting templates are not used under agile contracting

Q2: Most of the customers demand fixed bid contracts with fixed time, cost and scope variables. Since software development firms and their customers need legal contracts, this leaves the Agile practitioners to handle the apparent contradiction between the customers' desire for "certainty" with their own commitment to Agile values such as *responding to change*. Which Agile manifesto best describes the above scenario?

    A. Individuals and interactions over processes and tools

    B. Working software over comprehensive documentation

    C. Customer collaboration over contract negotiation

    D. Responding to change over following a plan

Q3: Which is one of the most popular and widely used agile frameworks among the following four?

    A. Agile Unified Process (AUP)

    B. Feature Driven Development (FDD)

    C. Crystal

    D. Scrum

Q4: SCRUM is the most popular and widely used agile framework in software development. Scrum is an iterative and incremental approach for completing complex projects. Scrum is an agile process that allows the team to focus on delivering the highest business value in the shortest time. Scrum has at its core the *sprint* – a term used for iteration. Scrum teams use specific roles, artifacts, and ceremonies. The three specific roles used in scrum are except:

A. Product Owner
B. Scrum Master
C. Scrum Owner
D. Scrum Team Member

Q5: SCRUM is the most popular and widely used agile framework in software development. Scrum is an iterative and incremental approach for completing complex projects. Scrum is an agile process that allows the team to focus on delivering the highest business value in the shortest time. Scrum has at its core the *sprint* – a term used for iteration. Scrum teams use specific roles, artifacts, and ceremonies. The four specific ceremonies conducted under scrum are, except:

A. Sprint Planning
B. Sprint Review
C. Sprint Retrospective
D. Weekly Scrum Meeting

Q6: SCRUM is the most popular and widely used agile framework in software development. Scrum is an iterative and incremental approach for completing complex projects. Scrum is an agile process that allows the team to focus on delivering the highest business value in the shortest time. Scrum has at its core the *sprint* – a term used for iteration. Scrum teams use specific roles, artifacts, and ceremonies. The three specific artifacts used in scrum are, except:

A. Agile manifesto
B. Product Backlog
C. Sprint Backlog
D. Burn-down Charts

Q7: Working pieces of the application are the only possible measurements for true status of the project. Every team member works towards achieving the acceptance of the product pieces created during sprint. The team is satisfied with creating the potentially shippable _____ which are conforming to the definition of done set by team and accepted by customer by acknowledging that it is bringing the business value.

A. Increments
B. Modules
C. Deliverables
D. Features

Q8: Extreme Programming (XP) has emerged as one of more popular agile methods, specific to software. XP is a disciplined approach to delivering high-quality software quickly and continuously. Extreme programming takes the best practices of software development to an extreme level. Which Agile manifesto closely describes the above methodology?

    A. Individuals and interactions over processes and tools
    B. Working software over comprehensive documentation
    C. Customer collaboration over contract negotiation
    D. Responding to change over following a plan

Q9: Extreme Programming (XP) has emerged as one of more popular agile methods, specific to software. Close teamwork to deliver working software at very frequent intervals, typically every 1-3 weeks. Continuous _____ and automation helps to deliver working software consistently over shorter period of time – small releases.

    A. Process Improvement
    B. Coding
    C. Integration
    D. Development

Q10: Extreme Programming (XP) has emerged as one of more popular agile methods, specific to software. Lots of testing is done on continuous basis which helps to identify defects at early stages. Defects can be fixed right away before they go any further. Developers don't start coding unless acceptance criteria for the requirements are not worked out. Best practices of _____ are followed throughout the development process.

    A. Test Driven Development (TDD)
    B. Acceptance Test Driven Development (ATDD)
    C. Model Driven Development (MDD)
    D. Unified Modeling Language (UML)

Q11: Extreme Programming (XP) has emerged as one of more popular agile methods, specific to software. Lots of testing done on continuous basis helps to identify defects at early stages. Defects can be fixed right away before they go any further. Developers don't start coding unless unit tests for the design are not worked out. Best practices of _____ are followed throughout the development process.

    A. Test Driven Development (TDD)
    B. Acceptance Test Driven Development (ATDD)
    C. Model Driven Development (MDD)
    D. Unified Modeling Language (UML)

Q12: Lean software development focuses the team on delivering value to the customer, and on the efficiency of the "Value Stream," the mechanisms that deliver that value. The main principles of Lean include:

A. Eliminating Documentation
B. Eliminating Inventory
C. Eliminating Waste
D. Eliminating Meetings

Q13: Kanban focuses on maximizing the throughput of a team. One of the ways it achieves this goal is through the application of (WIP) limits in each of the states of a work item. What is WIP?

A. Work In Production
B. Work In Process
C. Work In Pending
D. Work In Progression

Q14: Which one of the following is not one of the typical types of project life cycles?

A. Predictive
B. Supportive
C. Iterative
D. Adaptive

Q15: Instead of arguing which style of software development is better, an agile hybrid model is proposed and should be implemented by agile practitioner based on the environment in which it will be applied. Many organizations are successfully using hybrid models that incorporate elements of:

A. Agile and non-agile techniques
B. Agile and waterfall techniques
C. Agile and Unified Process techniques
D. Agile and non-adaptive techniques

Q16: Which of the following items under agile manifesto seems to be incorrect?

A. **Processes and Tools** over individuals and interactions
B. **Working software** over comprehensive documentation
C. **Customer collaboration** over contract negotiation
D. **Responding to change** over following a plan

Q17: Which one principle seems to be more appropriate under the well-known twelve agile principles?

    A. *Running software* is the primary measure of progress
    B. *Valuable software* is the primary measure of progress
    C. *Working software* is the primary measure of progress
    D. *Tested software* is the primary measure of progress

Q18: As per another agile principle, Business people and developers *must work together* _____ throughout the project:

    A. Daily
    B. Weekly
    C. Monthly
    D. As needed

Q19: Agile processes promote sustainable development. The sponsors, developers, and users should be able to *maintain a constant pace* indefinitely.

    A. Fast
    B. Quick
    C. Constant
    D. Reliable

Q20: At most care must be taken when applying new agile practices under existing organizational procedures, methods and processes. There can be resistance as well as welcome from known and unknown peoples and groups. Please remember the following key factor when applying new agile principles

    A. Agile methods are process-oriented rather than people-oriented.
    B. Agile methods are people-oriented rather than process-oriented
    C. Agile methods are tool-oriented rather than technique-oriented
    D. Agile methods are technique-oriented rather than tool-oriented

Answers:

Q1: C. Agile contracting methods are not very well defined because it is difficult to describe/outline challenges in contracting when agile methods are used under contractual software development environments.

Q2: C. In this situation, when we are talking about agile contracting and its challenges, the following agile manifesto best describes the scenario: Customer collaboration over contract negotiation.

Q3: D. SCRUM is one of the most popular agile frameworks. Other agile frameworks are Extreme Programming (XP), Lean, Agile Modeling (AM), Agile Unified Process (AUP), Dynamic Systems Development Method (DSDM), Feature Driven Development (FDD), and Crystal etc.

Q4: C. The three specific roles used in scrum are – Product Owner, Scrum Master and Scrum Team Member.

Q5: D. The four specific ceremonies conducted under scrum are – Sprint Planning, Sprint Review, Sprint Retrospective and Daily Scrum Meeting.

Q6: A. The three specific artifacts used in scrum are – Product Backlog, Sprint Backlog and Burn-down Charts.

Q7: A. **Potentially Shippable Increments.** Working pieces of the application are the only possible measurements for true status of the project. Every team member works towards achieving the acceptance of the product increment created during sprint. The team is satisfied with creating the potentially shippable increments which are conforming to the definition of done set by team and accepted by customer by acknowledging that it is bringing the business value.

Q8: B. In this situation, when we are talking about coding as the most essential and core activity, the following agile manifesto best describes the scenario: Working software over comprehensive documentation.

Q9: C. Continuous integration and automation helps to deliver working software consistently over shorter period of time – small releases.

Q10:B. Extreme Programming (XP) has emerged as one of more popular agile methods, specific to software. Lots of testing done on continuous basis helps to identify defects at early stages. Defects can be fixed right away before they go any further. Developers don't start coding unless acceptance criteria for the requirements and unit tests for the design are not worked out. Best practices of Test Driven Development (TDD) and Acceptance Test Driven Development (ATDD) are followed throughout the development process.

Q11: A. Extreme Programming (XP) has emerged as one of more popular agile methods, specific to software. Lots of testing done on continuous basis helps to identify defects at early stages. Defects can be fixed right away before they go any further. Developers don't start coding unless acceptance criteria for the requirements and unit tests for the design are not worked out. Best practices of Test Driven Development (TDD) and Acceptance Test Driven Development (ATDD) are followed throughout the development process.

Q12: C. Lean software development focuses the team on delivering value to the customer, and on the efficiency of the "Value Stream," the mechanisms that deliver that value. The main principles of Lean include: Eliminating Waste. Waste includes creating features not needed, building wrong things and thrashing.

Q13: B. Kanban focuses on maximizing the throughput of a team. One of the ways it achieves this goal is through the application of (WIP) limits in each of the states of a work item. WIP stands for Work In Progress or Work In process.

Q14: B. Typically there are three types of project life cycles: Predictive, Iterative and Adaptive Life Cycles.

Q15: A. Instead of arguing which style of software development is better, an agile hybrid model is proposed and should be implemented by agile practitioner based on the environment in which it will be applied. Many organizations are successfully using hybrid models that incorporate elements of agile and non-agile techniques.

Q16: A. It should be **Individuals and interactions** over processes and tools.

Q17: C. The correct principle is: *Working software* is the primary measure of progress.

Q18: A. Per agile principles, Business people and developers *must work together daily* throughout the project.

Q19: C. Agile processes promote sustainable development. The sponsors, developers, and users should be able to *maintain a constant pace* indefinitely.

Q20: B. Please remember the following key factor when applying new agile principles: Agile methods are people-oriented rather than process-oriented.

CHAPTER THIRTEEN

Level II Knowledge And Skills

The Agile practitioner examination includes 33 knowledge and skills areas. This chapter covers the next 11 knowledge and skills classified at Level 2. Be aware that ALL 33 knowledge and skills are included in PMI-ACP exam with equal importance. The 33 K&S are distributed over 3 chapters for simplicity.

The questions are based upon agile knowledge and skills, so this chapter will help you to prepare those questions.

> ➤ **Assessing and incorporating community and stakeholder values**
> ➤ **Communication management**
> ➤ **Continuous improvement**
> ➤ **Developmental mastery models (Tuckman, Dreyfus, Shu Ha Ri)**
> ➤ **Facilitation methods**
> ➤ **Global, cultural, and team diversity**
> ➤ **Incremental Delivery**
> ➤ **Knowledge Sharing / written communication**
> ➤ **Leadership tools and techniques**
> ➤ **Managing with agile KPIs**
> ➤ **Participatory decision models (convergent, shared collaboration)**

There are 11 knowledge and skills listed under this level II. Realistically speaking, expect at the least 1 or 2 questions about each item from the above list. There will be 60 questions based on total of 33 K&S.

Assessing and incorporating community and stakeholder values

There are various communities of practices (COP) in an organization. Similarly there are multiple stakeholders with their own values that they wish to get implemented in the product. The major challenging task for the team is to assess and incorporate those community and stakeholders values. The stakeholder values can become conflicting or mutually exclusive or dependent. It is crucial for the product owner to acquire the skill of reading between the lines and making all stakeholders happy about the inclusions or exclusions of features that may implement or omit the stakeholder values.

The stakeholders can provide their valuable feedbacks right from inception all the way till transition. There are multiple points like planning meetings, reviews, product demos, and retrospectives where the customer and agile team members can exchange values put in the product. Assessing and incorporating community and stakeholder values is the responsibility of entire agile development team. This must be the topmost priority for all agile team members. It's the worth that the project delivers to the business and stakeholders.

Communities of Practice (Networks)
"A community of practice (CoP) is a group of people who share a concern, a set of problems, or a passion about a topic, and who deepen their knowledge and expertise in this area by interacting on an ongoing basis."

Knowledge is both social and individual. Forming a group thus promotes learning and innovation. Creating a community of practice (CoP) is a way to share your knowledge with others who are passionate about the same topic. In return, you learn from their knowledge and experience. CoP members freely discuss the various situations they face. They share their aspirations. They identify their needs. They develop a unique, action-oriented perspective. Together, they discuss, innovate and develop a common practice in their field. CoPs can be small or large. CoPs can be internal or linked to partners outside the organization. CoPs can be virtual or physical. CoPs develop and must be tailored to their members' needs. CoPs are not like working groups. CoPs do not mainly aim to achieve a collective result. A CoP is a place where people collaborate. They learn from others. They share with them. CoP members manage their tacit and explicit knowledge in a given field as effectively as they can.

Communication management

According to PMI, ***Project communications management*** employs the processes required to ensure timely and appropriate generation, collection, distribution, storage, retrieval, and ultimate disposition of project information. This knowledge area provides the critical links between people and information that are necessary for successful project communications.

Look at the entire communication management from the perspectives of communications planning, information distribution, performance reporting, and manage stakeholders.

Communications planning:

- PMI definition: *Determining the information and communication needs of the projects stakeholders.*
- When agile teams talk about communications, they are usually talking about communications within the team.
- Agile puts a great deal of emphasis on the free flow of information between team members, between team members and the product owner, and even between the team and the direct customer.

Information distribution

- PMI definition: *Making needed information available to project stakeholders in a timely manner.*
- Agile teams keep their project status information up to date using large and visible information radiators that everyone in the team has access to and can update themselves.
- At all times, the agile team members know the location of these repositories of information and therefore they can manage their own work.
- The major benefit of these information radiators for the project managers is that everyone has instant access to real time information about the health of the project, release, or iteration.

Performance reporting:

- PMI definition: *Collecting and distributing performance information, including status reporting, progress measurement, and forecasting.*
- Performance reporting on agile projects is pretty simple. The team knows how big the project backlog is and they also know how much work they can complete in each iteration. Based on these two variables, the team members are able to predict how many features they will be able to complete before the end of the project, the release, or the iteration.
- Part of performance reporting involves keeping a high level project roadmap that helps team members to understand where the project is expected to be at certain point as it progresses to completion.
- Performance reporting is also useful for managing external dependencies.

Manage stakeholders:

- PMI definition: *Managing communications to satisfy the requirements and resolve issues with project stakeholders.*

- Managing stakeholders is really about managing the issues that come up during the life of the project.
- A significant benefit of agile is that nothing is hidden. This level of visibility gives the project manager the information they need to resolve problems and remove impediments.
- Issues are reviewed during the daily stand-up meetings and during various retrospective meetings.
- There will be always some issues that cannot be dealt by the team. In such situations, weekly or bi-weekly meeting with senior stakeholders to help the team resolve the issues is highly recommended.
- The most effective communication to manage stakeholders is to have face-to-face conversation rather than communicating by sending paper documentation, sending e-mails, leaving voice messages, or using audio/video conferencing.

Continuous improvement

A **continuous improvement process** (**CIP** or **CI**) is an ongoing effort to improve products, services, or processes. These efforts can seek "incremental" improvement over time or "breakthrough" improvement all at once. Delivery (customer valued) processes are constantly evaluated and improved in the light of their efficiency, effectiveness and flexibility. Some people see it as a meta-process for project management process.

Dr. Deming saw it as part of the 'system' whereby feedback from the process and customer were evaluated against organizational goals. This continuous process improvement responsibility traditionally used to be executed by 'management' but under agile, it's the responsibility of entire agile team and members.

Key points in continuous improvement processes:

- The core principle of CIP is the (self) reflection of processes. (Feedback)
- The purpose of CIP is the identification, reduction, and elimination of suboptimal processes. (Efficiency)
- The emphasis of CIP is on incremental, continuous steps rather than giant leaps. (Evolution)

One of the on-going rituals in each of iterations is to continuously look for areas of improvement using mini-retrospectives. These are quick and time-boxed to ten-to-fifteen minutes and the goal is to fulfill the following agile principle:

"At regular intervals, the team reflects on how to become more effective and then tunes and adjusts its behavior accordingly."

Developmental mastery models

The following 3 models will be described:

Tuckman, Dreyfus, Shu Ha Ri

Tuckman Model

Teams go through stages of development. Team formation usually follows easily recognizable stages, known as "forming, storming, norming, and performing." Psychologist Bruce Tuckman, who created this memorable phrase, later added a fifth stage, "adjourning" or "mourning." He used it to describe the path that most teams follow on their way to high performance.

These phases are all necessary and inevitable in order for the team to grow, to face up to challenges, to tackle problems, to find solutions, to plan work, and to deliver results. This model has become the basis for subsequent models. Here are those five stages of development.

Forming

> In this stage, most team members are positive and polite. Some are anxious, as they haven't fully understood what work the team will do. Others are simply excited about the task ahead. The team meets and learns about the opportunities and challenges, and then agrees on goals and begins to tackle the tasks. Team members tend to behave quite independently.

Storming

> Next, the team moves into the storming phase, where people start to push against the boundaries established in the forming stage. This is the stage where many teams fail.

> Storming often starts where there is a conflict between team members' natural working styles. People may work in different ways for all sorts of reasons. However, disagreements within the team can make members stronger, more versatile, and able to work more effectively as a team. The team members will therefore resolve their differences and members will be able to participate with one another more comfortably.

Norming

> Gradually, the team moves into the norming stage. This is when people start to resolve their differences, appreciate colleagues' strengths, and respect your authority as a leader.

Now that your team members know one another better, they may socialize together, and they are able to ask one another for help and provide constructive feedback. All team members take the responsibility and develop a stronger commitment to the team goal.

Performing

The team reaches the performing stage, when hard work leads, without friction, to the achievement of the team's goal. By this time, they are motivated and knowledgeable. The team members are now competent, autonomous and able to handle the decision-making process without supervision.

Adjourning

Many teams will reach this stage eventually that involves completing the task and breaking up the team (also referred to as Mourning). For example, project teams exist for only a fixed period, and even permanent teams may be disbanded through organizational restructuring.

Dreyfus Model

In the fields of education and operations research, the Dreyfus model of skill acquisition is a model of how students acquire skills through formal instruction and practicing. The original model proposes that a student passes through five distinct stages: novice, competence, proficiency, expertise, and mastery.

- In the **Novice** stage, a person follows rules as given, without context, with no sense of responsibility beyond following the rules exactly.
- **Competence** develops when the individual develops organizing principles to quickly access the particular rules that are relevant to the specific task at hand; hence, competence is characterized by active decision making in choosing a course of action.
- **Proficiency** is shown by individuals who develop intuition to guide their decisions and devise their own rules to formulate plans. The progression is thus from rigid adherence to rules to an intuitive mode of reasoning based on tacit knowledge.

To summarize, the five stages of increasing skill are as follows:

1. **Novice**
   - "rigid adherence to taught rules or plans"
   - no exercise of "discretionary judgment"

2. **Advanced beginner**
   - limited "situational perception"
   - all aspects of work treated separately with equal importance

3. **Competent**
   - "coping with crowdedness" (multiple activities, accumulation of information)
   - some perception of actions in relation to goals
   - deliberate planning
   - formulates routines

4. **Proficient**
   - holistic view of situation
   - prioritizes importance of aspects
   - "perceives deviations from the normal pattern"
   - employs maxims for guidance, with meanings that adapt to the situation at hand

5. **Expert**
   - transcends reliance on rules, guidelines, and maxims
   - "intuitive grasp of situations based on deep, tacit understanding"
   - has "vision of what is possible"
   - uses "analytical approaches" in new situations or in case of problems.

Shu Ha Ri

Originally, "Shu Ha Ri" is a concept describing the different stages of learning martial arts. This concept was applied in the Lean approach at Toyota.

"Shu Ha Ri" consists in three steps that a novice has to follow to acquire a skill or master a technique:

Shu: the disciple learns the basics by following the rules laid down by the master

Ha: having mastered the fundamentals, the disciple applies the rules but begins questioning them, understanding their subtleties and seeking exceptions to rules

Ri: the disciple who has mastered the rules can transcend and adapt them.

This simple model is being successfully used to support Agile adoption by the project team.

Facilitation methods

Definition of facilitation: The process of helping participants to learn from an activity. The literal meaning of facilitator is "one who makes things easy." Sometimes a facilitator is also called as a trainer.

What are some popular on-line facilitation methods?

- Video conferencing
- Online community
- Online collaboration

What are commonly used methods of group facilitation?

- **The world café:** New ideas may get developed and refined through informal conversations in café.
- **The story circle:** People gather in small groups to reflect upon and learn from the experiences of others. Storytelling is also an effective way to build trust between people.
- **Scenario thinking:** It is a powerful way to prepare organizations and teams to respond effectively to potential opportunities and threats. Thinking in scenarios is fundamentally a process of identifying forces of change.
- **Open space meetings:** It is a method by which participants determine for themselves the outcomes, agenda, and length of a group discussion.

Global, cultural, and team diversity

The agile teams are normally co-located small teams. Even then the team members may come from different work culture and there will be some team diversity. It is very important for the entire team to understand the culture and team diversity when working as a single cohesive agile team. There are various options such as cultural shows, diversity training, cross-cultural get-togethers etc. which can bridge the gaps if any among the team members. All team members are encouraged to differentiate and understand the meaning of terms:

- Co-located Team
- On-site Team and Customer
- Off-Site Team
- Remote / Work-from-remote
- Off-shore Team / Out-sources team
- Global Services Team

The agile team needs to understand the challenges in collaborating with each other amidst the cultural/language differences as well as team diversity. Globalization brings more challenges but the team must understand and reap the benefits in working with the global teams by maximizing local talents, time zone differences and localization. By understanding the differences between traditional teams and agile teams, the organization will be equipped to remove existing boundaries. This process is necessary to encourage collaboration within product teams.

Incremental Delivery

Incremental delivery is a key component of most software projects today – it allows us to deliver the *most valuable* elements of a system first, which allows our customers to start getting benefit from the system earlier. As additional features are developed, and additional use cases are enabled, they are delivered to the customers, who get incremental value from those features.

The phrase "Incremental Delivery" mainly refers to the Agile team's delivery of their product to their customer for acceptance. *Every* Agile project does this at the end of *every* iteration. But Agile teams would prefer that "delivery" should not stop there.

What is the purpose of Incremental Delivery?

- The purpose of incremental delivery is to get feedback on what has been developed to date.
- Demonstrating the product to one or a few customers and asking their opinion will gain us a certain amount of valuable feedback.

Knowledge Sharing / Written Communication

- **Knowledge sharing** is an activity through which knowledge (i.e. information, skills, or expertise) is exchanged among people, or within an organization, or even within industry groups.
- Organizations have recognized that knowledge constitutes a valuable intangible asset for creating and sustaining competitive advantages. Knowledge sharing activities are generally supported by knowledge management systems. However, technology constitutes only one of the many factors that affect the sharing of knowledge in organizations, such as organizational culture, trust, and incentives. The sharing of knowledge constitutes a major challenge in the field of knowledge management because some employees tend to resist sharing their knowledge with the rest of the organization.
- "Knowledge management" is about creating a work environment that encourages team work,
- collaboration, the sharing of knowledge, and continuous learning.

- **Peer Assist** is a method of cooperation, based on dialogue and mutual respect among peers. Peer Assist involves a meeting organized by a work team who are starting up a new project (the hosts). The hosts call on another group who already has experience with a similar project. They introduce the background and data of their project and their capabilities. They then express their specific needs.

- Once the situation is explained, both teams work together to identify possible solutions to the problem.

- **After Action Review (AAR)**: AAR's main purpose is learning by talking and thinking about a completed activity or project. Its goal is simply to state lessons learned, rather than to solve problems or criticize.

- AAR must be done in-house. If possible, it must be done right after the activity discussed. The exercise aims to capture the lessons before they are forgotten. All stakeholders in the process, and they alone, are invited to join the discussion group. Everyone must take part with an open mind.

- **Storytelling**: Stories have recently been rediscovered as a way to transfer knowledge. Stories allow us to describe employee relations or activities in a formal or informal way. The aim is to transmit tacit knowledge that an organization can use. Stories are a simple and accessible way to communicate complex ideas, key messages and lessons learned. Telling stories out loud engages people's minds, imaginations and emotions. This makes storytelling much more accessible than theory, and a very powerful way to transfer knowledge. But we must recognize the importance of analytical thought. We must use stories to complement other tools.

Knowledge Sharing Meetings:

FORUMS AND MEETINGS

Small meetings, discussion groups and large forums can all serve as opportunities for sharing knowledge and learning. But, for this to happen, they have to be organized with learning in mind. The process of the meeting, discussion or forum has to be well planned in advance. By forums and meetings, we are referring to everything from a large conference or congress, to round-table discussions that happen on their own or inside a larger conference, to armchair presentations or panel presentations, and any type of staff or regular meeting that brings people together. Meetings and forums can be useful learning and knowledge sharing opportunities

WORKSHOPS, TRAINING AND SEMINARS

In traditional courses, people listen to the presenter without interrupting. More and more, this approach is giving way to a much more dynamic and stimulating group learning process. This may involve a workshop, training session or seminar. The trend in learning activities is now for people to interact with their peers. People share what they know.

People discuss things. People benefit from each other's views and experiences. A presenter no longer leads these meetings. A facilitator does. The facilitator's mandate is to guide the various activities and discussions throughout the event. Several knowledge-sharing methods can be used in a seminar, training session or workshop. These methods can be tailored to your needs.

KNOWLEDGE FAIRS

Got a lot of information to share with a whole lot of people? Think an interactive presentation would be the ideal way to share your knowledge of a specific subject? Then it may be useful to organize knowledge fair. Knowledge fair is designed to present information on a chosen theme. You can use several technical means to present your information to the target group. They include showcases, panels; scale models and kiosks. You can also have all kinds of demonstrations and presenters.

Leadership Tools & Techniques

Learning Iteration-by-iteration: One of the agile leadership techniques is to learn to lead as the leader observes oneself becoming more competent and confident, iteration by iteration.

Value Provider: Another technique is based on the realization about how the leadership could provide value under new agile circumstances.

Servant Leadership Role: Most important change in agile leadership is to adapt to the tools and techniques under "servant leadership" role transitioning away from the conventional "command and control" style. Some of the characteristics under "servant leadership" approach are:

➢ Allow teams to self-manage.
➢ Assumes different leadership styles for different stages of team formation. A well-known model describes the stages of team formation: forming, storming, norming, performing and adjourning.
➢ Leads by serving: A leader who ensures that "other people's highest priority needs are being served".
➢ Possesses Self-awareness.
➢ Partnering with traditional functional/skill managers to create most effective teams possible.
➢ Give up on micro-management, since the team manages itself within the boundaries of iterative and incremental deliveries.
➢ Facilitates Collaboration by practicing multitude of facilitation tools with teams.
➢ Removes impediments

Managing with agile KPIs

The KPI stands for Key Performance Indicators (KPI). Here few KPIs related to agile are discussed and how to manage those KPIs.

Changing View of Project Success: Delivering a project "on-time and on-budget" is no longer adequate. In today's environment, the key question should be: "Did the project deliver value to the business?" Value is largely determined by how the system is embraced by the user community in the months and years after it is deployed.

Using Business Metrics: Project professionals are historically skilled and focused on managing the triple constraints of budget, time, and scope, but this is not enough. To deliver optimized project results that deliver long lasting benefits, project teams need to incorporate relevant value metrics into their project approach that are focused on business outcomes. Defining and using KPIs should become a standard skill for all project managers and business analysts.

A Critical Success Factor (CSF) is what is necessary for an organization or project to achieve its mission. A Key Performance Indicator (KPI) is a metric that is tied to a target to determine if we have met our CSF. KPIs are the effects of your actions. KPI should be explicitly tied to an objective If you can't describe the business goal it's monitoring, it's not a KPI; it's a metric. KPIs are metrics that are outcome oriented, target based, and graded.

The CMMI may provide guidelines to agile coach to define the KPIs for agile projects. CMMI has definite KPIs listed under each level, ranging from Level 1 to Level 5. Agile seems to be somewhere at level III.

Participatory decision models

Participative decision-making (PDM) is the extent to which employers allow or encourage employees to share or participate in organizational decision-making. A new kind of participative decision-making is communication through the computer, sometimes referred to as "decision-making through computer-mediated technology" such as chat room.

Key Point: Participatory decision making is a creative process to give ownership of decisions to the whole group, finding effective options that everyone can live with. A common form of participatory decision making is called consensus. This is a process that works to find *common ground and solutions that are acceptable to all* and best for the group.

How can the PDM be made more successful?

- Everyone must be committed to reaching a consensus view;

- The group must participate actively in the process and good facilitation must be used;
- Awareness of the common ground within the group is needed. This is useful for bringing the group back to if there are disagreements;
- Everyone must understand the process;
- It must be a substantial decision;
- Sufficient time must be allowed for the process.

SUMMARY

All these 11 knowledge and skills areas covered under level II are important, and carry equal weight in the exam. The student is advised to study these with same importance as previous ones.

Sample Practice Examination on Chapter XIII Level II Knowledge & Skills

Q1: To assess and incorporate stakeholder values, stakeholders are identified and their characteristics are collected as data. This helps a lot to do the stakeholder management and it also provides guidelines to manage stakeholder engagements. What is this called as where the stakeholder information is gathered?

    A. Stakeholder List
    B. Stakeholder Reference
    C. Stakeholder Register
    D. Stakeholder Dictionary

Q2: _____ is a group of people who share a concern, a set of problems, or a passion about a topic, and who deepen their knowledge and expertise in this area by interacting on an ongoing basis. This is a place where people collaborate. They learn from others. They share with them.

    A. Agile Blog
    B. Community of Practice
    C. Study Group
    D. Focus Group

Q3: The most effective communication to manage stakeholders is _____

    A. Face-to-face conversation
    B. Audio/Video conferencing
    C. Text and SMS messages
    D. Sending e-mails

Q4: As per PMI, the information distribution is *"Making needed information available to project stakeholders in a timely manner"*. The best tool Agile team use to keep their project status information up to date using large and visible _____ that everyone in the team has access to and can update themselves.

    A. Billboards
    B. Wikipedia
    C. Share point site
    D. Information Radiator

Q5: A **continuous improvement process** (**CIP** or **CI**) is an ongoing effort to improve products, services, or processes. This continuous process improvement responsibility traditionally used to be executed by 'management' but under agile, it's the responsibility of _____

    A. Product Owner
    B. Scrum Master
    C. Agile Team
    D. Agile Coach

Q6: One of the developmental mastery models uses a Shu Ha Ri model. It consists of three steps that a novice has to follow to acquire a skill or master a technique, except this one:

    A. The disciple learns the basics by following the rules laid down by the master
    B. Having mastered the fundamentals, the disciple applies the rules but begins questioning them, understanding their subtleties and seeking exceptions to rules
    C. The disciple who has mastered the rules can transcend and adapt them.
    D. The disciple only teaches the rules but never implements those.

Q7: Teams go through stages of development. Team formation usually follows easily recognizable stages, known as Tuckman's model. What is the correct sequence of the stages of Tuckman's development model?

    A. Forming, Storming, Norming, Performing, Mourning
    B. Norming, Forming, Storming, Performing, Mourning
    C. Performing, Norming, Storming, Forming, Mourning
    D. Storming, Norming, Forming, Performing, Mourning

Q8: The Dreyfus model of skill acquisition is a model of how students acquire skills through formal instruction and practicing. The original model proposes that a student passes through five distinct stages. Which sequence is right?

    A. competence, proficiency, novice, expertise, and mastery
    B. novice, competence, proficiency, expertise, and mastery
    C. novice, competence, expertise, proficiency, and mastery
    D. novice, competence, proficiency, mastery and expertise

Answers:

Q1: C. Stakeholder register is a project document including the identification, assessment, and classification of project stakeholders. This definition is provided in PMBOK Fifth Edition.

Q2: B. A community of practice (CoP) is a group of people who share a concern, a set of problems, or a passion about a topic, and who deepen their knowledge and expertise in this area by interacting on an ongoing basis.

Q3: A. The most effective communication to manage stakeholders is to have face-to-face conversation rather than communicating by sending paper documentation, sending e-mails, leaving voice messages, or using audio/video conferencing.

Q4: D. As per PMI, the information distribution is *"Making needed information available to project stakeholders in a timely manner"*. The best tool Agile team use to keep their project status information up to date using large and visible information radiator that everyone in the team has access to and can update themselves.

Q5: C. This continuous process improvement responsibility traditionally used to be executed by 'management' but under agile, it's the responsibility of entire agile team and members.

Q6: D. "Shu Ha Ri" consists of the FIRST three steps that a novice has to follow to acquire a skill or master a technique.

Q7: A. The correct sequence of the stages of Tuckman's development model is: Forming, Storming, Norming, Performing, Mourning.

Q8: B. The Dreyfus model of skill acquisition is a model of how students acquire skills through formal instruction and practicing. The original model proposes that a student passes through five distinct stages: novice, competence, proficiency, expertise, and mastery.

CHAPTER FOURTEEN

Level III Knowledge And Skills

The Agile practitioner examination includes 33 knowledge and skills areas. This chapter covers the last 11 knowledge and skills classified at Level 3. Be aware that ALL 33 knowledge and skills are included in PMI-ACP exam with equal importance. The 33 K&S are distributed over 3 chapters for simplicity.

The questions are based upon agile knowledge and skills, so this chapter will help you to prepare those questions:

> ➢ **Physical and virtual co-location**
> ➢ **PMI's Code of Ethics and Professional Conduct**
> ➢ **Principles of systems thinking (complex, adaptive, chaos)**
> ➢ **Prioritization**
> ➢ **Problem-solving strategies, tools and techniques**
> ➢ **Process analysis**
> ➢ **Regulatory compliance**
> ➢ **Self-assessment tools and techniques**
> ➢ **Stakeholder management**
> ➢ **Training, coaching, and mentoring**
> ➢ **Value-based analysis and decomposition**

There are 11 knowledge and skills listed under this level III. Realistically speaking, expect at the least 1 or 2 questions about each item from the above list. There will be 60 questions based on total of 33 K&S.

Physical and Virtual Co-location

Agile flourishes when agile team members work closely together in an environment that supports the process. Agile teams can be co-located or distributed teams. If at all possible, the team needs to be collocated – that is, physically located together. Co-location means putting teams together, preferably in same building; in fact on same floor with close proximity so they can see each other and literally they can walk to talk to anyone in the team. Normally the classification of work at the level of a software team falls into three broad categories:

Co-located: This is the most traditional way of working, where a group of people will be working together in an office. Co-located teams have an advantage in productivity, because communication is simple. Managers also feel that the co-located teams are easier to manage.

Outsourced: An outsourcing arrangement involves two or more separate teams, with responsibilities divided explicitly between the teams. For example, the "in" team might be located in Boston and do specification, and the "out" team might be located in India and do implementation and testing.

Global team: A global team is distributed geographically, but it does not have a fixed division of responsibilities between locations. Work goes to the team member who is best able to do it.

The following practices are encouraged when the agile teams are co-located:

- ✓ Communicating face-to-face
- ✓ Physically standing up in daily stand-up meetings rather than relaxing by sitting
- ✓ Using simple and low-tech tools for communications
- ✓ Getting clarification from other team members in real time (almost immediately)
- ✓ Being aware of what is going on in the team and what others are working on
- ✓ Seeking help from others with a task
- ✓ Supporting and mentoring others when needed

With collocation, the team gets the benefit of better and direct communication. This is much more effective than an e-mail.

For distributed or global or outsourced teams, the same face-to-face communication can be achieved using advanced but free internet tools like video conferencing, webcams, web-based desktop sharing, collaboration websites, chat, on-line meetings and instant messaging.

PMI's Code of Ethics and Professional Conduct

PMI's Code of Ethics and Professional Conduct means the "social responsibility of a project manager". The values that the global project management community chose as most important were: **responsibility, respect, fairness, and honesty**. This code of ethics affirms these four values as its foundation. Details about code of ethics and professional conduct are available and can be downloaded from PMI official website at http://www/pmi.org/

For more details, please read Appendix A, PMI's Code of ethics and professional behavior at the end of this book.

Principles of systems thinking

Basic Principles of Systems Thinking are:

- Systems' thinking is a tool for diagnosing organizational issues, understanding organizational dynamics, and creating change. It can help managers to be proactive instead of reactive and to shape the future of the organization.
- Systems thinking looks at organizations as organic entities.
- System thinking provides another lens for understanding people's behavior within organizations. It is a very different focus from that of leadership development, where the characteristic of one individual is seen to determine the fate of the entire organization or department.
- Principles of systems thinking help understand how organizations are impacted by internal and external factors that directly influence how they function.
- Principles of systems thinking use concepts from the field of system dynamics.
- Principles of systems thinking help understand that large systems in particular need systemic interventions, not just command and control leaders.

Prioritization

Agile Principle #2: Welcome changing requirements, even late in development. Agile processes harness change for the customer's competitive advantage.

Although the customer is always free to make changes, the agile team can't lose focus on getting product into production. Typically the customer changes are honored towards the end of iteration, and the iteration schedule / priorities are not changed /disturbed during the execution of that iteration. Prioritizing the backlog always ensures delivering the most important features next. Meeting the actual needs of stakeholders is more important than building the system to specification.

The process of prioritization can happen at two levels:

- Prioritization by Customer (involves product backlog)
- Prioritization by Product Owner (involves iteration backlog)

How does agile process harness changes at Customer level?

- Change is welcomed as an expected consequence of emergent requirements and product evolution. New requirements or changes can be added at any time to the project.
- Changes are added to the product backlog, resulting in a changed feature set and prioritization.
- Customer adjusts priorities as required by business needs, changes in the market, new regulations, and better understanding product.
- Customer prioritization of product backlog may be based on various factors or combination thereof:
  o Risk-based prioritization
  o ROI-based prioritization
  o Value-based prioritization
  o Cycle Time / Time-to-market

How does agile process harness changes at Development level?

- Agile teams practice continuous planning, always responding to an evolution of customer requirements. The prioritized list of Product backlog is further split into Release level backlog.
- The Release level backlog is further split into Iteration level backlog.
- The Product Owner with help from agile development team then prioritizes this list based on various factors such as:
  o Team Velocity
  o Complexity of user story to turn into deliverable increment
  o Spike – Architectural and Design
  o Epic Stories
  o Risk based

Problem solving strategies

One of the most effective problem-solving strategies is:

➢ Allow teams to solve the problem: The best people to solve the technical problem are not necessarily the project stakeholders and development managers. Rather, the team themselves can solve problems by iterating solutions together. Getting right brains in the war room together can solve any problem. Just trying to solve the problem or managing solution is not right approach; the best problem-solving strategy is to use the power of self-managed teams.

Various techniques for problem-solving can be used such as Brainstorming Sessions, Monte Carlo Simulation (what-if analysis), face-to-face communication, expert judgment, workshops, and root cause analysis.

Process analysis

Process analysis is a fundamental business tool and an essential component of lean operations and six sigma projects. Every business operation converts inputs into outputs. The inputs may be raw materials, data, labor time or financial capital, and the outputs may be a physical or intangible product or service.

Process analysis techniques are essential components of lean operations and six sigma. Process analysis is the science of analyzing a business process to ensure that it performs optimally with minimal bottlenecks and maximum productivity.

- The first step is process mapping, which is the creation of a powerful visual representation of the process. e.g. "swim lane" approach.
- Then the process can be analyzed methodically to identify the bottleneck, or the primary constraint that slows the entire process performance and limits the speed at which the total flow can operate.
- As per "Theory of Constraints", the primary focus must be on identifying the bottleneck.

Regulatory Compliance

Compliance means conforming to a rule, such as a specification, policy, standard or law. Other compliance frameworks (such as COBIT) or standards (such as NIST) inform on how to comply with the regulations. It is possible that agile may not be fully compliant with these regulatory standards.

To achieve the regulatory compliance, it is necessary to prove that there is an established documented process and that it is followed by the team/organization appropriately all the time.

How can agile project provide necessary regulatory compliance?

- It may be necessary to produce extra artifacts or more detailed artifacts than normally would.
- It may need to add extra features to agile solutions such as tracking financial information that wouldn't have normally been implemented.
- It may become necessary to produce specific reports to be submitted to the regulatory body.

- It may even need to submit agile team to audits, sometimes scheduled and sometimes not, to ensure regulatory compliance.
- It may be possible to scale the agile strategy to address regulatory compliance.
- It may be wise to get help from regulatory compliance experts.
- It may need to read the regulations and develop a strategy to conform to them in most agile manner possible whether those regulations are imposed or willingly adopted.

Self-assessment tools and techniques

Self-assessment is the process of "knowing yourself." It involves taking an inventory of your likes, dislikes, personal characteristics, values, wants, and needs. It is the first part of the career management process. Before you can decide what you want to be, you first have to discover who you are.

All agile managers must do self assessment on regular basis. They must ask the team members to evaluate manager. People are constantly changing, growing, and developing. Therefore, it is necessary for everyone to re-assess themselves periodically in relation to their career goals. There are many tools that are used for self assessment, such as the Myers and Briggs. Other tools are also available at schools, workforce developments, leadership workshops etc.

Why self-assessment is necessary?

- **Self-assessment** is the process of looking at oneself in order to assess aspects that are important to one's identity.
- It is one of the motives that drive self-evaluation, along with self-verification and self-enhancement.
- **Self assessment** lets you learn about your skills, interests, personality and values.

Stakeholder management

Stakeholder: Anyone who is a direct/indirect user, manager of users, senior manager, operations staff members, owner to funds the project, help desk/support staff member, auditors, program/portfolio manager. Stakeholders are the people involved in or affected by project activities and include the project sponsor, project team, support staff, customers, users, suppliers and even opponents of the project. Internal stakeholders can include business systems owners, executive management, program management, marketing, and sales. External stakeholders can include customers, users, partners, regulatory bodies, and others.

Stakeholder management is part of the communications management. It is very important to know what information is needed by individual stakeholder and how best the information can be conveyed to the stakeholders.

Agile principles focus on verbal/oral communication rather than written communication. Also the information gets posted on regular basis on Share point (or similar effective web media) so it is available to all stakeholders any time and all the time, they need to pull the information. Most of the information distribution is through automated notifications and in electronic/soft format.

Training, coaching and mentoring

Coaching, with a professional coach, is the practice of supporting an individual, through the process of achieving a specific personal or professional result e.g. life coaching, business coaching, sports coaching, personal coaching, career coaching, financial coaching, health coaching etc.

Mentoring: Mentoring is a learning relationship between two employees. **Mentors** are experienced employees who share their knowledge, experience and ideas with less experienced employees, or associates. **Associates** are people who have shown what they can do. Associates really want to acquire new knowledge and skills. Mentoring is not specific to a position. A mentor is not the employee's manager. Mentoring occurs outside any formal employer employee relationship. Mentoring looks to the future. Its aim is career development. Its aim is to give associates the general management and/or leadership skills that will prepare them to meet the demands, roles and responsibilities that lie ahead. Mentoring is based on mutual commitment, respect and trust. Mentoring gives mentors the chance to share their experience and expertise in a rewarding relationship. Mentors are also exposed to new ways of thinking and doing things.

Coaching: Coaching is not mentoring. In mentoring, employees are guided by the advice and experience of senior counterparts who "take them under their wing". Coaching specifically aims to develop new qualifications and skills in an employee. It aims to improve that person's learning and job performance, so that he/she can then reach organizational goals. The coach does not convey his or her personal vision to the employee. Coaching focuses solely on the employee's predefined needs as these relate directly to his/her job; however, this relationship does not necessarily mean that the person reports to the coach. Coaching aims to develop abilities to meet targeted goals in a given work situation.

Benefits and strengths of Coaching:

- Makes the employee feel more confident.
- Gives the employee real support and follow-up.
- Gives the employee the chance to learn from the coach's experience.
- Improves the employee's chances of success.

People like working on agile projects because agile team dynamics enable people to do great work in the best way they know. People on agile teams have opportunities to learn, to teach, to lead, to coach, to mentor and to be really part of a cohesive, self-managing team.

Coaching and mentoring within team means:

- Inspire employees,
- Empower employees,
- Build commitment,
- Increase productivity,
- Grow talent, and
- Promote success.

Both coaching and mentoring are an approach to management and a set of skills to nurture staff and deliver results. They are, fundamentally, learning and development activities that share similar roots. A good coach will also mentor and a good mentor will coach too, as appropriate to the situation and the relationship.

What are the differences between Mentoring and Coaching?

- **Focus**: Mentor focuses on individual whereas coach focuses on performance.
- **Role**: Mentor is a facilitator with no agenda whereas coach has a specific agenda.
- **Relationship**: Mentor has self-selecting relationship whereas coach relationship comes with job.
- **Source of influence**: Mentor has a perceived value whereas coach influences through position.
- **Personal returns**: Mentor enforces affirmation and learning whereas coach fosters teamwork and performance.
- **Arena**: Mentor mentors throughout life whereas coach is only task related.

Value-based analysis and decomposition

Agile methods strive for clarity at the level of operations. Value based management strives for clarity at the level of the business. SWOT Analysis is performed to identify strengths, weaknesses, opportunities and threats. This follows the risk management knowledge area in traditional plan-driven project management.

A good approach is to start with a vision statement, and then use functional decomposition to come up with the features that will be needed to achieve that overall vision. Functional decomposition becomes important on large projects, where it provides a hierarchical approach for organizing requirements based on possibly hundreds of user stories. Thus the functional decomposition provides an approach that aligns with an overall value statement.

Agile teams continually identify and articulate changes in the underlying assumptions and requirements regarding the overall project/product delivery. The constant analysis can be seen as the movement to adopt stakeholder value-based measures of project performance.

Teams can become more successful when they meet their objectives. Allowing teams to plan their selected features in detail, a granular level of decomposition means that tasks get better estimated, which reduces the possibility of team's over- or under-commitment.

The customer is always in the driver's seat, determining the value being created in the product as it emerges. The customer is free to request additional features, prioritize those under product backlog and decide the expected delivery, based on time-to-market conditions.

- The team works with the customer to prioritize the work.
- The team then delivers incrementally in order of priority.
- As the features are demonstrated and as the product emerges, the customer can regularly review and frequently validate the business impact of each feature.
- When sufficient value is reached in the features delivered in multiple iterations, the customer can request a product release.

SUMMARY

All these 11 knowledge and skills areas covered under level III are important, and they carry equal weight in the exam. The student is advised to study these just like the others.

Sample Practice Examination on Chapter XIV Level III Knowledge & Skills

Q1: If at all possible, the team needs to be located together. It means putting teams together, preferably in same building; in fact on same floor with close proximity so they can see each other and literally they can walk to talk to anyone in the team. What is this known as?

    A. Team Dynamics
    B. Team Binding
    C. Collaboration
    D. Collocation

Q2: The following practices are encouraged when the agile teams are co-located, except:

    A. Communicating face-to-face
    B. Supporting and mentoring others when needed
    C. Taking your own time to distribute information due to close proximity
    D. Participating in daily stand-up meetings by standing up

Q3: One of the most effective problem-solving strategies is:

    A. You solve every problem and tell the solutions to others
    B. Allow teams to solve the problem
    C. Let stakeholders and development managers solve the technical problems
    D. Leave the problem as is and it will get solved anyway eventually over project duration

Q4: Various techniques for problem-solving can be used such as described below, except:

    A. Brainstorming Sessions
    B. Monte Carlo Simulation (what-if analysis)
    C. Ad-hoc quick decisions
    D. expert judgment

Q5: PMI's Code of Ethics and Professional Conduct means the "social responsibility of a project manager". The values that the global project management community chose as most important were, except:

A. responsibility,
B. respect,
C. equality,
D. honesty

Q6: _____ thinking helps understand that large systems in particular need systemic interventions, not just command and control leaders.

A. Principles of systems
B. Lateral
C. Management by Objective
D. Dynamic Leadership

Q7: One of the agile principles says that, welcome changing requirements, even late in development. Agile processes harness change for the customer's competitive advantage. Although the customer is always free to make changes, the agile team can't lose focus on getting product into production. Typically the customer changes are honored _____ of that iteration.

A. Anytime during execution
B. Towards the end
C. By changing the schedule
D. By adjusting the priorities

Q8: Customer prioritization of product backlog may be based on various factors or combination thereof, except the following:

A. Risk-based prioritization
B. ROI-based prioritization
C. Value-based prioritization
D. Stakeholder-based prioritization

Q9: Process analysis techniques are essential components of lean operations and Six Sigma. Process analysis is the science of analyzing a business process to ensure that it performs optimally with minimal bottlenecks and maximum productivity. As per "Theory of Constraints", the primary focus must be on identifying the _____.

A. Performance
B. Waste

C. Bottlenecks

D. Limitations

Q10: **Compliance** means conforming to a rule, such as a specification, policy, standard or law. To achieve the _____ compliance, it is necessary to prove that there is an established documented process and that it is followed by the team/organization appropriately all the time.

A. Regulatory

B. Business

C. Legal

D. Provisional

Q11: Self-assessment is the process of "knowing yourself." All agile managers must do self-assessment on regular basis. They must ask/use the _____ to evaluate manager.

A. Vendors

B. Stakeholders

C. Self-assessment tools

D. Team members

Q12: Agile principles state that face-to-face meeting is the best for communications. Stakeholder management is part of the communications management. Agile principles focus on _____ communication rather than _____ communication.

A. Written, verbal

B. Verbal, written

C. Formal, informal

D. Advanced, simple

Q13: The practice of supporting an individual, through the process of achieving a specific personal or professional result can be commonly known as, except:

A. Training

B. Commanding

C. Coaching

D. Mentoring

Q14: Coaching and mentoring within team means the following, except:

A. Inspire employees

B. Build commitment

C. Increase dependency

D. Promote success

Answers:

Q1: D. If at all possible, the team needs to be collocated – that is, physically located together. Co-location means putting teams together, preferably in same building; in fact on same floor with close proximity so they can see each other and literally they can walk to talk to anyone in the team.

Q2: C. The following practices are encouraged when the agile teams are co-located:

- ✓ Communicating face-to-face
- ✓ Physically standing up in daily stand-up meetings rather than relaxing by sitting
- ✓ Using simple and low-tech tools for communications
- ✓ Getting clarification from other team members in real time (almost immediately)
- ✓ Being aware of what is going on in the team and what others are working on
- ✓ Seeking help from others with a task
- ✓ Supporting and mentoring others when needed

Q3: B. One of the most effective problem-solving strategies is: Allow teams to solve the problem. The team themselves can solve problems by iterating solutions together. Getting right brains in the war room together can solve any problem. The best problem-solving strategy is to use the power of self-managed teams.

Q4: C. Various techniques for problem-solving can be used such as Brainstorming Sessions, Monte Carlo Simulation (what-if analysis), face-to-face communication, expert judgment, workshops, and root cause analysis.

Q5: C. PMI's Code of Ethics and Professional Conduct means the "social responsibility of a project manager". The values that the global project management community chose as most important were: **responsibility, respect, fairness, and honesty.**

Q6: A. Principles of systems thinking help understand that large systems in particular need systemic interventions, not just command and control leaders.

Q7: B. Although the customer is always free to make changes, the agile team can't lose focus on getting product into production. Typically the customer changes are honored towards the end of iteration, and the iteration schedule / priorities are not changed /disturbed during the execution of that iteration.

Q8: D. Customer prioritization of product backlog may be based on various factors or combination thereof:

- o Risk-based prioritization
- o ROI-based prioritization
- o Value-based prioritization
- o Cycle Time / Time-to-market

Q9: C. Process analysis is a fundamental business tool and an essential component of lean operations and six sigma projects. The process can be analyzed methodically to identify the bottleneck, or the primary constraint that slows the entire process performance and limits the speed at which the total flow can operate. As per "Theory of Constraints", the primary focus must be on identifying the bottleneck.

Q10: A. **Compliance** means conforming to a rule, such as a specification, policy, standard or law. To achieve the regulatory compliance, it is necessary to prove that there is an established documented process and that it is followed by the team/organization appropriately all the time.

Q11: D. Self-assessment is the process of "knowing yourself." All agile managers must do self-assessment on regular basis. They must ask the team members to evaluate manager.

Q12: B. Agile principles state that face-to-face meeting is the best for communications. Stakeholder management is part of the communications management. Agile principles focus on verbal/oral communication rather than written communication.

Q13: B. The practice of supporting an individual, through the process of achieving a specific personal or professional result can be commonly known as training, instructing, coaching, mentoring, or guiding.

Q14: C. *Coaching and mentoring within team means:*

- ▪ Inspire employees,
- ▪ Empower employees,
- ▪ Build commitment,
- ▪ Increase productivity,
- ▪ Grow talent, and
- ▪ Promote success.

PART IV

Overview: PMI-ACP Domains and Tasks

Chapter 15 Domains and Tasks

CHAPTER FIFTEEN

Domains And Tasks

Agile project practitioners engage in a number of tasks in the course of working on projects in an agile environment. These tasks have been delineated and organized into six major domains of practice:

Domain I: Agile Principles and Mindset
Domain II: Value-Driven Delivery
Domain III: Stakeholder Engagement
Domain IV: Team Performance
Domain V: Adaptive Planning
Domain VI: Problem Detection and Resolution
Domain VII: Continuous Improvement (Product, Process, People)

While these domains and tasks are not used in the construction of the certification examination, they are important. These domains and tasks may form the basis of educational and training programs and materials. These may also provide guidance for professional development initiatives. Recognition of the tasks may help shape the ways in which Agile project management is understood across industries as organizations continue to adopt Agile frameworks in project management.

Reading these domains and tasks will help you to answer many questions in the PMI-ACP certification examination. It is strongly recommended that you read this chapter at least once before the examination. For details on every task under each domain, please visit the PMI website and read the PMI Agile Certification Examination Content Outline provided by PMI at their website: http://www.pmi.org/

Domain I: Agile Principles and Mindset

Under this domain, there are nine tasks:

- ❖ Advocate for agile principles across the team as well as between customers and the team
- ❖ Help ensure that everyone has a common understanding of values and principles of agile
- ❖ Support change at the system or organization level by educating the organization
- ❖ Practice visualization by maintaining highly visible information radiators
- ❖ Contribute to a safe and trustful team environment by allowing everyone to experiment
- ❖ Enhance creativity by experimenting with new techniques and process ideas
- ❖ Encourage team members to share knowledge by collaborating and working together
- ❖ Encourage emergent leadership within the team by establishing suitable environment
- ❖ Practice servant leadership by supporting and encouraging others

Domain II: Value-Driven Delivery

Under this domain, there are 4 categories.

- ❖ Define Positive Value
- ❖ Avoid Potential Downsides
- ❖ Prioritization
- ❖ Incremental Development

Under each category, there are multiple tasks, making total of 14 tasks under this domain.

Domain III: Stakeholder Engagement

Under this domain, there are 3 categories.

- ❖ Understand Stakeholder Needs
- ❖ Ensure Stakeholder Involvement
- ❖ Manage Stakeholder Expectations

Under each category, there are multiple tasks, making total of 9 tasks under this domain.

Domain IV: Team Performance

Under this domain, there are 3 categories.

- ❖ Team Formation
- ❖ Team Empowerment
- ❖ Team Collaboration and Commitment

Under each category, there are multiple tasks, making total of 9 tasks under this domain.

Domain V: Adaptive Planning

Under this domain, there are 4 categories.

- ❖ Levels of Planning
- ❖ Adaptation
- ❖ Agile sizing and estimation

Under each category, there are multiple tasks, making total of 10 tasks under this domain.

Domain VI: Problem Detection and Resolution

Under this domain, there are 5 Tasks.

- ❖ Create an open and safe environment by encouraging conversation and experimentation.
- ❖ Identify threats and issues by educating and engaging the team at various points in project.
- ❖ Ensure issues are resolved by appropriate team members and/or reset expectations.
- ❖ Maintain a visible, monitored, and prioritized list of threats and issues.
- ❖ Communicate status of threats and issues by maintaining threat list.

Domain VII: Continuous Improvement (Product, Process, People)

Under this domain, there are 6 Tasks.

- ❖ Tailor and adapt the project process by periodically reviewing and integrating team practices.

❖ Improve team processes by conducting frequent retrospectives and improvement experiments.
❖ Seek feedback on the product by incremental delivery and frequent demonstrations.
❖ Create an environment of continued learning by providing opportunities for people
❖ Challenge existing process elements by performing a value stream analysis and removing waste.
❖ Create systemic improvements by disseminating knowledge and practices across projects.

SUMMARY

The above mentioned seven domains and underlying tasks are not used in the construction of the certification exam. However the students are urged to read these because the questions in PMI-ACP exam will be based on these domains and tasks.

PART V

Overview: PMI-ACP Sample PMI-ACP Cert Exam

➢ Sample PMI-ACP Certification Exam

➢ Answers

Sample PMI-ACP Certification Examination

Q1: Agile information radiators mostly provide

    A. Radiation Information
    B. Environment Protection Agency Information
    C. Highly Visible Information
    D. Very Protective Information

Q2: Which is NOT one of the feedback techniques for products under Agile?

    A. Prototyping
    B. Surveys
    C. Demonstrations
    D. Evaluations

Q3: _____ delivery is a key component of most software projects today – it allows us to deliver the *most valuable* elements of a system first, which allows our customers to start getting benefit from the system earlier.

    A. Initial
    B. Iterative
    C. Incremental
    D. Internal

Q4: Many software companies give away 30-days free "evaluation" copy of their product. Under Agile this can be looked upon as one of the:

    A. Marketing Techniques
    B. Customer Testing tools
    C. Overstock Items
    D. Feedback Techniques

Q5: Kaizen method became famous by the book of Masaaki Imai "Kaizen: The Key to Japan's Competitive Success." Kaizen means

A. Continuous Progress
B. Continuous Integration
C. Continuous Improvement
D. Continuous Success

Q6: This can't be used as one of the tools & techniques for Value-based prioritization

A. Foreign Exchange Rate (FOREX)
B. Return on Investment (ROI)
C. Net Present Value (NPV)
D. Internal Rate of Return (IRR)

Q7: The defects in the agile software development cycle which are not caught in the earlier stages before deployments are known as:

A. Missed Defects
B. Escaped Defects
C. Requirements Defects
D. Design Defects

Q8: What is the purpose of a Daily Stand-up meeting?

A. To provide status report
B. To mark that employee is present for the day
C. To adapt work plans
D. To prioritize feature list

Q9: Which of the following Adaptability is not part of five key business objectives of Agile Project Management?

A. Market
B. Product
C. Process
D. People

Q10: In estimating the complexity and duration of iterations during agile project planning phase, iteration is assessed based on _____.

A. Function Points
B. Use Case Points

C. Story Points

D. User Stories

Q11: Which design concept helps agile developers in avoiding code duplication?

A. Refactoring

B. KISS

C. DRY

D. Technical Debt

Q12: The PMO is planning to adapt Agile. They used to get _____ at the project initiation phase of Waterfall model.

A. List of Product Backlog Document

B. Requirements Specifications Document

C. Technical Specifications Document

D. Systems Specification Document

Q13: Which of the following agile practices does NOT help in defect prevention and detection?

A. Test Driven Development

B. Acceptance Test Driven Development

C. Exploratory Testing

D. Performance Testing

Q14: Which term is used where Agile team only plans about this iteration and starts planning about next iterations only after reaching its predecessor iteration?

A. Iteration Planning

B. Progressive Elaboration

C. Synergy Planning

D. Precedence Planning

Q15: The variation between Ideal Time and Calendar Time is caused due to _____

A. Agile Estimates

B. Technical Debt

C. Work Interruptions

D. Daily Stand-up meeting

Q16: In Scrum, the sprint retrospective meeting facilitation is done by whom?

A. Product Owner

    B. Team Member

    C. Scrum Master

    D. Stakeholder

Q17: In XP, what is time-boxed for up to 4 weeks, and consists of full life cycle of analysis & design, code, verify & validate, and release of shippable product?

    A. Agile Project

    B. Agile Release

    C. Agile Iteration

    D. Agile Plan

Q18: Which meeting is used to demonstrate the functionality to stakeholders?

    A. Release Planning

    B. Iteration Planning

    C. Iteration Retrospective

    D. Iteration Review

Q19: The Product Backlog is originated in which Agile Practices?

    A. XP

    B. SCRUM

    C. FDD

    D. AUP

Q20: The User Story is originated in which Agile Practices?

    A. XP

    B. SCRUM

    C. FDD

    D. AUP

Q21: Value points represent the value of a story from the Customer's perspective. Which team performs Value Point Estimating?

    A. Customer

    B. Development

    C. Product

    D. SCRUM

Q22: What is NOT shown on the TASK/KANBAN Boards?

A. Work In Progress
B. Story Points Completed
C. Total Number of Iterations
D. Features

Q23: An avid agile practitioner should strive to

A. Deliver working products
B. Deliver defect free Software
C. Deliver Business Values
D. Deliver promised deliverables

Q24: What can be used to find issues in a process and determine how well a team is adhering to agile methods?

A. Process Improvement Plan (PIP)
B. Health Checks Questionnaires
C. Process Documentations
D. Combined Burn up and down charts

Q25: Scope Creep in Agile is best controlled by using:

A. Rolling Wave Planning
B. Iterations
C. Product Backlogs
D. All of above

Q26: Agile project managers may NOT run into lots of resistance from

A. Management
B. Business
C. Team Members
D. Customers

Q27: XP teams are advised to integrate the code once per _____ to resolve integration problems as soon as they occur.

A. Day
B. Week
C. Release
D. Build

Q28: Value Stream mapping is a recognized method used as part of which methodologies?

    A. Extreme Programming

    B. Six Sigma

    C. Rational Unified Process

    D. Agile Valuation

Q29: Velocity is the amount of work a team can complete in iteration. A typical example of team velocity can be:

    A. 20 use stories per iteration

    B. 20 story points per iteration

    C. 20 requirements per iteration

    D. 20 features per iteration

Q30: Cycle time, starts at fixed time with an idea and ends with a finished product to be delivered at predefined fixed time. What is NOT a suggested way to reduce cycle time?

    A. Removing waste

    B. Avoiding rework

    C. Decreasing duration

    D. Improving quality

Q31: AgileEVM is primarily used to measure _____ performance for agile projects.

    A. Team

    B. Process

    C. Cost

    D. Schedule

Q32: An escaped defect is a defect that was found by whom?

    A. Developer

    B. Tester

    C. Team Member

    D. Customer

Q33: Because risk and uncertainty influence product success, uncertain and risky items should be_____

    A. Same priority

    B. Low priority

    C. High priority

    D. No priority

Q34: The best approach to deal with risk-adjusted backlog under Agile is _____, the team and management would like to know earlier about the failures rather too late.

 A. Fail Safe
 B. Fail Fast
 C. Fail Early
 D. Fail Late

Q35: Agile teams avoid the biggest risk most traditional projects face—that of eventually

 A. delivering nothing
 B. delivering customer values
 C. delivering potentially shippable products
 D. delivering incrementally

Q36: Risk-based Spike is about exploring the _____ and probably throwing away everything that was researched and any prototypes developed.

 A. known known
 B. known unknown
 C. unknown known
 D. unknown unknown

Q37: A **spike** is a story that cannot be estimated until a development team runs _____ investigation.

 A. Only technical but for permanent use
 B. experimental but with fixed time allocated
 C. thorough but take your own time
 D. very extensive but time consuming

Q38: You won the lottery of 10 million. If you are following Net Present Value concept, what is your best bet, provided inflation is at 10%.

 A. Take 9 million right now.
 B. Take full 10 million after 1 year.
 C. Take 11 installments of 1 million paid every year.
 D. Donate ticket due to high inflation.

Q39: You are the agile project manager. Your company informed you that the regulatory compliance will happen in next 3-months. What should you do?

 A. Ask company to cancel the regulatory compliance
 B. Wait till the compliance people come, it may not happen at all.

    C. Coach the group over time so that when audit time comes you are prepared

    D. No need to do anything, since your company is very reputed to pass compliance by name.

Q40: Who is responsible for providing product backlog control across multiple projects?

    A. Customer

    B. Stakeholder

    C. Finance Controller

    D. PMO

Q41: Who should facilitate the iteration retrospective meeting and keep notes from the retrospective?

    A. Technical Writer

    B. Agile Project Manager

    C. Agile Team Member

    D. Product Owner

Q42: There were 4 features targeted for completion during Iteration #2. Unfortunately the third feature was not accomplished. After discussions with product owner, it was decided to defer this feature. What should be done?

    A. Add the deferred feature into next iteration backlog.

    B. Drop the feature #3 altogether since it wasn't completed.

    C. Put back the deferred feature on the product backlog.

    D. Do nothing.

Q43: Agile and waterfall principles and practices are

    A. Complimentary to each other

    B. Contradictory to each other

    C. Mutually Exclusive

    D. Not mutually exclusive

Q44: Agile development is a philosophy - canonical description of this way of thinking is called as what?

    A. Agile Process

    B. Agile Method

    C. Agile Manifesto

    D. Agile Practices

Q45: At what phase typically waterfall projects find whether or not they built a product the customer needs and wants?

    A. Architecture and Design
    B. Coding
    C. Testing
    D. Deployment

Q46: You are part of an agile team, and looking over your burn-down chart for last 3 iterations, you realized that you aren't going as fast as you'd hoped. What is the best option for you?

    A. Adding resources
    B. Pushing out the date
    C. Catch up the pace in next iteration
    D. Give your customer some options

Q47: Agile teams keep information radiators mostly

    A. In hidden places like closets.
    B. On Kanban / task walls visible to all.
    C. On individual working desks.
    D. On their own computers under personal folder.

Q48: A listener learns many things just due to presence, not necessarily participating. What kind of communication is this under agile?

    A. Active Communication
    B. Passive Communication
    C. Osmotic Communication
    D. Cosmetic Communication

Q49: Which agile principle correlates closely with value stream mapping?

    A. Customer value
    B. Eliminate waste
    C. Agile valuation
    D. Valuable delivery

Q50: While drawing a value stream map, typically the stream that carries value is called as part of "process" and then the non-value stream is called as _____

    A. Non-process
    B. Operation

C. Waste

D. Overhead

Q51: The initial velocity was decided to be 20 story pts. per iteration. As agile team started delivering, it was observed that the velocity has dropped. What is the best course of action?

A. Change the plan usually by reducing scope.

B. Change the people usually by recruiting subject experts.

C. Don't change anything since velocity will get adjusted automatically.

D. Agile project manager starts controlling and commanding the team closely to boost velocity.

Q52: This is NOT the suggested way to reduce cycle time, which may be time-boxed.

A. Avoiding rework

B. upping quality

C. root-cause analysis

D. decreasing duration

Q53: Agile projects are estimated _____ with detail and accuracy appropriate to the time horizon.

A. Top-down

B. Bottom-up

C. Progressively

D. Iteratively

Q54: Using AgileEVM, the project progress is generally measured at the end of each _____?

A. Release Level

B. Iteration Level

C. Delivery level

D. Product level

Q55: The further back in the software development process that defects are uncovered,

A. the less expensive they are

B. the more expensive they are

C. the same expensive they are

D. the non-expensive they are

Q56: Agile development team was extremely busy in delivering working software towards an end of iteration. Luckily a test team subsequently found major defect before customer noticed it. What is this defect called as?

  A. Missed defect
  B. Escaped defect
  C. No more defect
  D. Process defect

Q57: Superior ROI is the first reason for using Agile Development. What is ROI under agile?

  A. Return on Improvements
  B. Return on Investments
  C. Return on Iterations
  D. Return on Increments

Q58: Agile often employ

  A. Data Driven Testing.
  B. Test Driven Development.
  C. Waterfall Model.
  D. Only Unit Testing.

Q59: Under frequent validation and verification, which type of testing carries topmost priority under agile?

  A. Exploratory Testing
  B. Unit Testing
  C. Continuous Integration Testing
  D. Systems Testing

Q60: Agile processes are close to which level under CMMI?

  A. Level 1
  B. Level 2
  C. Level 3
  D. Level 4

Q61: In agile methodology, testing team members must be involved in the project from which stage?

  A. Early Stages
  B. Later Stages

C. No Stages

D. All Stages

Q62: In Test Driven Development, what is the sequence of activities?

A. Design, Code, Test

B. Code, Test, Refactor

C. Test, Code, Refactor

D. Test, Refactor, Code

Q63: What is kept under version control for agile projects?

A. Source Code only.

B. Documents only.

C. Both of above.

D. None of above.

Q64: Who needs access to version control repository?

A. Developers Only

B. Testers Only

C. Stakeholders Only

D. All above.

Q65: Paying down the debt under agile, means

A. Clearing the code

B. Refactoring the code

C. Retesting the code

D. Passing the code

Q66: Who writes acceptance tests in Acceptance Test Driven Development?

A. Development Team

B. Test Team

C. User Acceptance Team

D. Customer

Q67: What is the primary measure of success under definition of done?

A. Tested Software

B. Delivered Software

C. Working Software

D. Completed Software

Q68: The software isn't done,

A. If it can't potentially be shipped
B. If it isn't tested
C. If it isn't not under version control
D. If it isn't released

Q69: Under automated build, the source code is made production-ready

A. At end of every day
B. At end of every iteration
C. Whenever there is a change
D. Only when customer needs it

Q 70: Continuous Integration is primarily done so that the production ready code is available

A. Whenever there is a demo
B. When there is an installation
C. When customer needs it
D. Almost all the time

Q71: Automated builds can also automate deploying the potentially shippable software into

A. Development environment
B. Testing environment
C. Production environment
D. All of above

Q72: You aren't respecting the automated software build in continuous integration, if you don't

A. Break the build
B. Check in regularly
C. Check in on top of broken build
D. Comment out failing unit tests

Q 73: Who creates and owns both the vision and product roadmap from the Scrum team?
A. Product Owner
B. Scrum Master
C. Scrum Team
D. Sponsor

Q74: What is used to categorize requirements, to prioritize them, and to determine a timetable (schedule) for their release?

    A. Vision Statement
    B. Product Roadmap
    C. Project Requirements Plan
    D. Requirements Traceability Matrix

Q75: The user story map provides a useful tool for the entire team to get a _____

    A. Bigger picture through a high level overview
    B. Bigger picture through a detail level overview
    C. Detail picture through a high level overview
    D. Detail picture through a detail level overview

Q76: As per PMBOK fifth edition, which statement is correct?

    A. Rolling wave planning is a form of progressive elaboration.
    B. Progressive Elaboration is a form of rolling wave planning.
    C. Rolling wave and progressive elaboration are not related.
    D. Rolling wave and progressive elaboration are not important in agile.

Q77: Rolling Wave Planning is a multi-step, intermittent process like waves. What is the correct statement that describes rolling wave planning process in general?

    A. Provides details for near term planning and milestones for far out planning.
    B. Provides milestones for near term planning and details for far out planning.
    C. Provides both details and milestones for near term planning.
    D. Provides both details and milestones for far out planning.

Q78: At the beginning of the project, there is lots of uncertainty and things are not very clear. Over the time, as project progresses, team's knowledge about project expands as greater amounts of information become available. What is the name of this iterative process of increasing the level of details in agile planning?

    A. Detail Planning
    B. Progressive Elaboration
    C. Rolling Wave Planning
    D. Decomposition

Q79: Designers use them to push the user interface (UI) process and developers use them to get more tangible grasp of the website's functionality. Business stakeholders use those to ensure that requirements and objectives are met through the design and track functioning completeness. What is it called as?

A. Frameworks
B. Wireframes
C. Architecture
D. Use Cases

Q80: The project charter is a formal document used to justify, explain, define, and ultimately authorize a project. Who should be authorizing and signing the project charter?

A. Project Manager
B. Product Owner
C. Project Sponsor
D. Scrum Master

Q81: This is a fictional character that is created to represent the attributes of a group of the product's users. These are helpful to use as a guide when deciding on a product's features, functionality, or visual design. The agile team can identify possible end users of the product. What is this knows as under agile modeling?

A. Actor
B. Persona
C. Representative
D. Customer

Q82: DSDM grew out of the need to provide an industry standard project delivery framework for what was referred to as Rapid Application Development (RAD) at the time. DSDM methodology has evolved and matured to provide a comprehensive foundation for planning, managing, executing, and scaling agile and iterative software development projects. What is DSDM?

A. Dynamic Software Development Method
B. Dynamic Systems Design Method
C. Dynamic Systems Development Method
D. Dynamic Solution Development Method

Q83: Both Wideband Delphi and Planning Poker methods are effective estimation techniques under agile environments since estimates are made by _____

A. Subject Matter Experts (SME) who knew everything.
B. Project Planners with wide experience
C. Project Managers with expertise
D. Team Members who are committed to work

Q84: Planning Poker game is one of the two Agile Estimation Techniques. It is based on _____, where you choose few numbers and not all.

   A. Random Numbers
   B. Fibonacci Sequence
   C. Sequence Numbers
   D. Natural Numbers

Q85: As an agile estimation expert, you have called a meeting where you are betting that the team will be able to come up with a better guess than any one, single expert / individual. You put the user story to the group and allow brief discussion. The estimation calls upon the collaborative consensus in deciding story size during this agile estimation process. What technique are you using?

   A. Servant Leadership
   B. Planning Poker
   C. Agile Estimation
   D. Brainstorming

Q86: The airport authority uses the big display boards at airports providing most up-to-date information about all flights arriving, departing, delayed, and or cancelled. In agile projects, this concept is mainly used to let the team members understand that it is their responsibility to derive latest information from _____ and there won't be any kind of notifications regarding this.

   A. Information Gathering
   B. Information Radiator
   C. Information Beaming
   D. Communication Channels

Q87: Newer team space design considers co-location of team members so that their working with each other supports active and open collaboration. Agile flourishes when agile team members work _____ in an environment that supports the process.

   A. Remotely
   B. Independently
   C. Closely together
   D. Osmotically

Q88: Osmotic communication relies on team members overhearing conversations. A listener learns many things just due to presence, not necessarily participating. Active listening plays key role in communications. However the Osmotic communication will be successful only if the participant:

   A. Keeps only listening without active participation
   B. Keeps interrupting with irrelevant questions

C. Contributes into conversation when a topic of interest is brought up

D. Takes notes of all conversations and no communication

Q89: The initiative for "information radiator" in communications to agile team is to implement the ____ technology rather than _____ technology to retrieve the information related to agile project.

A. Pull, Push

B. Push, Pull

C. Interactive, Push

D. Pull, Interactive

Q90: Real time communication occurs throughout the project via use of "highly visible information radiators". Information radiators can include Kanban boards, white boards, bulletin boards, burn-down charts that show the iteration's status, and any other sign with details about the project, the product, or team. This concept is derived from _____

A. Project Communication Management

B. Airport Information Distribution

C. Information Management System

D. Lean Manufacturing

Q91: The three main models of Emotional Intelligence (EI) are Ability EI, Mixed Models of EI and Trait EI. The Trait EI model refers to an individual's emotional abilities in

A. Self-perceived abilities

B. Actual abilities

C. Self-perceived and actual abilities

D. Self-perceived or actual abilities

Q92: You are in the process of obtaining FOUR staff members from other functional department. The functional manager is concerned about the effect this will have on her operational goal and suggests that THREE members be assigned to your project. What technique are you engaged in?

A. Negotiation

B. Pre-assignment of staff

C. Acquisition

D. Acquire team members

Q93: Your software project is using developers from all over the globe. You are having difficulty organizing regular team meetings due to different time zones. What would be the best way to improve communication between your virtual team?

A. Only meet local team members in your office and tell them to brief others

B. Insist they all make themselves available at 9:00am your time zone every Wednesday.

C. Run multiple meetings on same topic so everyone gets same message

D. Use real time and recorded web based video conferencing.

Q94: You have decided that all your agile team members must move into their own space in the main headquarters to improve efficiency and team building. What is this commonly called as?

A. Assignment

B. Co-location

C. Team Space

D. War room

Q95: As an agile coach, your greatest challenge has been managing your agile team. You decided to gain extra skills to help yourself in this task. All of the following areas you must focus on except?

A. Negotiation

B. Communication

C. Remuneration

D. Leadership

Q96: You are having difficulty in understanding what a key stakeholder is saying during a business meeting. What technique could help you to understand better?

A. Repeat the message back to the stakeholder

B. Ask them to write everything down

C. Ask to postpone the meeting until you feel better

D. Asking them to speak slower

Q97: Velocity is one of the agile metrics. An example of team velocity can be:

A. 10 story points per iteration

B. 10 defects fixed per iteration

C. 10 increments integrated per iteration

D. 10 hours every day per iteration

Q98: One of the most important measures about time management in agile projects is the use of velocity, a very powerful tool for _____ on project timelines. This is what is used for measuring team's productivity and for setting expectations about delivery dates in the future.

A. Past performance

B. Historical Information

C. Current Status

D. Forecasting

Q99: Velocity can naturally increase with each sprint, as the scrum team finds synergy of working together over time, many things become clearer by using progressive elaboration and risk factors get reduced over time. However the following way should be avoided if possible in increasing the velocity:

A. Remove project impediments and avoid project roadblocks
B. Eliminate external and internal distractions
C. Keep consistent sprint lengths and work hours.
D. Swap skilled team members between projects.

Q100: Cycle time in agile is the elapsed time, where the cycle starts with an idea and ends with a finished product. To improve the agile performance, it is encouraged to reduce the cycle time by reducing the waste. Quality management plays an important role in reducing cycle time. What is not suggested way to reduce cycle time from quality management?

A. Avoid rework
B. Improve on quality
C. Perform root-cause analysis
D. Perform less testing

Q101: Cycle time is another metric used in measuring agile performance. Cycle Time needs to be measured between two points in the value chain. An empirical formula can be used to calculate cycle time as Cycle time = WIP/Throughput. In an agile environment if number of user story points in progress at a time are 50 and the velocity is 10 user stories per iteration. What is the average cycle time for user stories in this iteration?

A. Unknown
B. 5
C. 50
D. 10

Q102: Sample Kanban boards show various columns from left to right and list of ordered activities under each status columns. Once a task is completed, it is moved to the next column progressing to the right till its status is _____.

A. Tested
B. Approved
C. Done
D. Completed

Q103: The agile team is only allowed to work on finite number of tasks at a time. The Task Boards motivate agile team members to sign up for tasks exceeding / aggregating under one area (a specific column on Kanban board). These task boards also help in implementing _____

A. Resource Allocation
B. Resource Leveling
C. Work-In-Progress Limits
D. Upper Control Limits

Q104: To reduce wasted discussions in meetings, the meetings must be _____, since the meeting must remain focused in order to end within stipulated time period.

A. Time Sensitive
B. Time Boxed
C. Time Bound
D. Time Limiting

Q105: Release Planning is basically developing the project schedule at the ____ Level, whereas Iteration Planning is developing the project schedule at the ____ Level.

A. Strategic, Strategic
B. Tactical, Tactical
C. Strategic, Tactical
D. Tactical, Strategic

Q106: You are the Scrum Master conducting the daily stand-up meeting. The 15-minutes are over and there are 2 topics that need more attention or discussions. As a good Scrum Master, following the Scrum practices, what will you do?

A. Request the topics to be discussed on next working day scrum meeting
B. Ask the agile team members to ignore those since time is up
C. Extend the daily stand-up meeting with team consensus
D. You take those 2 topics to be resolved at personal level

Q107: While this methodology (at Toyota) usually delivers small improvements, the culture of continual aligned small improvements and standardization yields large results in terms of overall improvement in productivity. This philosophy differs from the "command and control" improvement program. The methodology that includes making changes and monitoring results, and then adjusting is popularly known as:

A. Process Improvement Plan
B. Quality Assurance

C. Kaizen

D. Divide-and-conquer

Q108: This is one of the most important aspects in the 5 Why approach - the *real* root cause should point towards a process that is not working well or does not exist. A key phrase to keep in mind in any Five Why exercise is _____

A. People do fail, processes do fail

B. People do fail, processes don't fail

C. People don't fail, processes do fail

D. People don't fail, processes don't fail

Q109: The Ninth Agile principle outlined in the Agile manifesto states, "At regular intervals, the team reflects on how to become more effective, then tunes and adjusts its behavior accordingly." Which meeting fulfils this principle most closely?

A. Sprint Planning Meeting

B. Sprint Retrospective Meeting

C. Sprint Demonstration Meeting

D. Sprint Stand-up Meeting

Q110: Value stream mapping supports the following agile principle:

A. Our highest priority is continuous delivery of valuable software

B. Working software is the primary measure of progress.

C. Simplicity the art of maximizing the amount of work not done is essential.

D. Continuous attention to technical excellence and good design enhances agility.

Q111: The agile team member is helping the customer in understanding the characteristics of the product as well as how to use the features. The customer is getting more insight about the testing that needs to be done before they can sign-off on the approval of those features. The agile team is developing the software with same common understanding keeping the customers in perspective. What is this approach known as?

A. Rapid Application Development

B. Test Driven Development

C. Acceptance Test Driven Development

D. Feature Driven Development

Q112: The risk and stakeholder engagement is highest at the beginning of the project. Riskier features are created and tested in early sprints. If at all something is going to fail, it's better to handle it at the beginning rather than keeping it towards the end, when there will be less time.

The management may prefer to know the bad news earlier in the project than it's too late. What strategy supports this approach?

A. Rapid Development
B. Risk Management
C. Stakeholder Engagement
D. Fail Fast

Q113: TDD is a software development technique that literally means "development driven by test cases". TDD evolved from the _____ methodology and gives an emphasis on technical excellence and good design.

A. Scrum
B. Extreme Programming (XP)
C. Lean Manufacturing (Kanban)
D. Feature Driven Development (FDD)

Q114: Under Test Driven Development (TDD), the team has written failing unit tests, showing the intent of what the new code is supposed to do. The development team, due to multiple factors, is able to do just enough to get the test pass. The team knows that the code needs to be revisited and will clean up the code later by _____ to make it lean, mean and clear.

A. Reviewing
B. Retesting
C. Refactoring
D. Researching

Q115: As per agile team's "definition of done", it means when it is "done", it should be able to go into production without any changes and work properly! If the If the feature can't potentially be shipped, that means it's not _____

A. Completed
B. Ready
C. Perfect
D. Done

Q116: An agile team does both simultaneously, but it's important to understand the difference between continuous improvements that is _____ related and continuous integration that is mainly _____ related.

A. Product, process
B. Process, product

C. Process, code

D. Quality, Automation

Q117: Having the customer prioritize the master story list or product backlog from a business perspective ensures the biggest bang for their buck. Then ask the agile team to prioritize the list to identify items with most _____ risk.

A. Process

B. Methodology

C. Technical

D. Failing

Q118: As per Risk Management, failing _____ allows the Scrum team to change course while there is still the opportunity, for instance, to modify the architecture and technology selection, or to adjust the team composition.

A. Furious

B. Early

C. Later

D. First

Q119: In **agile software** development, a(n) _____ is a story that cannot be estimated until a development team runs a time-boxed investigation, which will usually take place in between sprints and are often intended to be thrown away.

A. Epic

B. Use Case

C. Spike

D. Backlog

Q120: Net present value (NPV) is used to calculate the total of all cash flows (in and out) that can be directly linked to the agile project. If it is _____, then it is good. Otherwise, the management will reconsider the investment.

A. Zero

B. Positive

C. Negative

D. One

Answers:

Q1: C (Agile information radiators mostly provide Highly Visible Information).

Q2: B (Prototyping, Simulation, Demonstrations, Evaluations are examples of few feedback techniques for product)

Q3: C (Incremental delivery is a key component of most software projects today – it allows us to deliver the *most valuable* elements of a system first, which allows our customers to start getting benefit from the system earlier.)

Q4: D (Many software companies give away 30-days free "evaluation" copy of their product. Under Agile this can be looked upon as one of the feedback techniques).

Q5: C (The translation of kai ("change") zen ("good") is "improvement"…continuous improvement).

Q6: A (The tools and techniques for value-based prioritization are including but not limited to ROI, NPV, IRR, customer-valued prioritization. Exchange Rate is not one of the T&Ts).

Q7: B (The defects in the Agile software development cycle which are not caught in the earlier stages before deployment are known as Escaped Defects).

Q8: C (Team members share information in the Stand-up meetings, evaluate the work done and adapt to plan based on progress made.)

Q9: A (The five key business objectives of Agile Project management are continuous innovation, product adaptability, improved time-to-market, people and process adaptability.)

Q10: C (The unit of measure for iterations is story points)

Q11: C (Don't Repeat Yourself design concept is used to prevent code duplication)

Q12: B (The PMO is planning to adapt Agile. They used to get Requirements Specification Document at the project initiation phase of Waterfall model.)

Q13: D (The first 3 provide a way for testers to improve quality).

Q14: B (Progressive Elaboration is where Agile team only plans about this iteration and starts planning about next iterations only after reaching its predecessor iteration)

Q15: C (The variation between Ideal Time and Calendar Time is caused due to work interruptions).

Q16: C (In Scrum, the sprint retrospective meeting facilitation is done by the SCRUM Master)

Q17: C (In XP, Agile Iteration is time-boxed for up to 4 weeks, and consists of full life cycle of analysis & design, code, verify & validate, and release of shippable product)

Q18: D (Iteration Review meeting is used to demonstrate the functionality to stakeholders)

Q19: B (The Product Backlog is originated in SCRUM Agile Practices)

Q20: A (The User Story is originated in XP Agile Practices)

Q21: C (Agile recommends that value point estimation is completed by Product team, headed by product manager).

Q22: C (Total number of iterations is not shown on the TASK/KANBAN Boards)

Q23: C (An avid Agile practitioner should strive to deliver business results that are valuable to customers)

Q24: B (Health check questionnaire can be used to find issues in a process and determine how well a team is adhering to Agile methods)

Q25: D (Scope and hence creep in Agile is best controlled by using iterations, progressive elaboration, and product backlogs)

Q26: D (Agile project managers will run into resistance from management, from the business, and from the team)

Q27: D (XP teams are advised to integrate the code once per day to resolve integration problems as soon as they occur)

Q28: B (Value Stream mapping is a recognized method used as part of Six Sigma methodologies)

Q29: B (Velocity is the amount of work a team can complete in an iteration, usually given in story points. A typical example of team velocity can be 20 story points per iteration)

Q30: C (Decreasing duration is NOT the suggested way to reduce cycle time. If the cycle time is time-boxed, it has pre-assigned fixed start and fixed finish)

Q31: D (AgileEVM is primarily used to measure cost performance for Agile projects.)

Q32: D (An escaped defect is a defect that was found by customers)

Q33: C (Because risk and uncertainty influence product success, uncertain and risky items should be high priority)

Q34: C (The best approach to deal with risk-adjusted backlog under Agile is "fail fast" – the team and management would like to know earlier about the failures rather too late)

Q35: A (Agile teams avoid the biggest risk most projects face—that of eventually delivering nothing)

Q36: B (Risk-based Spike is about exploring the known unknown and probably throwing away everything that was researched and any prototypes developed)

Q37: B (A **spike** is a story that cannot be estimated until a development team runs experimental but with fixed time allocated investigation)

Q38: A (You won the lottery of 10 million. If you are following Net Present Value concept, your best bet, provided inflation is at 10%, is to take 9 million right now. All other options are less than NPV of 9 million)

Q39: C (You are the Agile project manager. Your company informed you that the regulatory compliance will happen in next 3-months. What should you do? - Coach the group over time so that when audit time comes you are prepared)

Q40: D (The PMO is responsible for product backlog control by looking across multiple product backlogs to coordinate cross-program initiatives across multiple projects)

Q41: B (The Agile Product Manager should facilitate the iteration retrospective meeting and keep notes from the retrospective)

Q42: C (If it was decided to defer this iteration feature, then put it back on the product backlog)

Q43: D (Agile and waterfall principles and practices are not mutually exclusive. Some organizations apply elements of both principles and practices)

Q44: C (Agile development is a philosophy - canonical description of this way of thinking is called as Agile Manifesto)

Q45: C (At "test" phase typically waterfall projects find whether or not they built a product the customer needs and wants)

Q46: D (You are part of an agile team, and looking over your burn-down chart for last 3 iterations, you realized that you aren't going as fast as you'd hoped. The best option for you is to have the conversation and give your customer some options)

Q47: B (Agile teams keep information radiators mostly in visible place like Task / Kanban Boards, Conference Rooms, Walls, War rooms etc.)

Q48: C (In Osmotic Communication; listener learns many things just due to presence, not necessarily participating)

Q49: B (Agile principle of Simplicity – eliminate waste, correlates closely with value stream mapping)

Q50: B (While drawing a value stream map, typically the stream that carries value is called as part of "process" and then the non-value stream is called as "operation")

Q51: A (The initial velocity was decided to be 20 story pts. per iteration. As agile team started delivering, it was observed that the velocity has dropped. The best course of action - Change the plan usually by reducing scope)

Q52: D (Decreasing duration is NOT the suggested way to reduce cycle time. If the cycle time is time-boxed, it has pre-assigned fixed start and fixed finish)

Q53: A (Agile projects are estimated top-down with detail and accuracy appropriate to the time horizon)

Q54: B (Using AgileEVM, the project progress is generally measured at the end of each Iteration level)

Q55: A (The further back in the software development process that defects are uncovered, the less expensive they are)

Q56: B (Agile development team was extremely busy in delivering working software towards an end of iteration. Luckily a test team subsequently found major defect before customer noticed it. This defect called as escaped defect)

Q57: B (Superior ROI is the first reason for using Agile Development. ROI under agile is Return on Investments)

Q58: B (Agile often employ Test Driven Development)

Q59: B (Under frequent validation and verification, Unit testing carries topmost priority under agile)

Q60: B (Agile processes are close to CMMI Level 2)

Q61: A (In agile methodology, testing team members must be involved in the project from Early stages so that they can provide early feedback, the entire agile development team must be involved in ALL stages)

Q62: C (In Test Driven Development, the sequence is Write Failing Tests first, then add code to pass the test and ultimately refactor the code to reduce technical debt by cleaning the code)

Q63: C (Both the Source Code and Documents are kept under version control for agile projects)

Q64: D (Developers, Testers and stakeholders all needs access to version control repository – since the source code files, test scripts and artifacts are under version control)

Q65: B (Paying down the debt under agile, means refactoring the code)

Q66: D (The customer writes acceptance tests in Acceptance Test Driven Development, the Test Team or UAT team normally helps clients to come up with acceptance tests)

Q67: C (Working software the primary measure of success under definition of done)

Q68: A (The software isn't done If it can't potentially be shipped)

Q69: C (Under automated build, the source code is made production-ready whenever there is a code change)

Q70: D (Continuous Integration is primarily done so that the production ready code is available almost all the time)

Q71: D (Automated builds can also automate deploying the potentially shippable software into all 3 environments of Development, QA/Testing and pre-production/production environment)

Q72: B (Respecting the automated software build in continuous integration, you check in regularly)

Q73: A. The Product Owner creates and owns both the vision and product roadmap from the Scrum team.

Q74: B. A product roadmap is used to categorize requirements, to prioritize them, and to determine a timetable (schedule) for their release.

Q75: A. The user story map provides a useful tool for the entire team to get a bigger picture through a high level overview and to **understand the big picture** to see the entire breadth of the system and its diverse set of users and uses.

Q76: A. as per PMBOK fifth edition, rolling wave planning is a form of progressive elaboration.

Q77: A. Rolling Wave Planning is a multi-step, intermittent process like waves. Rolling wave planning process in general provides details for near term planning and milestones for far out planning.

Q78: B. At the beginning of the project, there is lots of uncertainty and things are not very clear. Over the time, as project progresses, team's knowledge about project expands as greater amounts of information become available. This iterative process of increasing the level of details in agile planning is known as Progressive Elaboration.

Q79: B. Designers use them to push the user interface (UI) process and developers use them to get more tangible grasp of the website's functionality. Business stakeholders use those to ensure that requirements and objectives are met through the design and track functioning completeness. This is known as wireframes.

Q80: B: The project charter is a formal document used to justify, explain, define, and ultimately authorize a project. Project Initiator or sponsor should be authorizing and signing the project charter. Project sponsor should be at the level that is appropriate to procure funding and commit resources to the project.

Q81: B. Persona is a fictional character that is created to represent the attributes of a group of the product's users. These are helpful to use as a guide when deciding on a product's features, functionality, or visual design. The agile team can identify possible end users of the product.

Q82: C DSDM stands for Dynamic Systems Development Method.

Q83: D. Both Wideband Delphi and Planning Poker methods are effective since the people who are estimating are the people who are committed to the work. The estimates are NOT made by the people who are typical project planners or project managers or schedulers as used to be under plan driven project management approaches.

Q84: B. Planning Poker game is one of the two Agile Estimation Techniques. It is based on Fibonacci sequence and also calls upon the collaborative consensus in deciding story size during the agile estimation process. When we play planning poker for agile estimation, we look to harness the wisdom of crowds with regard to our estimates.

Q85: B. Planning Poker game is one of the two Agile Estimation Techniques. It is based on Fibonacci sequence and also calls upon the collaborative consensus in deciding story size during the agile estimation process. When we play planning poker for agile estimation, we look to harness the wisdom of crowds with regard to our estimates.

Q86: B. In agile projects, this concept is mainly used to let the team members understand that it is their responsibility to derive latest information about the project from the "information radiator" and there won't be any kind of notifications regarding this.

Q87: C. Newer team space design considers co-location of team members so that their working with each other supports active and open collaboration. Agile flourishes when agile team members work *closely together* in an environment that supports the process.

Q88: C. Osmotic communication will be successful only if the participant contributes into conversation when a topic of interest is brought up.

Q89: A. The initiative behind information radiator is to implement the "pull" technology rather than "push" technology to retrieve the information. This reduces the burden on communication channels and also avoids potential miscommunication. No one can blame anyone that they didn't receive information on timely manner, since everyone is responsible to not only obtain the latest information but also update the information as and when it changes.

Q90: D. This concept is derived from lean manufacturing or Kanban.

Q91: A. Trait EI model describes *self-perceived abilities* whereas "Ability EI" model refers to *actual abilities*. E.g. claiming to have finished 20-miles Chicago Marathon can be *self-perceived abilities* whereas in reality, running in a local 5-mile community mini-marathon is *actual abilities*.

Q92: A. This is an example of negotiations.

Q93: D. Use of virtual teams is common and provides many benefits as well as communication challenges. Use of electronic video conferencing is a great way to overcome some of the communication problems.

Q94: B. Co-locating team members where possible improves team performance.

Q95: C. Team management involves combination of skills in areas of communication, conflict management, negotiation, and leadership.

Q96: A. Part of effective communication is to ensure that the message from sender is decoded properly. An effective way is to repeat the key points back to get clarity.

Q97: A. Velocity is one of the agile metrics. An example of team velocity can be 10 story points per iteration.Q98: D. One of the most important measures about time management in agile projects is the use of velocity, a very powerful tool for forecasting long-term project timelines.

This is what is used for measuring team's productivity and for setting expectations about delivery dates in the future.

Q99: D. Velocity can naturally increase with each sprint, as the scrum team finds synergy of working together over time, many things become clearer by using progressive elaboration and risk factors get reduced over time. If possible don't swap skilled team members between projects, let the same team continue to work on entire sprint/release/project due to synergy of working together.

Q100: D. Cycle time in agile is the elapsed time, where the cycle starts with an idea and ends with a finished product. To improve the agile performance, it is encouraged to reduce the cycle time by reducing the waste. Quality management plays an important role in reducing cycle time. "Perform less testing" is not suggested way to reduce cycle time from quality management.

Q101: B. Here Cycle time = WIP/Throughput. In an agile environment if number of user story points in progress at a time are 50, this leads to WIP = 50. The throughput is normally defined as velocity which is 10 user stories per iteration, so Throughput = 10. The Cycle Time (average) = 50/10 = 5.

Q102: C. Sample Kanban boards show various columns from left to right and list of ordered activities under each status columns. Once a task is completed, it is moved to the next column progressing to the right till its status is "Done" done.

Q103: C. The agile team is only allowed to work on finite number of tasks at a time. The Task Boards motivate agile team members to sign up for tasks exceeding / aggregating under one area (a specific column on Kanban board). These task boards also help in implementing WIP Limits.

Q104: B. To reduce wasted discussions in meetings, the meetings must be Time-boxed, since the meeting must remain focused in order to end within stipulated time period.Q105: C. Release planning is basically developing the project schedule at the Strategic Level, whereas Iteration Planning is developing the project schedule at the Tactical Level.

Q106: C. If there is any topic that needs more attention or discussions, the scrum master may extend the daily stand-up meeting with team consensus or may request for another separate meeting with few selected people who may be directly involved/impacted.

Q107: C. While kaizen (at Toyota) usually delivers small improvements, the culture of continual aligned small improvements and standardization yields large results in terms of overall improvement in productivity. This philosophy differs from the "command and control" improvement programs. Kaizen methodology includes making changes and monitoring results, then adjusting.

Q108: C. One of the most important aspects in the Five Why approach - the *real* root cause should point toward a process that is not working well or does not exist. A key phrase to keep in mind in any Five Why exercise is "people do not fail, processes do".

Q109: B. The Sprint Retrospective Meeting fulfils this ninth agile principle most closely.

Q110: C. Value stream mapping supports this agile principle: "Simplicity - the art of maximizing the amount of work not done - is essential".

Q111: C. When the agile team is developing the product based on the concept that it must pass the acceptance criteria of the customer, it is known as Acceptance Test Driven Development (ATDD).

Q112: D. If at all something is going to fail, it's better to handle it at the beginning rather than keeping it towards the end, when there will be less time. The management may prefer to know the bad news earlier in the project than it's too late. This is known as fail fast. The team still gets time to correct it over rest of the project duration.

Q113: B. TDD is a software development technique that literally means "development driven by test cases". TDD evolved from the Extreme Programming (XP) methodology and gives an emphasis on technical excellence and good design.

Q114: C. Under Test Driven Development (TDD), the team has written failing unit tests, showing the intent of what the new code is supposed to do. The development team, due to multiple factors, is able to do just enough to get the test pass. The team knows that the code needs to be revisited and will clean up the code later by refactoring to make it lean, mean and clear. Always improve by refactoring and do small chunks of refactoring frequently.

Q115: D. As per agile team's "definition of done", it means when it is "done"; it should be able to go into production without any changes and work properly! If the If the feature can't potentially be shipped, that means it's not done. Delivering a feature in agile is meant to be "doing everything necessary to produce shippable code".

Q116: C. Continuous improvement is process related and it attempts to build high quality at every stage and step of agile development by using frequent validation and verification as well as process tailoring. Continuous integration is related to software code and artifacts and documents, whereby the code is always kept in production-ready state by using automated build process.

Q117: C. Having the customer prioritize the master story list or product backlog from a business perspective ensures the biggest bang for their buck. Then ask the agile team to prioritize the list to identify items with most technical risk.

Q118: B. As per Risk Management, failing early allows the Scrum team to change course while there is still the opportunity, for instance, to modify the architecture and technology selection, or to adjust the team composition.

Q119: C. In **agile software** development, a Spike is a story that cannot be estimated until a development team runs a time-boxed investigation, which will usually take place in between sprints and are often intended to be thrown away.

Q120: B. Net present value is used to calculate the total of all cash flows (in and out) that can be directly linked to the agile project. If it is positive, then it is good. Otherwise, the management will reconsider the investment.

PART VI

Overview: PMI-ACP Appendices

Appendix A   PMI Code of Ethics

The PMI® Code of Ethics and Professional Conduct

Vision and Purpose

As <u>practitioners </u>of project management, we are committed to doing what is right and honorable. We set high standards for ourselves and we aspire to meet these standards in all aspects of our lives—at work, at home, and in service to our profession.

This Code of Ethics and Professional Conduct describes the expectations that we have of ourselves and our fellow practitioners in the global project management community. It articulates the ideals to which we aspire as well as the behaviors that are mandatory in our professional and volunteer roles.

The purpose of this Code is to instill confidence in the project management profession and to help an individual become a better practitioner. We do this by establishing a profession-wide understanding of appropriate behavior. We believe that the credibility and reputation of the project management profession is shaped by the collective conduct of individual practitioners.

We believe that we can advance our profession, both individually and collectively, by embracing this Code of Ethics and Professional Conduct. We also believe that this Code will assist us in making wise decisions, particularly when faced with difficult situations where we may be asked to compromise our integrity or our values.

Our hope that this Code of Ethics and Professional Conduct will serve as a catalyst for others to study, deliberate, and write about ethics and values. Further, we hope that this Code will ultimately be used to build upon and evolve our profession.

Values considered

- Responsibility, Respect, Fairness and Honesty

Professional and Social Responsibility

Here are the four values considered under this topic:

- **Responsibility**

Description of Responsibility: Responsibility is our duty to take ownership for the decisions we make or fail to make, the actions we take or fail to take, and the consequences that result.

Responsibility: Aspirational Standards

As practitioners in the global project management community:

- We make decisions and take actions based on the best interests of society, public safety, and the environment.
- We accept only those assignments that are consistent with our background, experience, skills, and qualifications.
- We fulfill the commitments that we undertake – we do what we say we will do.
- When we make errors or omissions, we take ownership and make corrections promptly. When we discover errors or omissions caused by others, we communicate them to the appropriate body as soon they are discovered. We accept accountability for any issues resulting from our errors or omissions and any resulting consequences.
- We protect proprietary or confidential information that has been entrusted to us.
- We uphold this Code and hold each other accountable to it.

Responsibility: Mandatory Standards

As practitioners in the global project management community, we require the following of ourselves and our fellow practitioners:

Regulations and Legal Requirements

- We inform ourselves and uphold the policies, rules, regulations and laws that govern our work, professional, and volunteer activities.
- We report unethical or illegal conduct to appropriate management and, if necessary, to those affected by the conduct.
- We bring violations of this Code to the attention of the appropriate body for resolution.
- We only file ethics complaints when they are substantiated by facts.
- We pursue disciplinary action against an individual who retaliates against a person raising ethics concerns.

- **Respect**

Description of Respect: Respect is our duty to show a high regard for ourselves, others, and the resources entrusted to us. Resources entrusted to us may include people, money, reputation, the safety of others, and natural or environmental resources. An environment of respect engenders trust, confidence, and performance excellence by fostering mutual cooperation — an environment where diverse perspectives and views are encouraged and valued.

Respect: Aspirational Standards

As <u>practitioners</u> in the global project management community:

- We inform ourselves about the norms and customs of others and avoid engaging in behaviors they might consider disrespectful.
- We listen to others' points of view, seeking to understand them.
- We approach directly those persons with whom we have a conflict or disagreement.
- We conduct ourselves in a professional manner, even when it is not reciprocated.

Respect: Mandatory Standards

As <u>practitioners</u> in the global project management community, we require the following of ourselves and our fellow practitioners:

- We negotiate in good faith.
- We do not exercise the power of our expertise or position to influence the decisions or actions of others in order to benefit personally at their expense.
- We do not act in an <u>abusive manner</u> toward others.
- We respect the property rights of others.

- **Fairness**

Description of Fairness: Fairness is our duty to make decisions and act impartially and objectively. Our conduct must be free from competing self-interest, prejudice, and favoritism.

Fairness: Aspirational Standards

As <u>practitioners</u> in the global project management community:

- We demonstrate transparency in our decision-making process.
- We constantly reexamine our impartiality and objectivity, taking corrective action as appropriate.
- We provide equal access to information to those who are authorized to have that information.
- We make opportunities equally available to qualified candidates.

Fairness: Mandatory Standards

As practitioners in the global project management community, we require the following of ourselves and our fellow practitioners:

<u>Conflict of Interest</u> Situations

- We proactively and fully disclose any real or potential conflicts of interest to the appropriate stakeholders.
- When we realize that we have a real or potential <u>conflict of interest</u>, we refrain from engaging in the decision-making process or otherwise attempting to influence outcomes, unless or until: we have made full disclosure to the affected stakeholders; we have an approved mitigation plan; and we have obtained the consent of the stakeholders to proceed.

Favoritism and Discrimination

- We do not hire or fire, reward or punish, or award or deny contracts based on personal considerations, including but not limited to, favoritism, nepotism, or bribery.
- We do not discriminate against others based on, but not limited to, gender, race, age, religion, disability, nationality, or sexual orientation.
- We apply the rules of the organization (employer, <u>Project Management Institute</u>, or other group) without favoritism or prejudice.

- **<u>Honesty</u>**

Description of Honesty: Honesty is our duty to understand the truth and act in a truthful manner both in our communications and in our conduct.

Honesty: Aspirational Standards

As <u>practitioners</u> in the global project management community:

- We earnestly seek to understand the truth.
- We are truthful in our communications and in our conduct.
- We provide accurate information in a timely manner.
- We make commitments and promises, implied or explicit, in good faith.
- We strive to create an environment in which others feel safe to tell the truth.

Honesty: Mandatory Standards

As practitioners in the global project management community, we require the following of ourselves and our fellow practitioners:

- We do not engage in or condone behavior that is designed to deceive others, including but not limited to, making misleading or false statements, stating half-truths, providing information out of context or withholding information that, if known, would render our statements as misleading or incomplete.
- We do not engage in dishonest behavior with the intention of personal gain or at the expense of another.

Upholding Responsibilities to the Profession

This includes the following items, but not just limited to the following:

- Take ownership for the decisions made
- Accept appropriate responsibilities
- Fulfill the commitments undertaken
- Maintain the confidentiality of the PMP˚ and other credential exams
- Report possible violations of the PMI˚ Code
- Cooperate concerning ethics violations
- Disclose conflicts of interest
- Behave in a truthful and ethical manner
- Comply with all applicable laws, regulations, and ethical standards
- Respect intellectual property
- Provide truthful advertising of your qualifications and services

Upholding Responsibilities to the Customer and the Public

This includes the following items:

- Provide truthful representations
- Uphold work related policies, rules, regulations, and laws
- Negotiate in good faith
- Respect the property rights of others
- Respect confidentiality
- Avoid conflict of interest
- Accept no inappropriate payments, gifts, or compensation

Adhering to Other Responsibilities

This includes but not limited to the following items:

- Maintain appropriate legal and ethical standards
- Share ideas and research findings to the body of knowledge
- Promote interaction within the project management community
- Demonstrate transparency
- Be truthful
- Do not engage in behavior that will deceive or mislead others

The PMI Code of Ethics is available for download in PDF format from the PMI's website. Please visit http://www.pmi.org/

Appendix B   PMP Certification Body of Knowledge

A Guide to the Project Management Body of Knowledge (PMBOK Guide) - Fifth Edition can be purchased from PMI or any other bookstore or from on-line bookseller sites.

PMI also has Community of Practice (CoP) for Agile Certification on their website.

Members of PMI are allowed to download an electronic copy of PMBOK Fifth Edition in PDF format, free of charge for their personal use and not for public distribution.

Glossary

ACP

An acronym used by Project Management Institute for their certification exam known as Agile Certified Practitioner.

Active Listening

This is a way of listening and responding to another person that improves mutual understanding.

Adaptation

Adaptation is the agile teams' ability to adjust quickly to minimize further deviations in products and processes. Any approach should be agile and adapt over time.

Adaptive Leadership

This is the style of leading by serving; allowing teams to self-manage and adapt their process empirically. This also assumes different leadership styles for different stages of team formation.

Affinity Estimating

In this estimation method, team arranges stories horizontally on a wall in order of size, without talking or discussing anything. Team consensus is achieved by moving around the stories till accepted.

Agile

Often used as the abbreviation for Agile Software Development or agile methods. Agile is a generic term which refers to a collection of light weight software development methodologies that value and support evolving requirements through iterative development.

Agile Accounting

This deals with various accounting methods used in the agile development, such as burn rate and agile earned value management.

Agile Adapting

The process of adapting to agile, related to releases and sprints. A suitable methodology will be chosen.

Agile Analysis and Design

This is the process of analyzing the backlogs or user stories, prioritization based upon various criteria, and coming up design for agile software development.

Agile Communications

The communications tools and techniques used by agile teams.

Agile Contracting

This deals with various methods used in the agreement on the ways of doing business with customers. Few methods are fixed price fixed scope, fixed price per story point.

Agile Estimation

This is the process of sizing user stories and the various techniques used in the process.

Agile Frameworks

Agile methodologies used in agile project management. Examples of agile frameworks are SCRUM, extreme programming, feature driven development, and DSDM etc.

Agile Manifesto

A statement of the principles and values that support the ideals of agile software development.

Agile Modeling (AM)

Agile modeling is a collection of values, principles, and practices for modeling software that can be applied on a software development project in an effective and light-weight manner.

Agile Monitoring

Agile monitoring and control process related to releases and sprints. It follows Dr. Deming's PDCA cycle.

Agile Planning

Agile planning process related to releases and sprints. It follows Dr. Deming's PDCA cycle.

Agile Practices

This deals with various methods such as SCRUM, extreme programming, test driven development.

Agile Tooling

Tools like wall space and whiteboards for co-located teams. Tools like Wikis and web conferencing for distributed teams. These tools are used for communications among agile team members.

Agile UP

A short form used for Agile Unified Process.

ATDD (Acceptance Test Driven Development)

This is a software development technique that generates the acceptance criteria first and then develops the code to pass those acceptance test cases. Acceptance TDD helps developers build high-quality software that fulfills the business's needs reliably.

Backlog

Backlogs are essentially requirements and are managed in SCRUM to get converted into features.

Brainstorming

This is a creative process to bring new ideas/perspectives using collective wisdom within the agile team.

Budget Estimation

The Budget Estimation under agile project means to determine primarily the cost of your scrum team, per sprint, and the cost of any additional resources needed to complete a task, requirement, release or even a whole project. Typically this can be done using velocity and Earned Value Management techniques under agile project.

Burn down chart

A burn down chart is a simple easy to understand graphical representation of "work remaining" versus "time remaining". The graph that shows how quickly the user stories are completed and when can the team expect to be done.

Burn up chart

This is a flipped burn-down chart.

Chartering

The project charter is a formal document used to justify, explain, define, and ultimately authorize a project. The key elements of project charter are vision, mission and success criteria.

Coaching

Couching is the practice of supporting an individual through the process of achieving a specific personal or professional result. Life coaching, sports coaching are few examples.

Code of Ethics

PMI's code of ethics and professional conduct means the social responsibility of a project manager. The most important values are responsibility, respect, fairness, and honesty.

Collaboration

The agile team must focus on customer collaboration over contract negotiations. Business people and developers must work together daily throughout the project.

Colocation

This is the situation where the agile development team works at one place where all members are physically reachable within walking distance.

Communications Management

Communications management is the process used to ensure timely and appropriate generation, collection, distribution, storage, retrieval, and ultimate disposition of project information.

Community Values

There are four community values under agile modeling namely communication, simplicity, feedback and courage.

Compliance

In general, compliance means conforming to a rule, such as a specification, policy, standard or law.

Continuous Improvement

A continual improvement process, also often called a continuous improvement process (abbreviated as **CIP** or **CI**), is an ongoing effort to improve products, services, or processes. These efforts can seek "incremental" improvement over time or "breakthrough" improvement all at once. Delivery (customer valued) processes are constantly evaluated and improved in the light of their efficiency, effectiveness and flexibility.

Continuous Integration

This is the act of continuously taking changes developers make to their software and integrating them all together continuously throughout the day, cycle, iteration, release etc.

Control Limits

These are the upper control limits and lower control limits, based on six sigma and normal theorem of distribution.

Cost Estimation

The Cost Estimation under agile project means to determine primarily the cost of your scrum team, per sprint, and the cost of any additional resources needed to complete a task, requirement, release or even a whole project. Typically this can be done using velocity and Earned Value Management techniques under agile project.

Crystal

Crystal is a lightweight agile software development framework.

Culture

This is the term to refer to the betterment or refinement of the individual, especially through education. It also reflects the distinct ways that people living in different parts of the world classified and represented their experiences, and acted creatively.

Cumulative Flow Diagram

This diagram is used to track performance and identify where bottlenecks or waste appears in the process.

Cycle Time

Cycle time is the time where the cycle that starts with an idea and ends with a finished product. Agile development is for reducing cycle time by avoiding rework, better quality and eliminating waste.

Conflict Resolution

It is a wide range of methods of addressing sources of conflict and of finding means of resolving a given conflict. There can include negotiation, mediation, compromise, and collaboration etc.

Decomposition

The concept of breaking down requirements into smaller more manageable pieces is called decomposition. The two major approaches used for decomposition are top down and bottom up.

Demonstrations

Demonstration is an activity of showing and walking through live sessions to explain to end users about how certain key characteristics or behaviors of a newly developed product or process are functioning and/or utilized in most optimal way. This is also used as one of the feedback techniques.

Daily Stand-ups

A helpful meeting conducted by the team and for the team on daily basis in agile communications. Team members discuss briefly on what was achieved, what will be achieved and any roadblocks within last/next 24 hours.

Definition of Done (DOD)

Done mean 100 percent complete. This includes analysis, design, coding, testing and anything else. When it is "done" it should be able to go into production without any changes and should work. Agile team may have different definitions of done for a feature or for a sprint or for a release.

Earned Value Management (EVM)

Agile EVM is the measure of progress at the release level. This covers both the cost and schedule performance. Normally the number of story points planned verses completed for a release and the earned value brought in a release from customer's perspective is measured under Agile EVM.

Evaluations

Evaluations is the process of handing over a finished product to the users with the intention that the end users will explore the product and provide constructive feedback, suggestions and points for improvements.

Escaped Defects

An escaped defect is a defect that was not found by, or one that escaped from, the agile team during development and testing cycle. Instead the defect was found by customers.

Empowered Teams

These are the teams with small number of people with complementary skills who are committed to a common purpose, performance goals and approach for which they hold themselves mutually accountable.

Emotional Intelligence

This is ability, skill or a self-perceived ability to identify, assess and control the emotions of self, of others, and of groups.

Epic Stories

Epic Stories are those stories whose scope is so large as to make them difficult to complete in a single iteration.

Facilitation

This is the process of helping participants to learn from an activity. There are many facilitation methods such as video conferencing, online collaboration, open space meetings, and world café etc.

Feedback

Feedback is the response from users and stakeholders that provides value, drawbacks, affirmation constructive criticism, and suggestions for improvements.

Failure Modes

There are various failure modes and alternatives, however the best approach is fail fast under agile so the failure can be corrected.

Globalization

This is the process of international integration arising from the interchange of world views, products, ideas, and other aspects of culture.

High Performance Teams (HPT)

These are the teams built with common purpose, clear roles, accepted leadership, effective processes, solid relationships, and excellent communications.

Impediments

An *impediment* is anything that slows or blocks progress. It also means something immaterial that interferes with or delays action or progress. It can be a factor causing trouble in achieving a positive result or tending to produce a negative result.

Information Radiator

Highly visible means used for real time communication throughout the project.

Iteration Planning

The meeting for the agile team members to commit to the completion of a set of highest ranked product backlog items.

Incremental Delivery

Incremental delivery is the process of delivering most valuable elements of a system first, which will allow the customers to start getting benefit from the system earlier. The purpose of incremental delivery is to get customer opinion and valuable feedback at various stages.

Ideal Time

An ideal day (time) is the perfect day with no interruptions and can work for eight hours straight.

Internal Rate of Return (IRR)

This is a handy tool for evaluating and comparing projects, especially when there are no common factors to compare. It can also be viewed as discounted cash flow rate of return.

Innovation Games

Innovation games are powerful qualitative research and problem solving techniques focused on the use of collaborative play with customers, colleagues, partners and the community at large.

Kanban Boards

The white board used to display showing status of activities in highly visible way.

Knowledge Sharing

This is the process of disseminating the things learned and skills acquired by individuals for the benefit of team using various means such as audio, video, electronic, osmotic and other methods.

Leadership

Agile project management follows the servant leadership rather than command-and-control style of leadership.

Levels of Planning

Agile planning activities for large-scale development efforts normally rely on five levels of planning: Product Vision, Product Roadmap, Release Planning, Iteration Planning and Daily Planning.

Mentoring

Mentoring is a role of facilitator to reiterate affirmation/learning.

Metrics

Metrics means measurements. Anything that is related to measuring the performance, progress, and status of people, projects, processes and tools falls under metrics. This is a about quantitative analysis. Some examples of metrics are velocity, burn down charts etc.

Minimally Marketable Feature

It represents distinct and deliverable feature that must also provide significant value to the customer.

Net Present Value (NPV)

The present value is today's value of an amount of money in the future. This is a technique used to find the viability of the project in financial terms; a positive NPV is favorable.

Negotiation

It is the process of creating something together by bonding around a shared task and establishing new ways of working together.

Osmotic Communication

A form of communication that relies on team members learn by overhearing conversations.

Organization Compliance

Organization compliance is one of the common themes or dimensions of organizational citizenship behavior.

Positive Value

Positive values are the additional benefits a customer may derive by using agile methods. These can be those values from the Agile Manifesto or the five core values (commitment, focus, openness, respect, and courage) for scrum teams.

Process Tailoring

Process tailoring is extracting from established set of processes, tasks or artifacts so as to best suit a project to achieve its objectives.

Planning Poker

This estimation method is based on Fibonacci sequence and uses team consensus to estimate efforts after detail team discussions.

Prototyping

Prototyping refers to an activity of creating an incomplete version which is replica of final product with the intention of getting valuable feedback from users early in the project.

Prioritization

The process of selecting few items with higher priority over others based on certain criteria such as customer value, risk, priority, and complexity etc. Prioritizing features helps the agile teams deliver critical features, even before full project gets completed.

Product Roadmap

This is high level document depicting evolution of product over time and defining scope as well as providing timeframe for each delivery.

Project Charter

This is the official document describing the vision, mission and success criteria for a project.

Participatory Decision

This is a creative process to give ownership of decisions to the whole group, finding effective options that everyone can agree on.

Principles of System thinking

System thinking is a tool for diagnosing organizational issues, understanding organizational dynamics, and creating change.

Project Standards

These can be those international standards followed by agile team in their agile project management. These may include ISO, PMI, SEI-CMMI, and others.

Professional Conduct

PMI's code of ethics and professional conduct means the social responsibility of a project manager. The most important values are responsibility, respect, fairness, and honesty.

Progressive Elaboration

It means that over time the work packages are elaborated in greater details. This is the process of planning for a project in phases as the project progresses and things become clearer.

Personas

These are just like actors under traditional use cases. These are real people, with real problems, and system is expected to meet their needs.

Product Quality

It is the degree to which the original requirements are met.

Quality Standards

These can be those international standards followed by various quality standards organizations as well as based on quality theories prevalent in project management and software development. These may include ISO, PMI, SEI-CMMI, Unified Process, Dr. Deming's Cycle, TQM, Six Sigma, PDCA and others.

Relative Sizing

This is a simple principle based on sizing the user stories relatively to each other and then measuring the velocity.

Release Planning

The meeting for the agile team members to commit to a plan for delivering an increment of a product value.

Relative Prioritization

The process of selecting few items based on priority. This is done by performing relative comparison against a predefined base item.

Relative Ranking

The process of selecting few items with higher priority over others based on customer value. This is done by ranking the items relative to each other.

Risk Management

Risk management is the process and knowledge area about identifying, assessing and responding to risks.

Risk Adjusted Backlog

This is the approach that tries to identify and mitigate the risk at an earlier stage in the agile project. Because risk and uncertainty influence product success, uncertain and risky items should be high-priority when the backlog prioritization process happens.

Risk Burn down Graphs

This is a technique used in managing risk on agile projects. In this graph, the sum of risk exposure values are plotted against the iterations and it is expected to see a linear drop in risk over the course of the project.

Risk-based Spike

This is a about exploring the known unknown and probably throwing away everything that was researched and any prototypes developed.

Regulatory Compliance

Regulatory compliance describes the goal that corporations or public agencies aspire to achieve in their efforts to ensure that personnel are aware of and take steps to comply with relevant laws and regulations.

Return on Investment (ROI)

The ratio of amount obtained back (returns) to the amount invested (investments). Under agile, superior ROI is desired meaning "getting more done".

Retrospectives

This is kind of review meeting. It is an excellent way for the agile team to analyze, adapt and improve its processes. The iteration and release retrospectives are very common among agile team members.

Soft Skills

These are skills related to interpersonal communication.

Self-assessment

This is the process of looking at oneself in order to assess aspects that are important to one's identity. Self-assessment lets you learn about your skills, interests, personality and values.

Servant Leadership

The main focus in this style is leading by serving; not by command and control. The servant leader is someone who ensures that other peoples' highest priority needs are being served.

Simulation

Simulating is the imitation of some real thing, state of affairs or process. Simulation entails representing certain key characteristics or behaviors with the intention of getting valuable feedback from users early in the project.

Stakeholder Expectations

Just like any other project, the stakeholder expectations will be that the agile team will deliver all requirements/scope on time and under budget, with available resources and of best quality with minimum risks. The team will be able to adapt to the changes throughout the project.

Stakeholder Involvement

Stakeholders are anyone with an interest in the agile project. Their involvement is needed throughout the project right from vision till releasing product.

Stakeholder Management

Project Stakeholder Management includes the processes required to identify the people, groups, or organizations that could impact or be impacted by the agile project. This may include identifying stakeholders, creating Stakeholder Management Plan, managing and controlling Stakeholder Engagement.

Stakeholder Needs

This involves understanding the stakeholders, their real requirements, problems in defining the needs, resolving the conflicts and getting consensus on the final product as needed by multiple stakeholders.

Stakeholder Values

There are values under agile project management which carry topmost priority and entire process is targeted towards identifying, improving and implementing stakeholder values. The values must be provided by stakeholders and may align with project charter and/or vision.

Story Points

This is simple point-based system where one story is used as a base with some points and all other user stories are compared relative to this base story.

Story Maps

This mapping is a way to help lots of small stories tells a bigger story that describes software and systems.

Team Space

Open workspace for co-located teams and virtual open workspace for distributed teams.

Time-boxing

The concept of setting aside a fixed block of time for an activity or meeting and then ending at a particular time regardless of how much have been finished.

Test Driven Development (TDD)

This is a software development technique that generates the tests first and then develops the code to pass those tests. The software development is driven by test cases that should pass, and then refactor the code to make the test pass again. TDD helps ensure the software's technical quality.

Trend Analysis

This refers to the concept of collecting information and attempting to spot a pattern or trend in the information.

Team Commitment

Commitment is the act of committing or pledging. Teams need three forms of commitments to be most successful: commitment to each other and each other's success, commitment to the team and team's success, commitment to the organization and organizational goals.

Team Collaboration

Collaboration describes a process of value creation that the traditional structures of communication and teamwork can't achieve." Team collaboration follows a process and the purpose is to create value. Teams need to connect and share with each other to have effective team collaboration.

Team Diversity

Team Diversity is the significant uniqueness of each individual on a team. This should not only include the usual diverse selections such as religion, sex, age, and race, but also additional unique personality characteristics. All of these differences can affect team interactions and performance.

Team Empowerment

In an empowered team, each teammate has a voice in group decisions. The team self-organizes around a leader instead of reporting to a manager, and may make changes to their project or product at will. An organization structured around empowered teams will have a relatively flat hierarchy and a high proportion of well-educated, highly trusted employees.

Team Formation

Teams initially go through a **"forming"** stage in which members are positive and polite. Some members are anxious, as they haven't yet worked out exactly what work the team will involve. Others are simply excited about the task ahead.

Time Estimation

The Time Estimation under agile project means to determine the effort, length, cost, or priority of a task, requirement, release or even a whole project. Typically this is referred to Activity Time estimation using affinity diagram or playing poker under agile project.

User Stories

Agile user stories are short descriptions of features; the customer wants or values most.

Verification and Validation (V&V)

The process of making sure that right product is built and the product is built right way.

Velocity

This provides a measure as how rapidly a team can create working features. The amount of work a team can complete in an iteration, usually given in story points per iteration.

Value Stream Analysis

This is performed mainly to eliminate waste by following the techniques of value stream mapping. The analysis involves studying existing process flow, representing current state using standard symbols and then drawing a future state by eliminating waste to make it optimized.

Variance

This is the difference between an expected result and actual result. In agile project management, the cost variance and schedule variance is measured.

Variations in Agile Methods

This mainly describes the differences among various methodologies used under agile.

Value Stream Mapping

This is a lean manufacturing technique used to analyze and design the flow of materials and information required to bring a product or service to a customer.

Value-based Analysis

The phase of analyzing project requirements/scope where emphasize is given on total value or customer value is known as value-based analysis.

Value-based Prioritization

The process of selecting few items with higher priority over others based on customer value. Prioritizing features helps the agile teams deliver value to customer sooner.

WIP Limits

The team is only allowed to work on finite number of things at a time. WIP means work in progress.

Wide Band Delphi

This estimation method is also known as "wisdom of crowds" and it is a consensus-based technique for estimating effort.

Wireframes

Wireframe focuses on what a screen does, not what it looks like. The main focus lies in functionality, behavior, and priority of content.

References

Books

Cohn, Mike. 2011. Agile Estimating and Planning. Prentice Hall.

Cohn, Mike. 2010. Succeeding with Agile. Addison-Wesley.

Highsmith, Jim. 2009. Agile Project Management. Addison-Wesley.

Guckenheimer, Sam and Neno Loje. 2011. Agile Software Engineering with Visual Studio. Addison-Wesley.

Crowe, Andy. 2012. The PMI-ACP Exam. Velociteach.

Shore, James and Shane Warden. 2007. The Art of Agile Development. O'Reilly.

Rasmusson, Jonathan. 2011. The Agile Samurai. Pragmatic Bookshelf.

Cockburn, Alistair and Jim Highsmith. 2007. Agile Software Development. Addison-Wesley.

Selected Web Sites / Organizations

www.AgileSherpa.org

SixSigmaForum.net

www.Agilealliance.org

www.scrumalliance.org

Agileleadershipnetwork.org

www.leanssc.org/

Vivek Vaishampayan, PMP, MCTS, PMI-ACP

Agiletraining.com

AgileExams.com

martinfowler.com

xprogramming.com

mountaingoatsoftware.com

rallydev.com

versionone.com

Index

T

U

V

W

Printed in the United States
By Bookmasters

Printed in the United States
By Bookmasters